Praise for Unlimited Abundance
and Quantum Success

"Are you ready to take a quantum leap in your experience of abundance, success, and happiness? Sandra Anne Taylor's brilliant book, Unlimited Abundance, *is packed with expert advice and guidance to show you how. NOW is the time to take the leap!"*

— **Robert Holden**, author of *Shift Happens!* and *Higher Purpose*

"Many books say they will change your life, but few really do. Unlimited Abundance *is one of those rare few. Sandra Anne Taylor covers everything from the science of energy and consciousness to the neurobiology of self-confidence. This is a quintessential guidebook to great success and happiness, filled with dozens of simple and practical techniques that are effective and easy to implement. So don't miss this book—it really can change your life!"*

— **Marci Shimoff**, *New York Times* best-selling
author of *Happy for No Reason*

"For going on 20 years, Quantum Success *has been rocking people's worlds by bringing abundance and prosperity front and center into their reality. If you're looking for true transformation that is profound and long lasting, this new edition,* Unlimited Abundance, *is the game changer you've been searching for. Read it now!"*

— **Radleigh Valentine**, best-selling author of
Manifesting Your Magical Life

"I am delighted to provide my enthusiastic endorsement for Sandra Anne Taylor's book, Unlimited Abundance, the expanded and updated version of her New York Times bestseller, Quantum Success. Sandra's profound insights and empowering approach delve even deeper into activating abundance and guiding readers toward embracing their limitless prosperity and fulfillment. This book explores crucial topics such as the influence of brain frequency on manifestation, the distinction between resistant and receptive affirmations, the power of neurotransmitter affirmations in building neural pathways of self-esteem, planting intentions in the energetic realm, and much more.

"Through practical wisdom, inspirational exercises, and transformative guidance, Unlimited Abundance stands as a guiding light for those striving to unlock their full potential and manifest abundance in every aspect of life. I wholeheartedly recommend this book to anyone committed to creating a life of abundance and joy, as it illuminates a path toward boundless prosperity and well-being."

— **Dr. Darren Weissman**, best-selling author of
The Power of Infinite Love & Gratitude and
developer of The LifeLine Technique®

"Sandra Anne Taylor's Unlimited Abundance, *based on her* New York Times *bestseller,* Quantum Success, *is brilliant! Not only does it teach principles that help you align with the energetic forces of the Universe, it offers absolutely inspired ways to connect with the amazing assistance of the spirit world. And I can tell you from personal experience, when you tap into that incredible unseen force, your life will never be the same!"*

— **John Holland**, international best-selling
author of *Bridging Two Realms*

Unlimited Abundance

Also by SANDRA ANNE TAYLOR

Books

The Akashic Records:
*Unlock the Infinite Power, Wisdom, and Energy of the Universe**

The Hidden Power of Your Past Lives:
*Revealing Your Encoded Consciousness**

Secrets of Attraction:
*The Universal Laws of Love, Sex, and Romance**

Secrets of Success:
The Science and Spirit of Real Prosperity, with Sharon A. Klingler*

Truth, Triumph, and Transformation:
*Sorting Out the Fact from the Fiction in Universal Law**

*28 Days to a More Magnetic Life**

Your Quantum Breakthrough Code:
*The Simple Technique That Brings Everlasting Joy and Success**

Audio Programs

Act to Attract Audio Seminar Program
(nine-CD audio program and workbook)

Act to Attract Meditations and Affirmations (CD and audio downloads)

Attracting Success (CD and audio downloads)

Energy Breakthrough Meditations (CD and audio downloads)

Healing Journeys (CD and audio downloads)

Card Decks

The Akashic Tarot, with Sharon Anne Klingler*

*Energy and Spirit Oracle**

*Energy Oracle Cards**

*Past-Life Energy Oracle**

The Priestess of Light Oracle, with Kimberly Webber*

*The Quantum Oracle**

*Available from Hay House

Please visit: Hay House USA: www.hayhouse.com®
Hay House Australia: www.hayhouse.com.au
Hay House UK: www.hayhouse.co.uk
Hay House India: www.hayhouse.co.in

Unlimited Abundance

Align Your Life with the Unseen Forces of Success

SANDRA ANNE TAYLOR

HAY HOUSE LLC

Carlsbad, California • New York City

London • Sydney • New Delhi

Published in the United States by: Hay House LLC: www.hayhouse.com®
Published in Australia by: Hay House Australia Publishing Pty Ltd: www.hayhouse.com.au
Published in the United Kingdom by: Hay House UK Ltd: www.hayhouse.co.uk
Published in India by: Hay House Publishers (India) Pvt Ltd: www.hayhouse.co.in

Cover design: Barbara LeVan Fisher
Interior design: Bryn Starr Best

**Cataloging-in-Publication Data
is on file with the Library of Congress**

Tradepaper ISBN: 978-1-4019-7695-8
E-book ISBN: 978-1-4019-7696-5
Audiobook ISBN: 978-1-4019-7697-2

10 9 8 7 6 5 4 3 2 1
1st edition, May 2006
2nd edition, September 2024

Printed in the United States of America

This product uses responsibly sourced papers and/or recycled materials.
For more information, see www.hayhouse.com.

For the wonderful children in my life,
Vica, Jenyaa, and Ethan Taylor,
and Devin Staurbringer.

Your laughter is the music of success to me.

CONTENTS

Bonus Content: Audio Download Instructions xii
Track List for the Unlimited Abundance *Affirmations and Meditations* . .xii
Author's Note on the Updates to the New Edition .xv
Introduction. xvii

PART I: THE SEVEN UNIVERSAL LAWS OF SUCCESS 1

Chapter 1:   The Law of Manifestation. 3
Chapter 2:   The Law of Magnetism 11
Chapter 3:   The Law of Pure Desire 27
Chapter 4:   The Law of Paradoxical Intent .35
Chapter 5:   The Law of Harmony 45
Chapter 6:   The Law of Right Action 55
Chapter 7:   The Law of Expanding Influence 63

PART II: THE SIX PERSONAL POWERS OF SUCCESS 71

Chapter 8:   The Power of Letting Go. 73
Chapter 9:   The Power of Consciousness. 95
Chapter 10:   The Power of Energy. 107
Chapter 11:   The Power of Intention 117
Chapter 12:   The Power of Choice. 127
Chapter 13:   The Power of Love. 137

PART III: THE FIVE MAGNETIC ENERGIES OF SUCCESS 147

Chapter 14:   The Energy of Confidence 149
Chapter 15:   The Energy of Optimism 157
Chapter 16:   The Energy of Purpose 169
Chapter 17:   The Energy of Presence. 177
Chapter 18:   The Energy of Appreciation 183

PART IV: THE FOUR STEPS TO SUCCESS 195

Chapter 19:   Commit to Your Goal 197
Chapter 20:   Set Up a Step-by-Step Plan 203
Chapter 21:   Take Action Every Day 209
Chapter 22:   Let Go of Attachment without Stopping the Action . . . 215

PART V: THE THREE UNSEEN ASSISTANTS TO SUCCESS 223

Chapter 23:   Your Higher Self 225
Chapter 24:   Angels, Guides, and Loving Spirits 237
Chapter 25:   The Divine Presence 245

PART VI: THE TWO OBSTACLES TO SUCCESS 253

Chapter 26:   Engaging in Limiting Beliefs 255
Chapter 27:   Giving Up Too Soon 265

PART VII: THE ONE PATH TO SUCCESS 273

Chapter 28:   Living with a Joyous, Successful Consciousness 275

Conclusion 291
Index of Energy-Shifting Truths and Techniques 301
Suggested Reading 303
Acknowledgments 305
About the Author 307

BONUS CONTENT

Audio Download Instructions

Thank you for purchasing *Unlimited Abundance* by Sandra Anne Taylor. This product includes a free download! To access this bonus content, please visit www.hayhouse.com/download and enter the Product ID and Download Code as they appear below.

Product ID: 6958

Download Code: audio

For further assistance, please contact Hay House Customer Care by phone: US (800) 654-5126 or INTL CC+(760) 431-7695 or visit www.hayhouse.com/contact.

Thank you again for your Hay House purchase. Enjoy!

> ### Track List for the *Unlimited Abundance* Affirmations and Meditations

Affirmations for Self-Empowerment: This track can be listened to at any time. Embrace each statement as a new intention to redirect your energy.

Relaxation and Memory Release: This process provides a deep, whole-body relaxation that increases tranquility and brings a peaceful sense of well-being. The visualization following the relaxation allows you to release the memories of stressful situations, whether they happened recently or long ago.

Rescripting Beliefs for Truth and Self-Empowerment: This meditation takes you back to childhood to shift the energy of the potential source of your misinformation. When you release and rewrite your old limiting beliefs, you will send clear and positive messages to the Universe that you believe in yourself and in your power to create great things.

Your Sacred Identity: This guided meditation creates profound peace and powerful vibration by connecting you with Divine Consciousness, the source of all Universal love, blessings, and solutions.

Clearing the Road Ahead: This meditation process is designed to eliminate the obstacles on your road to happiness and real achievement and to open the way to your highest power and ultimate success.

Planting Your Destiny Garden: This process helps you to visualize your goals and plant the seeds of your desires throughout your life and the world. To prepare for this process, you can simply imagine what you want to achieve, or you can place words or pictures of your goals on a piece of paper. These will represent the beautiful blossoms of your desires that this process will plant and nurture in the energetic realm.

Attracting Success: This process will allow you to project the highest, most magnetic energy of your higher self, broadcasting a strongly attractive vibration across time and space and drawing your desired results to you. This highly attractive resonance will reverberate throughout your life and attract your ideal solutions from the energetic realm.

Attracting Love: This guided visualization brings out the highest, most magnetic energies of your higher self. These vibrations of truly self-loving confidence are then sent out into time and space to connect with and attract your most resonant and ideal love.

AUTHOR'S NOTE ON THE
UPDATES TO THE
NEW EDITION

I'm excited and delighted to offer you this new, greatly expanded, and updated edition of my *New York Times* bestseller, originally titled *Quantum Success*. This new title was chosen to highlight the book's many updates. My wish is for you to feel unlimited and abundant in *all* areas of your life, not just the single focus on finances that might immediately come to mind for some people when they think of the word *success*. There are so many wonderful life experiences that enhance joy. Whatever you desire—whether it's abundant health, wealth, love, friends, happiness, or even leisure time—you deserve it and *can* achieve it when you align your life with the unseen forces of Universal manifestation.

For those of you who have read the original *Quantum Success,* rest assured that so many techniques and profound discoveries have been added here. I'm sure you will benefit deeply from all the new material contained within these pages.

There's been a lot of misunderstanding about attraction. In this update, I endeavor to clarify some common yet wildly misleading conclusions about manifestation that have taken place over the years. By understanding such things as cognitive creation; brain-frequency influences; life-force resonance; and the more subtle energetic nuances of projection, entanglement, and interaction, you can shift frustrating old patterns and create radiant new results. These vital, active elements are an ongoing part of our everyday journey, and they can empower you to reroute your life in entirely new directions.

Please read through the Introduction for more information about the updates. Also check out the index at the end of the book, which is designed to help you easily find the detailed information and powerful techniques that you can utilize to not only enhance your life but also accelerate the achievement of your desires. I have used every single technique I describe in this book, and I can say, without reservation, they have increased joy, focus, purpose, and unending appreciation in every area of my life!

INTRODUCTION

My life completely changed when I was introduced to quantum physics nearly 30 years ago. I had been in a private psychological practice and consistently witnessed repeating patterns of behavior and attraction. But I soon discovered that the principles of energy and consciousness could be applied to any personal situation to bring about amazing results.

This science is liberating because it gives you far more control over your future than you may have ever realized. It's empowering because it allows you to take specific energetic action now to determine the direction of your destiny. No matter what you may have experienced in the past, when you learn to tap into these amazing Universal forces, you'll arrive at the real source of abundance and success.

THE VIBRATIONS OF ABUNDANCE

Most people believe that the circumstances of their lives are based on random and uncontrollable occurrences, such as their history, their status, or their family income. But while some of these elements may be influential, the truth is that we can direct our life experiences through our own energy and our interaction with the forces and laws that govern nature.

There are several energetic patterns in the physical world that have powerful applications to humankind. In fact, the science of personal energy and the mechanics of consciousness are the two most important natural factors affecting the outcomes of your goals. Once you actively employ these elements within your life, you'll see profound changes taking shape. In fact, significant natural principles help to forge our life experiences, compelling us to look more closely at the science behind them.

Quantum physics reveals that the world is made up of amazing unknowns, such as dark energy and dark matter, which are being researched with great expectation for the answers they hold regarding energy, frequency, and the nature of the Universe. Human intention and consciousness are also made of pulsating, energetic vibrations that we can direct both inward and outward to have great personal influence. They can shape the destiny of each individual as well as the entire species. In fact, your future is taking shape right now! In order to facilitate that, I have added eight meditation and affirmation audios as a bonus download in this book. Please see pages xii and xiii for descriptions and download instructions.

These energetic truths—along with the techniques described in this book—are so empowering that they can quite literally change your life. Even if you've never been aware of them before, the unseen forces and Universal Laws of attraction and manifestation impose their influence on everything from your career and finances to your health and relationships.

In quantum physics, the uncertainty theory reveals that you live in a state of unending possibilities. The world exists in a constant state of flux where even a small shift in energy can create an immediate and far-reaching change in reality. Although most of the power in the Universe isn't visible, it can still be used to great effect. You may not be able to see an atom, but you can certainly witness the effects of an atom bomb—and your own personal unseen vibrations have very dramatic effects as well. But to take control of the power there, you must be willing to explore some new possibilities and take a journey through inner space.

LEAVING PRESENT PATTERNS BEHIND

Many people feel as if they're on a treadmill: constantly on the move but going nowhere. They're tired of running from task to task, job to job, or even from one relationship to another, always feeling like something's missing. Many feel isolated, empty, and stuck, longing for change but not knowing how to make that happen—so they just keep repeating the same old patterns over and over again.

If this sounds familiar, and your current circumstances seem like just another frustrating trip down memory lane, take heart. You do have the power to create a different life. In fact, quantum physics reveals that you're at the very center of a world of unlimited power and potential—in this very moment. The Universal forces are at work in your life and can completely turn things around.

I've used these principles in every aspect of my own life. They've helped me go from being a high school teacher to a counselor to an international speaker and author. After two failed marriages, I'd pretty much given up on love, but then I decided to apply the techniques that I talk about in this book to that pursuit. Within a year, I met my husband, a truly supportive, loving, wise, and humorous man who has enhanced my life beyond words.

Perhaps my most amazing experience in terms of these astounding precepts has been the story of my two wonderful children. People called my husband and me "crazy" for wanting to adopt two unrelated preteens from a Russian orphanage. But I knew that the powers of energy and consciousness were absolute and if I took the right steps in employing them, we'd attract the very best kids—and we did! It was a long and involved process, an extraordinary story that's so remarkable in the occurrence of "magical" events that it would take another book to tell it all. But everything turned out perfectly, and it changed all our lives in immeasurably happy ways.

I've also taught these principles for nearly 30 years to individual clients and in seminars all over the world. Since the beginning, I've heard countless success stories from people who've applied the techniques to both their private and professional lives. One man who started a software business in his garage was offered more than $7 million for his company just a few years later. Another fought depression and anxiety to get out of a low-level food-service position and open his own restaurant. He's become so successful that he was asked to create a national franchise.

In Australia, after I'd presented at an event, I was approached by a woman pushing a stroller. She told me that a couple of years previously she'd taken my seminar on how to attract love. At that time, she was alone, but she very much wanted a family. After learning about the forces and then implementing the techniques, she met the love of her life. She'd come back to thank me and to introduce me to her beautiful new baby.

It's so gratifying to receive emails and hear stories of so many individuals manifesting abundance in all different areas of their life: getting promotions or new jobs, finding love, or starting a business or a family. Some have even reported losing weight and looking younger! Whatever these people were working on, they were all empowered by their understanding of the science of success. They saw within their own lives that a shift in energy and consciousness could make anything happen.

Some of the techniques discussed here will be entirely new, while others may sound familiar but have nuanced differences. It's the Universal power and your own life-force energy that are the source of your real solutions.

JOURNALING YOUR JOURNEY TO SUCCESS

An important part of your self-exploration is keeping a Success Journal. The word *journal* originally meant a written record of the experiences on a journey. Your pursuit of success is a voyage in itself, and your written record will help you get from here to your ultimate destination. Your entries can act as a personal road map, keeping you on track and redirecting you toward your goals.

Your Desired Destination

As you go through the chapters, there will be several suggestions about what to record in your Success Journal, but the first entry you need to make is about where you want to end up. Take some time now to draw up your wish list, writing down everything that you desire. In your experience of unlimited abundance, do you have a new look, a million dollars, a new home, a blissful romance, a raise, or an entirely new career? Take note of every single thing that your heart dreams of. Continue to add to this list whenever you think of something else you long for.

Intentions

When you've completed this initial catalog, turn every item on it into a specific intention. For example, if a million dollars is on your wish list, you'll write: "I intend to be (or I am becoming) a millionaire." If you're looking for a new romance, write: "I am attracting a wonderful, caring partner who brings long-lasting love to me now." As you'll see, an important part of your journey will be to consistently turn your desires into *intentions* and your hopes into *affirmations*.

This focus connects you with the Universal forces, aligning your consciousness and vibration with the energetic realm. In fact, you should focus your intention regularly, not on just the thing you desire but also on the emotional experiences of your daily life. Try to consider both the emotional and practical intention of each task. This lifts your energy to a higher vibration. A clear purpose, like confidence or joy, goes a long way toward creating an irresistible resonance.

Affirmations

Affirmations are powerful statements that reinforce the reality of your personal power and your desires. While some people dismiss them as being too simplistic, they can be a very dynamic part of energy production. If you're not consciously *affirming*, it's entirely likely that you're unconsciously *negating* and creating dismal energy. Repeating affirmations helps you keep your focus on what you *do* want rather than what you *don't* want.

At the end of each chapter, you'll find a few pertinent affirmations. Pick the ones that resonate with you the most and read them often. You can also write them down and place them where you'll see them repeatedly. Make sure that you include basic statements of self-acknowledgment no matter what you're working on.

The energetic action of affirmative thinking and self-talk is thoroughly explained in Chapter 15. Pay close attention to the difference between *resistant* and *receptive* affirmations. Understanding this subtle shift can change the very vibration of your life. Also take special note of the section on Cognitive Creation in Chapter 2. This important piece of scientific information explains how and when your thoughts manifest reality and why they sometimes don't. This understanding—along with the energetic aspects of affirmation—can be real game changers in your pursuit of success. (Even the Easy Alpha Affirmations in Chapter 2 are a neat little energy trick.)

In addition to the statements at the end of the chapters, I have included an audio titled "Affirmations for Self-Empowerment" in the bonus download. You can also add new affirmations of your own into your Success Journal as you begin to work on new issues. Focus on positive intentions concerning yourself, your goals, your value, your power, or your world. Affirm yourself and your life every day. You deserve your own high regard, and when you learn to give that to yourself, the Universe will bless you in countless ways.

COUNTDOWN TO SUCCESS

Quantum physics demonstrates that great shifts of energy can occur in a single moment. This is true for your life, too—at every second, you're participating in the creation of your life-force energy. The energetic realm is always waiting to respond to your vibrations, so get ready to step into the future with new tools and more power than you ever thought you had. This is one science experiment you don't want to miss!

The energetic world represents a reality that happens on every level, from the cellular to the nonlocal, impacting things in far-distant space and often having no regard for linear time. And your energetic reach is just as powerful. Use the forces to shift your own vibrations and you'll find health and happiness right down to your very cells—and you'll be creating an irresistible magnetism for joyous achievements in the time to come.

This book is divided into seven parts, each section having one less chapter than the part before. This is a countdown of sorts, moving through the seven most important influences on the experience of abundance and personal success. From the Seven Universal Laws of Success to the Six Personal Powers, all the way down to the One Path to Success, your application of these techniques will bring increasing value and powerful momentum to the pursuit of your dreams.

In the nearly 20 years since I wrote *Quantum Success*, I have taught many new energetic practices and meditative processes that have helped countless people to dramatically shift both their present experience and their future outcomes. I have tried to include all those new techniques throughout this revision, and you can find an index at the back of the book listing these powerful practices. It is my most sincere desire that you utilize all these approaches—though some may seem strange at first. Trust in your own process; believe in yourself and in your deserving of all the best the world has to offer.

Open your heart and mind to your own energetic power and get ready to start your countdown now. Make these principles an active part of your daily life, and your life will take off like a rocket on the path toward unlimited abundance! You'll soon find that your lifestyle, career, personal relationships, and virtually everything else will begin to change. You'll see that nothing is impossible when you align your life with these vital unseen forces of success and manifestation. Your soul is connected to the powerhouse that charges all creation, and it's time to open yourself to that Universal current—that pulsating energy that directs your destiny. When you do, you'll find, as I have, that your life has been blessed beyond your expectations!

PART I

The Seven Universal Laws of Success

You live in a miraculous world. Truly wonderful things are happening all around you, and you can bring that enchantment to all that you do and all that you'd like to achieve! If you feel that your desires have been elusive up till now, you need to know that a world of power and energy is waiting to help make your dreams a reality.

What may seem random is actually the workings of the energetic world, the results of resonant patterns. Consciousness and energy are perpetually vibrating in an endless celebration of cause and effect, and your choices feed that process every day.

It's important to know how complex these laws are. There's more than one "law of attraction," and each one encompasses a different type and source of vibration. By understanding the subtler nuances of each law, we can either activate or resist that law's natural tendencies in the world. The energy is mutable. We always have the power to align with the most beneficial forces at play in our Universe.

The quantum world pulsates with power and endless possibilities! You're a vibrating force in this world, a creative consciousness that directs both your own destiny and that of all humankind. You are—at this moment—engaged in an exquisite act of personal and global creation. When you take control of the cosmic energy within and around you, the Universal Laws become a source of power, helping you create a wellspring of happiness, success, and value beyond belief!

Chapter 1

The Law of Manifestation

The First Universal Law of Success

The primal cause is mind.
Everything must start with an idea.
Every event, every condition, every thing
is first an idea in the mind.

— ROBERT COLLIER

The mechanics of your mind reveal fascinating possibilities—not merely in the capacity to work out complex problems and learn new information but an ability that transcends logic and moves into the realm of physical creation. This is the power of your consciousness, and it's the major source of your destiny creation.

The first Law of Success, the **Law of Manifestation**, demonstrates how things come into being. In quantum physics, *consciousness creates reality*—and this applies to your personal world as well.

Modern science explores many theories of consciousness-created reality. One is cosmological, explaining how the Universe came into being. It says that our world is far too complex to have reached this stage of development merely through a random series of coincidental events, so it must be the result of conscious intention. Another theory has to do with how physical reality is constructed out of the raw material of the Universe, and yet another explores how our individual consciousness chooses one of the infinite possibilities that are available to us at each moment of time. Even the theory of observer-created reality, which has to do with how particles and waves are measured, indicates that intention and consciousness are very real forces in the world.

These theories are intriguing, but it's your *personal* reality that we'll examine here. The individual application of observer creation reveals that what you notice about yourself and your life becomes present. Think about this for a moment: What do you tend to notice about yourself—and your life? Are those observations negative or positive? What kind of reality do you think you'll create based on those conclusions?

These are significant questions, and it would be helpful to answer them in your journal. But this is only the beginning where your destiny manifestation is concerned since *your consciousness creates your reality.* To understand how, it's important to find out what your "consciousness" is and how it acts as a creative force in your life.

If you want to see this power, all you have to do is look around you. Setting aside the discussion of higher consciousness–created reality and what you see in the natural world, it's easy to see the power and the presence of personal consciousness in your daily life. As I pause right now, I witness it everywhere: The spirit of a street artist from Venice, Italy, reveals itself to me in a painting that hangs on my wall. The energy of my favorite author speaks to me as I read myself to sleep at night. The inspiration of a stained-glass artist and dear friend shines for me as sunlight streams through one of her beautiful creations hanging in my window. The consciousness of a furniture builder supports me and that of a home builder protects me. And I'm amazed by the layers of intention that figure into the experience of hearing my favorite music fill the house in response to me simply speaking the artist's name into the air. In these and a million more ways each day, I'm influenced by the creative force of others, and I am a witness to the vast beauty and value that human consciousness has created.

It's important to truly open ourselves to the real fullness of consciousness-created reality in every sense of its meaning. From a child's paper airplane to a nationally computerized power grid, everything begins in the power of the mind. And this is not limited to material things; this is the fundamental reality of all manifestation. Everything exists in consciousness first. And while not all of it produces beneficial results, every bit of it produces something. Consciousness created the World Trade Center, and consciousness destroyed it.

In terms of your personal life, your success—or lack of it—manifests in your consciousness first. If you can look around you and see only problems and difficulty, that's largely a product of your mind. If you see abundance and achievement—even if it may seem small, that's a force of yours as well. Almost everything that you manifest is in the boiling pot of your present consciousness and energy, creating the concoction that you'll later call your life. The **Law of Manifestation** is clear: your consciousness creates your reality, and you simply can't manifest something that isn't formed in your heart and mind first. To experience abundance, you need to acknowledge the abundance vibrating in yourself and in your life right now.

WHAT'S YOUR CONSCIOUSNESS CREATING NOW?

The phrase "your consciousness creates your destiny" by no means translates to mean "you *consciously* create your destiny." The fact is that most of us are completely unaware of how we script the circumstances we find ourselves in. Most people don't even know *that* they create their own experiences. They perceive life as a series of random events having no apparent cause or meaning. Rarely does it occur to them that what they experience is something they've largely but unwittingly set up for themselves, perhaps even unknowingly *expecting* it!

For this reason, one of the first requirements of the Law of Manifestation is to investigate exactly what it is you're focusing on. This is your *consciousness direction*. The following questions are designed to help you get in touch with this important aspect of your destiny creation. While you'll be exploring the many layers of manifestation in the following chapters, this exercise will help you start to become more aware of your present consciousness direction.

JOURNAL FOR SUCCESS

Answer these questions in your Success Journal. Review them often to investigate your consciousness creativity on a regular basis.

- What are you most conscious of—that is, what do you tend to think about the most? Are you more conscious of what you have or what you lack? What's right or what's wrong? More conscious of the beneficial or difficult in your life?

- What do you *expect* to experience? How does that differ than what you *hope* to experience? Be honest about this. What do you *expect* your day to be like? This daily consciousness is a large part of manifestation.

- What's your most important career goal? How much time do you spend each day consciously focusing on the activities that would lead to your desired outcome? Are those activities enjoyable to you?

- What's the most prevalent habit, pattern, or even addiction in your life? How much time do you spend each day engaging in this habit? How conscious of it are you when you're engaged in it? What conscious action do you want to take regarding this behavior?

- Do you tend to focus more on the positive actions you can take during your day or the potential problems that could come up? Does your thought process tend to be more negative or positive?

The answers to these questions are important indicators of your consciousness direction. Do not fault yourself if you discover an underpinning of negative consciousness. You have within you an unlimited power to design your destiny the way you want it. In fact, you can work on it right now. But just as an architect can't design a masterful building with his eyes closed, you can't become the architect of your dreams until you open your eyes to all your choices.

BECOMING CONSCIOUS

Do you ever stop to notice what you're thinking about? How often do you consider the consequences of your choices *before* you make them? Many people are clueless about why they do what they do—or even what it means. They move through whole decades at a time, reacting out of an unconscious and largely unconsidered approach to life. These are what I call the "consciousness zombies," trudging through life day after day in an unaware state. They follow their habits and react out of emotion, doing what's required and not much more. But if this sounds like your approach in the past, don't worry. You have the power to awaken from the ranks of the undead. You can choose a different, higher, and brighter consciousness and move on to a better life than you've ever experienced—perhaps even better than you've ever dreamed of.

> Consciousness is always a choice. It's the choice to bring your awareness to the present moment, the decision to see and prioritize that which is truly important, that which is genuinely honoring and value enhancing in your life. Your constant question must be: What am I doing or focusing on right now? And the question that follows is: What might this action or consciousness be creating for me?

I have a client who readily admitted that she spent most of her day thinking about food, always wondering what, when, and how much she was going to eat each day. She considered herself "fat" even though she was a healthy size, and she exercised regularly in a struggle to control her obsession. No matter whether she lost or gained a few pounds, it didn't change the fact that she was always longing to eat and unhappy with her looks and her weight—a negative consciousness of self for sure.

She had similarly bad feelings about her career. She made just enough money to get by in tedious jobs that were always just okay, while doing a little freelance writing on the side. She hadn't realized that her negative focus on her weight issues and her job problems had created a consciousness wave she was riding on, and things weren't going to change until she began to become more conscious of her own true value and the value of her job.

We worked on letting go of her obsession and created a sane approach to eating. She began to affirm self-acceptance at any weight, and she also raised her consciousness about her career priorities. I encouraged her to replace her thoughts about food with a positive thought or creative action concerning her writing career. This shifted both her focus and her motivation, and it was just what she needed to get results. It took some time, but she not only let go of her obsession with food and her body, she saw her freelance writing career become more successful. In time, she was able to quit her old job and make even more money doing something she loved.

You, too, can take control of your own destiny manifestation. To shift your consciousness creation, you need to be much more aware of the positive than the negative—and of your value and priorities. Let go of the old rolling patterns of negative approaches. Instead, choose to focus your thoughts on the good things that you already are and have, as well as those that you're going to attract. Always take deliberate action in the direction of your goals instead of engaging in unconscious reactions and distractions.

In the next chapter, we'll discuss specific techniques that will enable you to make significant consciousness shifts, but you can start awakening to your options right now. Remember, if you don't like what you're creating, you can always change what you're conscious of. When you catch yourself focused on the negative, you need to know that your mind is likely to create a consciousness wave of negative results. Shift that focus no matter what it takes, and you'll soon see the powerful and positive outcomes that a truly optimistic consciousness can create!

Affirmations to Enhance Manifestation

Pick any of the following affirmations that resonate with you, and read them often, Write them down, and place them where you'll see them repeatedly. This will help adjust your consciousness direction toward the positive direction of your choosing.

✦ Every day I am becoming more aware of what I prioritize and what I tend to focus on. I prioritize my positive self-view and my own goals, and I am willing to take action in these directions now.

✦ I am choosing to be more and more conscious of all that I have to appreciate. I focus on the value in my life, and I am grateful.

✦ I am resourceful and creative, and I have the power to create a great destiny. I am choosing to believe in myself more and more each day.

✦ I take time to notice what I'm focusing on. I know that my consciousness creates my reality. I always have the option to choose an optimistic mindset.

✦ I consciously choose to create many moments of hope, joy, and peace throughout my daily life.

✦ ✦ ✦

Chapter 2

The Law of Magnetism

The Second Universal
Law of Success

Every person is surrounded by a thought atmosphere. . . .
Through this power we are either attracting or repelling.
Like attracts like and . . . we attract just what we are in mind.

— ERNEST HOLMES

While the first Law of Success concerns what you *create*, the second one, the Law of Magnetism, concerns what you *attract*. These two forces together have the greatest impact on your destiny: the first has to do with the power of your consciousness; the second has to do with the power of your personal energy.

Many patterns of energy are at work in the world today. Amazingly powerful yet unseen forces have very real and predictable outcomes, and we have become accustomed to things that would have seemed utterly impossible not long ago. Phone signals can travel from the earth to a satellite and then back to the other side of the planet with ease. Modern CAT scans and MRIs use energy to create images of the body. Microwaves cook food, sensors ensure security, and lasers remove tumors.

The list of ways in which modern humans have harnessed, directed, and utilized energy is almost endless. All the above phenomena—and countless more—have very significant physical results, but the influences aren't limited to medicine, communications, and technical gadgetry. The energetic workings of the Universe impact each one of us in ways that most people are never aware of—even to the point of the individual experiences of happiness and success.

> The **Law of Magnetism** says that we will attract the same kind of energy that we put out *about ourselves*. It's based on the quantum-physical principle that everything—including every person—projects unique vibratory information. Our own personal energy moves within us, from us, and all around us literally all the time. Whether we're aware of it or not, each of us is a part of a vast exchange and expansion of this force that takes place in the Universe every moment of every day.

Each of us projects a signature vibration that moves outward from us and connects with others of like resonance, largely determining both whom and what we'll attract in life. Like a little radio station, we are constantly broadcasting signals about our self and our life. The people and situations that match those signals are the ones that will tune in to us and be drawn into our life experience. In truth, what we call *chemistry*—whether it's romantic or professional—is actually more of a resonance, a matching of signals and personal vibrations. If success is what you're after, it will be important to understand how your energy is created—and what it may be broadcasting about you even now.

YOUR ENERGETIC CALLING CARD

In the Victorian era, calling cards were used to announce the arrival of a visitor or friend, and letters of introduction were sent ahead to pave the way and help someone new connect with others of like society. It was a formal process, but one which let the recipient know that the bearer was well connected and highly regarded.

Your personal resonance does much the same thing. Long before you arrive at an experience in life, your energy has sent messages about you to the people you'll be interacting with. It announces you to everyone, revealing that part of you that others relate to on an unconscious but very compelling level: your true energetic nature. If you don't like the society or circumstances you've attracted so far, or if you've had difficulty finding the success or relationships you desire, you might want to investigate what you've been putting into your energetic calling card.

Luckily, this personal frequency is something that you can change. Once you figure out what makes up your vibrational resonance, you can take active steps to improve your magnetic frequency and change all that you attract.

There are three major ways that your personal resonance is created:

1. Through your cognitive energy, or the vibrations of your thoughts

2. Through your emotional energy, or the vibrations of your feelings

3. Through your physical energy, or the vibrations of your body

This third factor is perhaps the easiest to direct. If you get regular muscle movement, eat well, and get enough sleep, your physical energy will be generally appealing. But let's take a closer look at the first two methods on this list.

COGNITIVE ENERGY: Your Brain Frequency

While it's true that our cognitive patterns are the fundamental source of the emotional quality of our lives, there is a lot of confusion about how that happens and what exactly our thoughts are creating. The exact details of this process can be revealed in a deeper understanding of *frequency.* Understanding what, when, and how your thoughts create is a crucial element of the unseen forces at play in your life.

The core of this incredible phenomenon can be found in your *brain frequency.* Being in a calm brain frequency gives you creative power over your life, but being in a higher state of analysis and agitation can take you out of alignment with your creative power and derail the pursuit of your goals.

Brain Frequency	Cycles per Second	Common Activities
Beta	15+	Continuous thought and analysis Worry, overanalysis, agitation Conscious thought, analysis, study, investigation
Alpha	7–14	Sleep, meditation, relaxation, dreaming Inspiration, meditation, hypnosis, intuition, mediumship Visualization for specific manifestation and creativity
Theta	4–7	Sleep, unconscious Trance, deep meditation, deep hypnosis
Delta	1–4	Sleep, deep unconsciousness

Let's take a look at the energetic details of brain frequency and activity to understand what's really going on. As indicated in this brain frequency chart, there are four basic levels of brain frequency.

- The slowest level is called *delta*, where your brain frequency averages between 1 and 4 cycles per second. This delta level is a state of deep unconscious and sleep where very little brain activity takes place.

- The next level is called *theta*. The common brain frequency in this state ranges from 4 to 7 cycles per second. Though this is a very deep level, some brain activity such as deep relaxation and meditation, deep hypnosis, and even trance can take place here. Like delta, theta is an unconscious and sleep state, though the Dalai Lama is said to have been conscious in the theta state.

- The next level of brain frequency is *alpha*, which ranges from 7 to 14 cycles per second. Alpha also happens during sleep and meditation. This is the most creative and most powerful level of brain frequency. It's the best level for meditation, relaxation, inspiration, and manifestation. In fact, this is the *only* level where you have the power to create *specific* results in your life. That's why creative visualizations are best started with relaxing induction techniques. It's the combination of a quiet mind, a relaxed body, and an alpha brain frequency that generates a truly magical visual resonance that gets results. This vibrational truth is the key to understanding and directing your cognitive creation.

- The next level of brain is *beta*, and the frequency vibrates at 15 cycles per second and higher. This is the level of conscious thought, analysis, study, and investigation. The frequency increases as thoughts become more worrisome, anxious, or agitated. If you tend to live in patterns of overanalysis, brooding, fear, or rage, your brain frequency moves into high beta. It's important to know that once you move into beta frequency, it becomes impossible to create *specific* results—whether for good or for bad.

Let's take a look at the energetic reasons and the deeper meanings of this phenomenon. The alpha brain frequency aligns with the peaceful yet very powerful creative flow of Universal vibration, where synchronicity, inspiration, and magical events are a part of the natural resonance of manifestation. But when brain frequency moves up into beta level, it creates a more analytical energy, one that disconnects your own vibration from that universal flow. In fact, as beta levels go higher into worry and anxiety mode, it splinters your life-force vibration, making it impossible to funnel valuable energy into single-minded *specific-outcome* intentions.

This brings clarity to two important yet misinformed assumptions that people have been making for years. Let's look at each one in turn.

- *If I worry about something often enough, my worry will make that event happen.* I can say from firsthand experience that this simply isn't the case. For over 20 years, I worked in a private psychological practice where most of my clients suffered from severe anxiety and phobias. Most of these people worried daily about major catastrophes and fatal or debilitating events. Of all my clients who engaged in these ongoing panic-stricken patterns, only one person ended up experiencing the thing she was afraid of—just one out of thousands of private and group clients!

  Why is this the case? The agitated vibration of beta level brain frequency—especially in a highly worried state—makes it impossible to create the specific result, no matter how much those results are focused on or how often those thoughts are repeated.

- *If I just think about what I want often enough, it will in time come true.* Here again, we are locked into the undeniable influence of brain frequency. It's fine to think about or visualize your desired end results when you're relaxed and in the alpha level of brain frequency. However, if you obsess about that outcome and think about it every day—if your thoughts are filled with need or desperation—you will very quickly move your brain frequency up into the agitation of a high beta level. In that state, your energy is utterly incapable of creating the specific outcome you're desiring and obsessing about. Not only that, your obsession and need stimulate the negative energies of the Law of Paradoxical Intent, sabotaging your intentions and making it doubly difficult to achieve your goal.

Unfortunately, the emotional reality of cognitive creativity remains true. Even if you can't create *specific* outcomes at beta level, you certainly can—and will—create an agitated or even miserable life-force energy when you're in a highly repeated negative focus.

The bottom line of cognitive creation comes down to the nature of the thoughts you engage in and the resulting emotions those thoughts create. If you're simply engaged in logical processing about the tasks of your daily life, there's not likely to be a lot of emotional content, so the energetic projection would be neutral. But if you're worried, stressed, or brooding about something, your life-force projection will attract fragmented responses from the Universe. On the other side of that coin, if your thoughts are peaceful and trusting, your resonance vibrates with open receptivity to the loving flow of Universal abundance. Ultimately, it's all about brain frequency, which is based on the type of thoughts you most consistently think.

The truth of your cognitive creation is that in order to create something valuable, you must relax into an alpha level. In order to activate alpha brain frequency, you must quiet your mind and think peaceful, trusting, positive thoughts. This reveals the key to your creativity, which is based in your frequency—your brain frequency!

The Thought's the Thing

It's clear that the first way you project your energy out into the world is through your cognitive power. Your thoughts rarely stop, so they're continually churning out vibrational messages in your energetic field. And since they're also the source of your emotional energy, they're doubly important in your pursuit of success.

Thoughts of confidence bring feelings of trust and hope, while those of inadequacy bring feelings of dread or despair. Which of these emotional vibrations is more likely to attract wonderful outcomes to you? Clearly the positive results you're looking for will come much more readily from a preponderance of peaceful emotions and positive thoughts. And even if that beneficial approach may seem foreign to you right now, it's never too late to achieve!

"Positive thinking" has become a cliché. But if you're like most people, your thought process may seem rather random and spontaneous; something that you passively experience rather than consciously direct. Maybe you've never been taught to think positively, or maybe the direction your mind takes depends on the situation you're in or the people you're with. One thing's for sure: if you want to increase the quality of your life, the best place to start is taking control of your thoughts!

Again, do not berate yourself for your negative thinking; just choose to notice it and change it as often as possible. Of course, it is natural to have fleeting worries and fear, but at its base, pervasive negativity is toxic to the energy of achievement. Fear of failure creates the energy of a self-fulfilling prophecy: thoughts of self-criticism draw despair and defeat. These repeating negative loops are your greatest obstacles to genuine present happiness, destroying optimism and hopeful expectation, increasing two miserable vibrations that attract equally miserable results. Life moves in the direction of your dominant thought, and your energy is the reason why.

Easy Alpha Affirmations

The alpha level of brain frequency is the most effective way to create a positive reality, so doing affirmations at this level is a powerful way to project an irresistible life-force resonance. To engage in this activity, you can relax and listen to the audio "Affirmations for Self-Empowerment" in the bonus download at any time. But there's also an even easier and quicker way to achieve this shift in consciousness.

Most people don't realize this, but there is a physical movement that immediately switches your brain frequency into alpha level. All you have to do is raise your closed eyes as if you're looking upward yet keep your head facing forward. (This is part of the physical position I teach in my book *Your Quantum Breakthrough Code*. That book teaches an easy process to break addictions and other unhealthy thought and behavior patterns.) I recommend trying that process if something you're dealing with just won't let go, but in the meantime—and any time—you can use the following, very short, very simple alpha affirmation technique. All that's required is a few deep breaths, a smile, and a mini-affirmation while raising your closed eyes to the ceiling.

These are the steps:

1. Close your eyes and take a deep breath.
2. On the exhale, raise your eyes and smile.
3. Say just one mini-affirmation.
4. Take another deep breath, relax your eyes, continue smiling, and let go with the exhale.

Your mini-affirmation could be a very simple phrase like:

- Feeling peaceful.
- Feeling grateful.
- Calm and confident.

- Love this day.
- Strong and empowered.
- Feeling happy.

. . . or any short affirmative phrase you desire.

5. After saying your short affirmation, continue to smile and sense a gentle feeling come up. Take another deep breath, relax your eyes, and notice your whole body relaxing.

6. Let yourself spend a moment feeling a sense of peace and tranquility growing within and all around you.

I came up with this process recently when I unexpectedly lost a very dear friend who was a profoundly important and inestimably loving part of my life. For weeks I walked around as if I were in a fog. I felt like an empty vessel without joy, purpose, or any sense of power. It was truly painful.

After a few weeks of this, I asked for inspiration and was given the idea for this process, and it worked immediately! While it didn't cause me to feel jubilant and sing with joy, it did make me feel more like myself again, more peaceful, more empowered, and more purposeful than I had felt since my friend got sick.

Since that time, everyone who's learned this easy process has told me they noticed a shift in energy upon their first try—and every subsequent one as well. So, breathe, smile, close and raise your eyes, and say a simple two- or three-word affirmation. It's the easiest and quickest shift you can make to turn your life-force energy around and bring happy results!

SUCCESS STORY: Shifting Cognitive and Energetic Resonance

I once had a client named David who lived his life with a pervading sense of fear. He was constantly worried about what other people thought, judging himself and assuming that others would do the same. Although he could function well enough to keep his job, his fears always prevented him from moving forward. He was smart and creative, and he often had good ideas but never had the confidence to present them. After 20 years at the same job, he found that he could make enough money to get by—but unless he made changes, he'd never earn any more.

David knew that he had to do something. Fear was his prevailing emotion, and worries of judgment and rejection were his primary thoughts. His emotional/cognitive energy was constantly churning out signals of gloom and doom, causing him to be miserable and attract more of the same. But although he'd been living like this for quite some time, he was determined not to stay stuck in this pattern.

He made a list of all the things he worried about and a corresponding list of positive options that would change his emotions as well as his energy. He persistently worked on letting go of the old worries, and he consciously chose to replace them with peaceful, trusting, and confident conclusions instead. He also added deep breathing and relaxation to physically support his mental changes. The bonus download includes "Relaxation and Memory Release," a variation of the deep muscle relaxation David used, but any form of meditation will also help you achieve alpha level brain frequency.

Bit by bit, David became less fearful and much more relaxed. He began to feel positive emotions he hadn't felt in years, emotions such as peace, hope, and even happiness—something he'd become accustomed to living without. The process of shifting his thoughts in order to calm his feelings took some time, but eventually he could sense his personal energy changing, too. He became confident, more productive, and willing to take greater risks—and his employer began to take notice.

Within 18 months of learning about the dynamics of energy creation, David got the first of several promotions. A few years later, I received pictures and a note from him. His company letterhead indicated that he was now a vice president, and the pictures that he sent were of his newly acquired vacation home on Hilton Head Island, South Carolina.

In less than four years, he'd totally reversed decades of energy stagnation. And because of the work he was willing to do to shift the resonance of his own thoughts and emotions, he was finally able to achieve the lifestyle and happiness that he had deeply desired for so long.

EMOTIONAL ENERGY:
Your Feelings Broadcast

Your emotional resonance is by far your most powerful energetic expression. Your daily feelings broadcast loud and clear signals about who you are and what you expect from the world. If you're chronically fearful, for example, you project that and will likely attract more situations that will cause you to be afraid. If anger is predominant, you're sending out signals expecting hostility, and you're likely to attract that energy back.

But if you choose a lighter, happier attitude, you broadcast the message that you expect the world to be a joyous place, and both your energy and your expectation will bring more of that to you. Confident and peaceful feelings about yourself will send out a very magnetic vibration, attracting people and experiences that bring an even deeper sense of serenity to your life. This is your *resonant reality*; what you send out *about yourself* will most certainly come back to you.

Your predominant feelings energize your destiny creation by virtue of their powerful presence in your heart and mind. *For good or bad, the more emotionally charged an experience or issue is, the more power it generates.* For this reason, a shift to more positive sentiments is a basic requirement of the Law of Magnetism. It's an energetic truth that the quality of your present emotional life will determine the caliber of your life experiences. In this the law is strict: the Universe will return your own joy, love, and happiness to you; it will return your fear, anger, and unhappiness as well. But don't give up—even if negativity has been your most frequent experience. No matter what you've been through or how long you've been stuck in difficult emotions, you still have the power to shift to higher, more attractive feeling energy. In fact, you have the power to do that now.

But where do emotions come from? What's the source of this powerful energy that you engage in all the time? Underneath every single emotional experience is a stimulating source. Whether the feeling is anger or love, misery or joy, depression or excitement, boredom or bliss, every blossom or thorn of sentiment has one originating seed—and that seed is thought.

TEE FOR YOU

Whatever your situation in life, you don't have to stay stuck in the old patterns any longer. It's time to understand your own Thought/Emotion/Energy connection, which I call your TEE Equation. The TEE Equation represents how the first level of your energy is created, and this is the formula:

Thoughts + Emotions = Energy

The power of your most dominant thoughts plus the force of your most frequent and intense emotions equals the resonance of your personal energy field. This is the pulsating vibration that broadcasts your individual signal and determines what you're likely to attract to your life.

If you're dissatisfied with what you've drawn in—either personally or professionally—it's time to work on changing your energy by shifting your present thoughts and emotions. You have the power to do this. In fact, you *have* to make it a priority. You simply can't keep adding negative thoughts to negative emotions and expect to generate positive results.

JOURNAL FOR SUCCESS

In order to get a handle on this aspect of your destiny creation, keep a record of your thought patterns in your journal. (If your journal is too big to carry all the time, just keep a little notebook with you or use a notes app on your phone.) As you jot down your most commonly experienced ideas, you'll find that you tend to think about the same issues over and over, repeating the same old conclusions about them.

After you've written down your negative thoughts, describe the emotions being created. If you find that negativity is the predominant energy of your thoughts and feelings, then create the intention to at least let them go. When you catch yourself thinking something negative, simply affirm: *I can let this go. I don't have to think this way any longer. I choose to release worry and judgment and engage in trust instead.*

When you feel an unpleasant emotion taking over, stop for a moment to investigate what you were thinking about just before having that feeling. Then consciously choose to release the thoughts. You can also reduce the power of the feeling by physically moving, doing some deep breathing, shaking out your muscles, and just affirming: *Release. Release. Release.*

Over time, you can replace those negative thoughts with more optimistic, self-honoring conclusions, but at the very least choose to let them go now. In Chapter 8, you'll learn about the seven major toxic thought forms, which will give you a better grip on this shift. But for now, let yourself start to be aware of the patterns and choose to let go.

It's extremely important to become aware of the energetic frequencies that you send out each day. Instead of responding unconsciously, broadcasting cognitive and emotional energy that you don't want representing you in the energetic realm, you must become very aware of your ongoing options in thoughts and feelings. It may seem difficult at first, but it's crucial when you want to project the energy of success. It's very empowering to know that you yourself can send out new waves of information that define you to the world—and by becoming conscious of them, you can determine what you get back. These energetic vibrations are within your power to alter in any given moment. By transforming just one predominant negative thought, you'll make a major shift in your life-force energy. As you continue to make these shifts within, everything around you will begin to change, including your present peace, trust, and happiness. Then, as a result, the future outcomes of your desires won't be far behind.

Affirmations for Dynamic Magnetism

✦ I determine what I think. I energize my life with positive thoughts and peaceful emotions at every opportunity. It is my ever-present choice.

✦ I am now choosing a peaceful, self-accepting attitude about myself and my life. My optimism about my future grows every day. I deserve to be happy.

✦ I am becoming more and more conscious of the kind of energy that I create each day. I notice any opportunities to let go of old patterns, and I choose more positive approaches in all that I think and do.

✦ Through my own energy, I have the power to make my life better in every way. I know that as I choose to create healthier, happier thoughts and emotions, I will attract even more joyful people and results to me.

✦ I choose to believe that I have all the talent and resources I need to magnetize all that I desire. I deserve the best and I open my heart and my life to receiving it!

✦ ✦ ✦

Chapter 3

The Law of Pure Desire

The Third Universal Law

Desire is possibility seeking expression.

— RALPH WALDO EMERSON

The next two laws are driven by your intentions or motivations. Underneath every drive and every desire is the real reason for your pursuit. Although you may not even be aware of what it is, this will either accelerate or block your desired outcome by virtue of its energetic nature.

In order for you to align yourself with the powerful forces of the third Universal Law, your intention must be pure—not manipulative, fear-based, or desperate. In other words, your motivations must be genuine, healthy, and honoring to yourself and others. This law and the next one are all about *why* you're going after your goals in life. If you've never thought about it before, now is the time to consider why you do the things you do.

The **Law of Pure Desire** says that when you're driven by a pure intention—one that's free of fear, doubt, and desperation—you can rely on some sort of beneficial outcome. Freedom from fear completely shifts the energy of your motivation from a negative, resistant vibration to a positive, receptive one. When you move from the energies of longing and desperation to those of hope and expectation, you activate two vital components of this law.

Motivations that are founded in fear or filled with doubt and urgency can only create a dark energy around your desire. Such emotions originate in neediness, sending out waves of repulsive energy. Fear's negative signal is clear, and the message is: *I'm incapable. I'm undeserving. I'm lost.* This kind of resonance then attracts situations and people that bring painful evidence that your negative conclusions are true.

Emotions of fear and doubt could eclipse all the positive energy boosters that you could project, sabotaging the important components required by the third Universal Law. The engine of pure desire is ignited by an honest and honoring intention, but it's fueled by the positive energies of hope, excitement, enthusiasm, and belief. Your intention must be infused with these feelings if it's going to move freely forward in the Universe.

Some people say that if you use the word *hope*, you're reminding yourself that you don't already have that which you long for. Well, guess what—your subconscious mind knows the truth and can't be tricked, and your intention to give up hope is one of the most self-sabotaging energies you can ever engage in.

Your life requires hope for energetic sustenance and purpose. It empowers you. It lifts the soul and opens the heart, and it's the source of your enthusiasm and excitement. Without hope, you can't get excited about your life—or keep your passion for your goal high enough to keep going when faced with obstacles.

Excitement and enthusiasm are like amplifiers on a sound system, energizing the process of your desire. But you won't maintain these powerful emotions if you don't have genuine hope and the true belief that your dream can and should become a reality for you. In addition, the loss of hope can be one of the biggest causes of depression and despair, two dark energies that nothing bright or beautiful can get through.

That's what happened to my client Maria, who longed to find a partner who would truly love her. She had dated a number of men in her 20s and 30s, but each relationship eventually fell apart. Now she was facing midlife alone and in the depths of depression.

When Maria's hopes for real love were lost, she constructed the belief that she could never find someone who truly cared for her. Her life started swirling in the emotions of resignation and futility. I explained how she had trapped herself in a web of conflicting intentions, and we immediately started working on changing that negative energy.

CALMING CONFLICTING INTENTIONS

It's not uncommon for people to have two very different feelings about their desires. On the one hand, you may tell yourself that you want to be successful—that's the first driving intention. On the other hand, a defeating experience or an old limiting belief may lead you to assume that it isn't possible—and that also becomes an energetic intention.

In this case, your desires are both desperate and disparate (or opposite), and these intentions fight each other in the energetic realm. Intellectually, you're expressing: *I want; I desire.* Yet your emotional energy is screaming out: *It's hopeless! It can't happen!* Which beliefs will the Universe serve?

Energetically, your negative emotions tend to be more highly charged, and therefore, they're much more compelling in the process of attraction. The more despondent and desperate you become, the more the Universe will have to honor your belief in the hopelessness of it all.

This is precisely what happened to Maria. She had believed in herself and had hope about the future. But each romantic loss caused those feelings to change. She had a sense of being defeated that was so negatively emotionally charged, it became her new intention.

In truth, Maria was far from beaten. It took work, but we were able to uncover her original belief in herself—and in her deserving. We also created new hope by affirming the limitless possibilities still available in the Universe. Although the desired outcome seemed very remote at first, Maria mustered up the courage and willingness to do whatever it took to create the happy, optimistic energy she needed. With patience and perseverance, she was able to break through. She used the Attraction Intention and other techniques in this book, and she finally found the truly loving, life-long partner she had been longing for.

Don't define yourself by your history or even by your present circumstances. You are capable of creating great things! If you find yourself feeling defeated, you must rekindle your hope and renew your beliefs. Choose positive expectations and confidence in yourself, or else you, too, will get caught in the web of conflicting intentions, trapped in an inertia of energy and activity that can lead to empty or even negative results. The old saying is not just a cliché, it's an energetic truth: whether you think you can or think you can't, you're right.

FROM DESIRING TO DESERVING

It's not enough to desire something; it's also necessary to know that you *deserve* it. This is the next important component of the Law of Pure Desire. For your wishes to be pure, you must genuinely believe that you are worthy of what you want.

Your sense of deserving is usually something that you're taught when you're very young. It's given to you in how you're treated (or mistreated), in judgment or in praise. It's fundamentally tied to the amount of approval and affection that you received when you learned who you are. Even now, you're likely to be holding on to the conclusions that you made long ago about what you deserve and why—and those beliefs are major influences on your present process of attraction. To help release any misinformation from parental influences, try the meditation audio "Rescripting Beliefs for Truth and Self-Empowerment" included with your bonus download.

If you were taught in any way that you don't deserve the happy experiences of life, including love, success, wealth, and approval, then you were wildly misinformed. You may still be living according to the lies and distortions of the fearful people who influenced you, but as a thinking adult, you have the ability— even the responsibility—to change that now. In fact, the journal investigation around this issue can be a pivotal price in changing the very trajectory of your life.

JOURNAL FOR SUCCESS

To better understand the real source of your feelings of worthiness and deserving, answer the following questions in your journal:

- In what ways have you been told—by your parents or others—that you do or do not deserve?

- Do you believe that you don't measure up in some way, that there's something in you that's lacking? If so, what is it?

- Do you feel that you have to *do* something, *prove* something, or in some way *be* something different in order to be worthy? If so, what?

What do your answers reveal about you? If they say that you're undeserving in any way, you need to know that they do not demonstrate your truth. In fact, your false sense of unworthiness is completely based on the skewed psychology of someone else's fear, self-loathing, or need for power. And whether that "someone else" was a parent, teacher, social influence, or anybody else, you do not have to embrace their false version of your truth any longer.

YOUR DIVINE LEGACY

Your real deserving isn't based on what you've been told by your parents or anyone else. Your worthiness isn't determined by how much money you make, your college degree, how old you are, or what you weigh. Instead, its real origins go back to your Divine legacy.

> Your life pre-existed the lies of your present history. Your value, power, and worthiness resonate from your true original source. They come from your Divine heritage, the unconditionally loving energy of your eternal parent. With this as your source, your value never varies and never falters; there's no condition to fulfill, nothing you have to do. As a child of God, you've always been—and always will be—truly deserving of all the wonderful things that the abundant Universe has to offer.

I once counseled a client who was having trouble at work. She was overloaded with responsibilities and didn't get the acknowledgment or the remuneration that she felt she deserved. I suggested that she saturate herself with a few affirmations repeated many times each day, including: *I deserve my own respect and the respect of others; I deserve to be happy; I deserve to be treated well.* She wasn't desperate about it but merely repeated them peacefully. And as she did, she would breathe deeply and open her heart to the truth of her soul's worthiness.

She called me a few weeks later, elated about how much better she felt. In fact, she felt so much better about herself, she was able to let go of her urgent needs around work. In time, she noticed that people were also treating her differently. In a very peaceful and organic way, she eventually did get her good evaluation at work, her letter of commendation, and a nice raise! All the acknowledgment she longed for came when *she* finally gave heartfelt acknowledgment to herself.

JOURNAL FOR SUCCESS

It's now time to redefine yourself—and your worthiness—according to the fundamental truth of who you really are: an eternally beloved child of God.

Write some releasing statements in your journal to counter the toxic assumptions you uncovered by answering the earlier questions, and add affirmations about deserving unconditionally. Repeatedly let go of any old conditions or distortions that don't support this new understanding. These limitations are the false prisons that keep you from your accomplishments.

When you free yourself from that prison, you'll be free to let go of even more—finally creating a liberty of heart and mind that allows you to receive all that you desire.

THE ART OF SURRENDER:
When You Want It, Let It Go

It may sound like a cliché, but no amount of need or desperation will help you hold on to anything. It only creates severe energetic restrictions that you'll have to eventually break through. Ridding yourself of such needy beliefs and conditional worthiness are the rudimentary steps in achieving the greatest liberation of all: freedom from attachment, the final component of the Law of Pure Desire, which is accomplished through the art of surrendering.

By doing so, you're giving up neither the goal nor the desire. Instead, you're surrendering your *attachment*—your desperate need to make it happen. It's impossible to have a pure desire when you're feeling desperate because you're motivated out of fear and urgency rather than trust. But loosening your grip is the ultimate engagement in trust, both in the future and in yourself. It acknowledges your ability to create happiness for yourself in the present no matter what may happen in the future. The real necessity of this deeply peaceful approach becomes alarmingly clear when you investigate the next law, which shows that desperation and urgency can significantly sabotage your intention to achieve.

Affirmations for Pure Desire

+ I am a worthy and valuable person, always deserving of abundant wealth, fulfillment, and real happiness.

+ I pursue my goals to enhance an already happy life, one that I choose to make more peaceful and joyous every day.

+ I know that the Universe is abundant and what I desire is available to me. I am excited about the bright new future that I created for myself even now.

+ I know that I deserve true happiness and wonderful experiences. I open my heart and my life to a deeper sense of my own deserving, and I am ready to receive.

+ Every time I look in the mirror, I affirm and acknowledge my power, my value, and my worthiness. I live in the truth of my eternal soul, and I expect the best.

✦ ✦ ✦

Chapter 4

The Law of Paradoxical Intent

The Fourth Universal Law of Success

The quantum field is just another label for the field of pure consciousness or pure potentiality. And this quantum field is influenced by intention and desire.

— DEEPAK CHOPRA

While surrendering is just one of the components of the Law of Pure Desire, it's the energetic axis around which the fourth Universal Law revolves. This principle reveals exactly what happens when we allow urgency and need to become our major motivations. The desire for success is a natural and healthy endeavor, but it's our emotions around *why* we want it that determine its energetic nature.

Trust is an easy, fluid vibration that brings results; desperation is a broken, agitated vibration that stops them cold. When it comes to our pursuit of success, where does our fear and urgency come from? It originates in our dissatisfaction with what we have and who we are. In fact, many of our desires are driven by dissatisfaction, making us obsess about what we feel we need. We're willing to go into debt, lose time with our families, and work unending hours just to achieve that hoped-for outcome.

But what happens while we're desperately waiting to get what we want? We're projecting a terribly unattractive energy because we not only feel dissatisfied but also deprived. We're constantly obsessed with what we lack, and our constant focus on what we don't have actually *increases* what we *don't* have!

The process goes on and on, locking us in abrasive energy and negative vibrations of emotion. In this state, your personal energy field often vibrates with palpable agitation, longing, and despair. You may be sending out such an unsettled and unhappy life force that the Universe can't possibly respond with anything positive in return. This is the unyielding truth of the fourth Universal Law: *desperation is bound to push away the very thing that you long to achieve!*

> The **Law of Paradoxical Intent** reflects the **Law of Magnetism** in reminding you that the Universe returns your own emotional energy. If you're desperate to make something happen, that agitated vibration will actually push it away, blocking the very people and situations that might bring your desired outcome. So you either attract nothing at all—or you attract an outcome that is equally agitating. Your desperation, therefore, creates the paradox—or the opposite—of your original intent, leading you in difficult directions instead of success.

The Universe wants you to achieve all that you desire, and when you align yourself with the forces and laws of success, it will do everything in its power to help you on your way—but desperation and urgency are deal-breakers. This isn't because the Universe wants to prolong your yearning. In fact, just the opposite is true: it wants you to enjoy your life and engage in a different, higher vibration *now*—and stop waiting for vague potential happiness to come in a distant future. The fact is, the most magnetic energy happens when you let go of urgency and engage in trust, when you rid yourself of despair and choose peace in the present instead.

You simply can't be happy when you're living in chronic dissatisfaction. When you're obsessed with what you *don't* have, you draw even more lack; you show the Universe that you're willing to forego present contentment by setting up a list of goals that you must achieve in order to be happy in the future.

In fact, until you have those things, you feel a nagging sense of *un*happiness. You feel as though something's missing, and you can't relax until you fill that void. Instead of enjoying your life and valuing what you are and have in the present, you spend your time longing for something else and constantly striving to get it.

This is a very serious mistake where the laws of energy and consciousness are concerned. *When you give away today's happiness to embrace misery about tomorrow's uncertainty, you shut down your willingness to receive. You shift from a mentality of appreciation to a consciousness of lack and need—and when you make that choice, you lose your power to be happy now and to succeed in the future.*

This is no light matter. What happens when you filter everything you have through wanting something else? You project a very unattractive energy of misery. Your need for something else to make you happy will always cause you to perceive your present situation as just not good enough. The core of your life-force energy vibrates with messages of "not enough," filled with feelings of despair, grief, and longing, which are highly charged emotions that attract very difficult results. This abrasive energy sabotages your success. It's an irresistible force, and there's no way to get around the power of this law. If you pump out a broadcast of despair, your efforts will draw back desperate situations and deeper feelings of hopelessness.

The inescapable truth is that *all* your feelings are charged with positive or negative vibrations. The uplifting ones create flow and beneficial results, while dissatisfaction creates blockage and problematic results. But you can change your emotions (and your resonance) by switching what you think about and what you focus on as your priority. You must let go of urgency and engage in thoughts of trust in order to open the doors of magnetic attraction. Shift your concentration from what you lack to all that you have to appreciate in order to create a consciousness of success.

Obsessing about what's missing in your life causes you to channel your energy into missing more, and if you're always complaining about what you don't have, it will only create more to whine about. You need to put your passion into noticing your present positives. This will help you experience your desired feelings *right now,* allowing you to magnetize more of those sensations in the future. This is called vibrational entrainment, and it's a must for being in harmony with this law. Think about the appreciation that you'll have at the fruition of your goals, and choose to feel that gratitude for what you already have in your life right now.

GETTING PAST THE PARADOX:
Understanding Constructs

Many people find letting go of urgency to be very difficult because they've attached so many emotional experiences to the hoped-for outcomes of their desires. They worry whether they could handle it if their dreams never come true; they fear that their desires are out of reach, and they'll never be able to accept themselves or their lives if that happens. But when you're engaging in these energies of paradoxical intent, the underlying predominant thought about your goal is: *I can't be happy without this.* And with that as your central belief, the inability to be happy becomes your reality.

This is a function of our mental *constructs.* We create a construct when we connect a state of mind to an external event. Our basic constructs revolve around our happiness, value, self-acceptance, or security—and to these and other emotional states, we often unknowingly attach the achievement of very specific goals. We then become *driven* to attain those goals in order to ensure that desired state of being.

Constructs always read according to the format, "If A, then B." Here are some of the most common constructs that people engage in:

- "I need to be married in order to be happy."
- "People would accept me more if I had more money, a better house, etc."
- "I can accept myself only if I lose weight."
- "If I get a promotion or a better job then my life will be secure."

You can see the toxic connections that these conclusions present. They lay a foundation of striving and desperation that can destroy our present potential for peace and joy. As a result, such driving assumptions, even if they're unconscious, go on to destroy our desires. When we believe we'll never be happy without our desired end result, the belief itself is so very disturbing that it's already creating the very misery we're trying to avoid!

Constructing a New Approach

We must reverse these negative constructs and replace them with more positive affirmations and intentions, such as:

- "I can find many things to be happy about right now."
- "I am learning to accept myself just as I am."
- "I deserve to love and appreciate myself at any age and any weight, and I choose to do that now."
- "I create my own security; I am strong and resourceful."

Just by reading these statements, you can feel how these positive constructs create a more receptive and successful approach.

I had to learn the hard way about toxic emotional attachments and the power of positivity when I was looking for a publisher for my first book, *Secrets of Attraction*. I had been teaching the principles of quantum physics and romantic attraction to clients seeking relationships for many years with amazing results. Eventually, I started teaching the ideas in seminars, and everywhere I went, people asked me where they could get a book on the subject. There was nothing at that time that applied the natural laws to romantic relationships, so I decided to write about it myself. I self-published a small book that I gave to my clients and sold at my seminars, but people started buying copies for their friends and asking if it was available anywhere else in the country. When the demand kept increasing, I decided to look into traditional publishing.

That decision spawned a great deal of emotion within me, rekindling a deeply held desire about becoming a writer, a longing that I had forged when I was very young. I deeply believed in the information, and I rewrote and edited the small volume that I'd self-published, adding an outline for several more chapters to be put in the book proposal. I became very excited about getting my book published, but I was also generating an undercurrent of anxiety and urgency about making it happen.

I actually had no trouble getting agents—but they certainly had trouble finding publishers. My first agent was very enthusiastic, certain that she'd get a sale right away. She sent it to the "big" publishers in New York City, and they all had pretty much the same reaction. It was dismissed as just another book about love, rejected because "there are already too many relationship books out there." Yet I knew that despite the countless books on love, not one of them had addressed the quantum physics of attraction!

Almost every week I got a new rejection, and I found myself going deeper and deeper into despair. After being turned down about a dozen times, my first agent said that she had nowhere else to go, so I got another one, who tried another half dozen publishers—with exactly the same results. In time, she gave up, too.

At first, this sent me into a spiraling depression. My childhood dream of being published seemed to be on the skids. I wallowed in depression and self-pity for a while, but I finally realized that I was engaging in the energies of paradoxical intent. In spite of my hope, I'd unknowingly embraced the belief that I couldn't be happy if I didn't make this happen, and I couldn't call myself an author without a publisher. I had created a construct that went right down to my self-definition! It was so extreme, I knew I had to do something about this!

Every day, I meditated on releasing my paradoxical intentions. I had to let go of my desperate need, but every time I affirmed that it would be okay if I didn't get published, I started to cry. I realized that I was grieving for the potential loss of my dream, but I was determined to get back to being happy in the present. I meditated each day for several weeks, allowing myself to mourn, continuing to release the need and to define myself as complete just as I was.

In time, I was able to *genuinely* surrender. I came to the conclusion that I'd continue to submit my book to publishers myself. In the end, if I were meant to self-publish and sell them myself at my seminars, then I'd do that joyfully. I'd pursue my dream and see the value in that experience alone, all the while living with satisfaction! I shed no more tears because I had truly let go.

The interesting thing about the Law of Paradoxical Intent is that truly and finally letting go of the desperation is what brings the results—and my case was no exception. Within a few months of surrendering, I met someone who suggested that I send my book to Louise Hay herself, and she gave me her address. (Now you may ask, "What are the chances of meeting such a connection?" But when you truly move to peaceful surrender, the world opens up for you and the chances become very high indeed.)

The process of that submission took several months, but since I'd let go of the urgency, I didn't have the same anxiety as before. In fact, I was so relaxed that I even forgot I'd sent it in. A few months later, though, I got a letter from Louise welcoming me to the Hay House family. My book had been accepted—and I was ecstatic!

My dream of being published had come true, but that was only the beginning. I now realize that *this* was the company I was meant to be with, the one I resonated with the most. As depressed as I was over all those early rejections, I now understand that they were protection from the Universe. I have been blessed with the loving family and genuine support I've found at Hay House. I get to work with the most wonderful people in the business, those who are intent on bringing messages of hope, purpose, and peace to the world!

In addition, my books are published in 32 languages worldwide. I've received countless letters and e-mails from people based in dozens of countries who wanted to tell me how these principles have changed their lives. Those messages mean more to me than I could ever express; they're the manifestation of a profound desire that I had since I was young. But I had to choose to let it go, and I firmly believe it was that choice that shifted everything for me!

That process of submissions and rejections took nearly two years, and I was miserable until I finally released it and learned how to be content in the present and trust in the future. Now I know what a blessing those rejections really were. Sometimes the Universe doesn't give us exactly what we want when we want it because there's something better down the road. It may be just a happier outcome, or it may be more helpful for our personal growth or for our process in learning how to embrace our present life with peace—even while working on our future goals.

In my case, all these reasons were true. Not being chosen in that first year gave me the opportunity to deal with my own issues of urgency and control. I had to face my own paradoxical intent head-on, and I had to learn to live in trust and self-established happiness. It was consistently choosing present joy that brought the results I wanted—not the other way around!

The **Law of Paradoxical Intent** points out the underlying paradox of personal achievement: you can get what you want by knowing that you don't need it to be happy! It forces you to shift your focus from a desperate intention to a peaceful pursuit. Never send out the energy that you're willing to wait to be happy—choose to be happy now and just be willing to wait for the results. Claim your happiness, your value, and your definition without needing a particular achievement before you can live with peace and joy. Desperation is absolute poison to the resonance of success, so be clear about your intentions and fearless in your motivations. Pursue your goals because you want them to enhance an already happy life, not because you'll be miserable without them.

True success is a state of mind, and it doesn't depend on any one event. Be careful not to construct unhealthy expectations that limit your happiness, your value, or your purpose. When you base such things on external events, you dismiss your present power and block your future goals. But when you engage in the unseen forces of trust and surrender, you'll find yourself on a present path of peace that will lead you to your dreams in magical and unexpected ways.

JOURNAL FOR SUCCESS

Use your journal to investigate the motivations behind your desires. Answer the following questions to find out what your emotional attachments are.

- What are your underlying *needs* that may be poisoning your process? If you obsess about your *need* for your goal, you're focusing both your energy and your consciousness on what's missing in your life.

- What are you making your goal really mean? Is your goal about defining yourself or making you happy— or are you willing to pursue it for its own sake? Make the choice to define yourself—and make *yourself* happy—all at the present time, all while working on your goal.

Be patient, and trust in the Divine timeline. You live in a Universal tapestry where the picture of your destiny comes together according to the threads of your energy, consciousness, and intention. Let yourself weave your future with positive energy; creative consciousness; and pure, unconflicted intentions about all things. Never obsess about only one option or solution, and let the desperation go. Many things can enhance your happiness, and when your central goal is to live with present optimism and trust, your other desires will be met.

Affirmations to Release Paradoxical Intent

- ✦ I know that the Universe is abundant; all that I desire is available to me.

- ✦ I release desperation. I relax and live with patience, persistence, and present peace of mind.

- ✦ I am letting go of lack and choosing to see all the value and blessings already in my life from now on.

- ✦ I release urgency and live with trust. I know that as I let go of despair, my peaceful energy attracts my desires to me.

- ✦ I am practicing the art of surrender. As I trust and let go, I open my heart and my life to wonderful and unexpected blessings that continue to come my way.

✦ ✦ ✦

Chapter 5

The Law of Harmony

The Fifth Universal Law of Success

*Keep your thoughts and feelings in harmony with your actions.
The surest way to realize your purpose is to eliminate any
conflict or dissonance that exists between what you're thinking
and feeling and how you're living your days.*

— DR. WAYNE W. DYER

In quantum physics, Bell's theorem of nonlocality demonstrates how the action of one particle here can affect the action of another particle separated by a great distance. This is no less true on a personal level because we live in a Universe where all things are connected. Nonstop energy vibrates within and around us all the time, connecting us with each other and with the constant flow of Universal energy and events. When we're in harmony, we move into an unending stream of synchronicity, bringing the blessings of the abundance that is active everywhere in the world. But when we're *out* of harmony, we take ourselves out of this bountiful current and get stuck on the shore, watching the blessings go by.

In this way, our harmonizing energy is the key to the magical phenomenon of synchronicity, which is that place where energies are so perfectly aligned that a world of fantastic possibilities opens up. It provides that blend of surprising coincidences that sparks real results. When this happens, we find just what we need in the right place at the perfect time. People show up who can help us along, information is given to us just when we need it, and inspiration seems to come out of the blue. Harmony is the confluence of currents where intention meets outcome in almost mystical ways. But it isn't magic, and it's certainly not random. Harmony is all about alignment—aligning energies, consciousness, and even intentions.

The **Law of Harmony** says that when you consciously choose to create balance and align yourself with the Universe, your intention and energy open the floodgates of Universal abundance, allowing you access to all the insight, power, and blessings that the world has to offer. In order to achieve this sublime state, your energies must be in tune with the vibrational sources within and around you. Align your energy with yourself, with others, and with the Universal flow.

SELF-HARMONY

All laws—and all solutions—start with the self. The key to harmonizing with yourself is establishing *balance* in your thoughts, emotions, and activities, which is achieved through your daily choices. The way you live your life—from your seemingly inconsequential thoughts to your most momentous decisions—will determine the amount of harmony in your personal energy.

Balanced thoughts aren't scattered or worried; they're calm, centered, and focused on the task at hand. This mental state starts with self-acceptance and moves on to equanimity with the vagaries of life. It may sound strange, but the kind of equilibrium that creates harmony comes from staying centered in two seemingly opposite intentions: *taking complete responsibility and letting go of control.*

Real self-responsibility means that you're 100 percent account-able for the mental and emotional quality of your life. You're in charge of your thoughts and emotions and your reactions to your life experiences. This may seem like a difficult task, so it's import-ant that you see it more as a process. We're always in the midst of living, creating, attracting, and responding. When we make more honoring choices in our thoughts and activities, then our frequency rises and our consciousness shifts. As time goes on, our higher choices become more spontaneous and encourage even greater harmony.

One of the best ways to jump-start this harmonic process is to intervene on your self-criticism. Balanced thoughts vibrate with love—even if the subject of those thoughts is yourself. Your own self-acceptance is the key to a higher consciousness and more attractive energy. No matter what you've been taught, you deserve your own high regard, so whether you engage in chronic self-doubt to utter self-loathing, this pattern has got to change. *You may be convinced it is true, but your self-criticism must stop! You can't be both in harmony and in hatred with yourself.*

And you can't be in harmony with others as long as your thoughts are telling you to fear or control them. Every being is an active part of the Divine flow of abundant opportunity, and you deserve to see yourself as connected and equal. This is absolutely crucial to both your consciousness and your energy changes. To live in balance with the world and tap into that magical river of abundance, you must start with harmony with yourself then extend that peaceful approach outward.

Peaceful Priorities

This law calls for you to seek a tranquil mind and heart because all blessings flow from this gentle vibration. This isn't just some simplistic "positive thinking" theory; it's absolute energetic truth. The more conflict that you experience in your thoughts and feel-ings, the more discord you'll attract in the outside world.

The most harmonic—and most successful—emotions are peace, love, acceptance, and an enthusiasm for your own life. If you can't learn to bring these core emotions into a prominent place in your daily existence, then you'll continually be striving for peace, battling your inner turmoil and the outer world as well. To avoid this, you need to get back in balance. Your cognitive center *must* be self-acceptance, and your emotional center *must* be self-love and self-care.

This kind of peaceful foundation makes it much easier to balance your personal activities, both in time and priorities. Life requires your attention in many areas, such as career and family, and you may find your activities drawing you out of balance, causing you to put most of your energies into one concern, often letting the others go.

But there's an inherent energetic problem in unbalanced priorities because you're sending out signals that say you're willing to give up something important. These are clear vibrational messages that can only attract people and situations that will require you to give up even more. And if you consistently put *yourself* last, you'll only find yourself coming in last where the fulfillment of your desires is concerned. There's no getting around it: t*the Universe always returns your self-priority to you.*

Harmony in action displays a healthy respect for yourself, your loved ones, your career, and your own personal goals. It's a balancing act to be sure, but it's well worth the effort. To create the highest harmonic resonance, you need to become truly conscious of how you spend your mental, physical, and emotional energy.

There are, of course, times when extremes can't be avoided, but you must do your best to bring your consciousness to them, always being mindful of weaving in some self-care. If your life is overburdened with endless tasks and you're running around from appointment to appointment, your vibration will be fragmented and agitated, attracting more difficulty and turmoil from the world. If your days are spent in the constant distraction of indulgent or addictive activities, this creates a thick, resistant energy in your harmonic resonance, blocking what could be fluid movement toward your dreams. The bottom line is, when you're out of balance, you're out of harmony, and your vibrations are out of tune with the Universal flow.

The harmonic choice is one of tranquility—that is, peace over conflict, trust over fear, and value over judgment—and you can make this decision at every opportunity. Even if things seem out of control in your life, release the tumult in your mind and let go of the fear in your heart. Allow yourself to choose peace, trust, and value instead. Close your eyes, let go, and breathe deeply. Choose trust and feel the shift in consciousness that even this single moment of conscious choice creates.

JOURNAL FOR SUCCESS

Use your journal to release your negative thoughts. If you're feeling depressed, write down what you're thinking, and then write a more positive assumption. If you're fearful, affirm that you're switching to trust; if you're angry, use your journal to write about it and get it out. This will help you consciously create a greater peace in your emotional state. Ventilate your raw energy, and then release the situation to the Universe. Bless it and *truly* let it go.

HARMONY WITH OTHERS

Harmonic resonance begins with the self, then vibrates outward to connect with every other living being. A beautiful vibrational symphony occurs when people are in harmony with each other. You're at the center of that song, and through it, you can create beautiful music in every part of your life. But in order to be a part of the glorious sound—and not just sitting in the audience—you must harmonically align your own energies with those of others.

To achieve real harmony, it's important to arrive at a place of equal acceptance for yourself and others, neither seeking their approval nor denying them yours. This is essential if you want to remove yourself from the destructive energies of conflict. You can't enlist help from the Universe if you're working against it, so your intention must be to seek unity instead of separation and to acknowledge similarities instead of differences. This isn't just a simplistic and idealistic worldview; it's a fundamental energetic necessity if you truly want to create the energy to succeed.

Your view of others can't be extricated from how you see yourself. This is a primary part of your personal reality and your consciousness. You can't consider the world to be an arena of constant competition without developing an unhappy present or a fear-based approach to the pursuit of your goals. As long as you see others as a potential threat to your happiness, you're destined to live in dread and act out of desperation and urgency—or you'll simply shut down.

When you know that you are equally powerful and the source of your solutions, no one can be a threat to you. Living in the higher energies of love and acceptance of self and others will attract people who support rather than threaten you. The fact is that in your refusal to accept others, you give your power to them. Your energy says, "You have the ability to make me angry or afraid; you have power over me and my emotions."

But when you make the choice to accept yourself and others, you regain your strength. You take control of your emotions and your energies, creating a higher, more peaceful consciousness, one that aligns with the flow of Universal intention. Your choice to accept others demonstrates that you're willing to work together to bring harmony to yourself, each other, and the world—so the more acceptance you have, the more influence you have in the energetic realm. Refusing to accept others not only reduces your power but also invites people and situations that will challenge you even more. It's important to know, however, that accepting others doesn't mean being passive or tolerating dishonoring treatment. In fact, engaging in that type of response only causes resentment, which turns into hatred and further separation.

Hatred sends out hostile jabs of jagged energy, a resonance that may succeed in hurting others but doesn't stop with them. Those barbs of negative vibration snatch up even more negativity from the Universe, gathering momentum and returning far greater hostility back to you. Even if you do it only for your own sake, you must let go of judgment and move past the fear. Honor yourself and others and choose love, patience, and tolerance instead.

Real harmony is achieved when you perceive others with a deeper understanding. Bring your consciousness to every situation to maintain your authentic power while weaving in a compassionate approach. As more and more people choose to see their shared humanity and connected consciousness, their empathy widens the harmonic flow. This creates a profoundly joyous energetic unification, a harmony of understanding that raises your own vibration—and that of everyone involved.

HARMONY WITH THE UNIVERSE

There's no limitation as to when or where your energies vibrate; there's no time or space within this Universe where your influence isn't felt. All that you do, say, and think moves outward from you in a frequency that has your name on it. In time, it will blend with other similar wavelengths, and those accumulated vibrations will then expand and come back.

Harmony with the Universe begins when you connect with the source of the Universe itself—that great Consciousness that created all reality. If you truly want to harmonize your energy with every positive vibration in the world, this is all you have to do: *connect with Divine Consciousness.* It's present all the time and closer than you think.

It's interesting how people want to dismiss or even resist this powerful force when it comes to applying it to their personal pursuits. Perhaps Divine Presence is a foreign concept, maybe it evokes fearful memories, or is too abstract or dogmatic. Whatever the reason, many individuals have a real resistance to calling upon this power, and as a result, they cut themselves off from the major source of their solutions. Whether you want to call this grand creative Consciousness God, Loving Source, Creative Force, or just Universe, it's up to you. All that matters is that you open up to your undeniable connection with it.

> You're a sacred soul, existing as a manifestation of Divine Intention. The Higher Intelligence of all creation vibrates within and around you at all times. The more you align your own energies with this all-powerful heartbeat, the more you move yourself into the flow of Universal blessings. The more you genuinely acknowledge this part of your identity—on both a conscious and energetic level—the more clarity you'll bring to all that you do. When you live in harmony with the loving intention of the Universe, you see clearly, intend purely, and act creatively.

Start to acknowledge this power within by affirming: *I am one with the Loving Source. I connect with the Divine Presence in all things; I acknowledge the Divine within myself and in all people. I open my heart and life to this truth and I attract endless blessings from this all-powerful, all-loving Source. I am grateful.*

MEDITATION: Your Sacred Identity

This process will help you harmonize your energies with the Universe. Do this as you go to sleep or take a few minutes out of your day to just relax and remind yourself of this most loving Force within your life. You can also listen to the meditation audio "Your Sacred Identity," included with your bonus download, as you're falling asleep. Just let yourself focus on the words, and if your mind wanders, gently bring it back to your intention to feel the Divine connection deep within your heart.

Gently visualize the sun's light and warmth flowing through you, making you feel relaxed and tranquil. Relax your body and your mind, and gently drop your consciousness into your heart center. You begin to notice a very powerful presence there that has a brilliant source of light all its own. This is the beacon of Divine Love bringing you a sense of calm security and filling your heart center with sublime peace. This place is the still point of eternal light, the seat of your soul, the connection where the all-loving spirit of the Divine embraces and enfolds you in unconditional, perfectly loving light.

Feel this light; breathe in this light; be this light. Allow yourself to experience the energy of peace and Divine Love and light filling you up. Like an eternal well, an unending fountain of illumination fills you with wisdom and joy. Every drop brings clarity and calm, and every vibration brings encouragement and love.

This is the blessed realization of Divine Presence, an ever-present gift from your perfect, eternal Source. There's never a time when this perfect light is not with you or when God's power and presence cannot be invoked. Allow yourself to sense the radiant energy vibrating in your own sacred heart; your heart connecting with Divine Heart, your love with Divine Love, your intention with Divine Intention. This is your sacred connection . . . willing, waiting, and available to you at all times, in all places, for all things. Open yourself to its wonderful energy; know that this loving Presence is with you every moment of every day.

Your choice to harmonize with yourself, others, and the loving energy of the Divine casts a magical spell on all the areas of your life. It's the center of synchronicity, the source of miraculous energy that turns conflict into peace and hardship into happiness. Return to this tranquility whenever you get the chance. Allow Divine brilliance to vibrate in every cell of your body and every part of your consciousness. Know that you are One.

Affirmations for Living In Harmony

✦ I always take responsibility for my thoughts, choices, and emotions. I know the emotional quality of my life is up to me.

✦ I choose to lead a balanced and happy life. I release concern and conflict and live in trust and honoring in everything I do.

✦ I accept myself and others as equal. I acknowledge the Divine light within us all.

✦ I am one with the Universe. I open myself to the flow of love and blessings that are coming my way more and more each day.

✦ Abundant wealth and happiness flow freely all around me. I peacefully receive all that I desire.

✦ ✦ ✦

Chapter 6

The Law of Right Action

The Sixth Universal Law of Success

We must be the change we wish to see in the world.

— MOHANDAS K. GANDHI

The Law of Magnetism and the Law of Right Action are closely connected. They both work on the exchange of energy, but there are subtle differences. Magnetism deals mostly with how you treat yourself, while Right Action includes not only that approach but also extends to the *treatment* of others and the world. This can be an interesting dilemma because many people mistakenly believe that they can't prioritize both themselves and others. They think that in order to treat yourself well, you have to be selfish—or to treat others well, you have to sacrifice yourself. But the Law of Right Action indicates that this doesn't have to be the case, and balance is the key.

Your energetic output accrues, and all of it—whether it's directed toward yourself or others—creates a kind of destiny bank account. The thoughts or actions you engage in, your interactions with others—whether good or bad—become a part of your investment. If you only buy in to negativity toward yourself or others, then that's what will pay out.

The **Law of Right Action** says that your energy is self-perpetuating in the world. Value, honor, and dignity will increase in your life to the same degree that you promote them within yourself and in the environment around you. On the other hand, if your own actions work to tear down the value, honor, or dignity of yourself or others, then in time that destruction will return to you. According to this principle, there's one core question that you must ask yourself about every choice: *Is this honoring to myself and others?*

This is the pivotal point of all your energetic options. Throughout your life, you're always making choices that will either enhance your sense of honor or deplete it. This is true in your daily decisions, your chronic self-talk, and your interactions with others. Your days are filled with unending options, and the choices that you make will be energetically responsible for directing your destiny either toward greater happiness or increasing disappointment.

The energy of honoring is one of the most magnetic and attractive frequencies that you can broadcast. When you choose it, you can feel it in your gut and emotions, but when you make a dishonoring choice, you can also sense that something's wrong. Even if things temporarily turn out well, it just doesn't ring true. Although no hard-and-fast rules define honoring action, you'll know it in your heart. Every time you think a thought, make a decision, speak a word, or take a course of action, you'll know inside whether you're projecting the kind of honoring energy that will bring value back to your life.

I once had a client named Casey who worked in quality control for a large chemical company. Not long after she accepted her position, she found that her supervisor had been changing data on the toxicity levels before they were sent to the boss. At first it seemed insignificant, but it still made Casey uncomfortable. She was hesitant to say anything because she feared confrontation and her supervisor had been critical, expressing unfounded dissatisfaction with Casey's work.

Eventually, however, Casey had to confront her supervisor, who told her not to make waves. It was only a few little changes, she said, and swore that it would never happen again. She persuaded Casey that it would be pointless to bring it up to the boss at that time.

Things settled down for a while, but several months later, Casey learned that her supervisor was once again fabricating information—and she again convinced Casey to keep her mouth shut, convincing her that was the only way to keep her job. Casey didn't want to stay with this company any longer, but she was hesitant to leave before she had another source of income. She continued working while looking for a new job, and that's when the depression set in.

Casey was miserable when she came to see me in therapy. She was thoroughly dissatisfied with her current job, was resentful about her supervisor's lack of respect and integrity, and couldn't seem to find the kind of job she wanted. The largest contributor to her depression was that she'd been willing to sacrifice her own integrity and self-respect because she had been acting out of fear. She dishonored herself, the boss, the clients, and the business by allowing the false information to continue. But she stayed and continued the deceit because she feared what would happen if she spoke up.

Once we discussed the Universal Laws and her own energy, Casey knew what she had to do. She went in and told her supervisor that things would have to change. It was very difficult, but she said that she needed more respect, and she knew that she deserved it. She also told her supervisor that the boss had to be told about the changed reports.

Casey's honoring paid off. The boss appreciated her courage and her honesty, and he even forgave her. In fact, the boss came up with an immediate solution: he made Casey a supervisor herself—with a promotion and salary to match—and he gave her the job that her old supervisor had.

In this case, the honoring choice was risky but clear. In many situations, the right decision is not so easy to find—and not so easy to do. It's important to remember that it never dishonors another to honor yourself. Some people may have become accustomed to having a sort of power over you, and unlike Casey's boss, they may not be so willing to accept your new decision to honor and prioritize yourself. They may try to shut you down or get upset or angry, yet your request to be honored does not dishonor them. It merely calls on them to choose the honoring path as well.

RIGHT ACTION FOR THE PLANET

Choosing the honoring path is not limited to what effects ourselves and others; it must extend to the world around us. We must make choices that support the environment and protect the planet, including the air we breathe and the water we drink. As individuals and as humankind we must take responsibility for the type of environmental legacy we are leaving for our descendants.

This comes down to the personal choices we make about whether to recycle and expands to community and government choices that support environment-based programs. Such decisions may not seem important in the bigger scheme of things, but when we understand the energetic cause and effect of each considered choice, we know that across the globe even the minor actions do add up. Each individual has the power to change the global direction, and together our accumulated intentions can shift the present reality as well as the future experiences for generations to come.

Whatever the issue, to make honoring choices you must listen to your heart and look for the choice that resonates with your own sense of personal dignity. Right Action may not always be the easiest thing to do, but it's always the very best energy for everyone involved. When in doubt, refer to the following guidelines.

Guidelines for Engaging in Right Action

- Always take responsibility for yourself, your decisions, your emotions, your energy, and your behaviors. Your integrity, your self-priority, and your right to express yourself are important parts of your energetic projection.

- Make choices that promote your mental, physical, and emotional health. In every situation, ask what feels honoring to you, then follow that path.

- Seek genuine empowerment from within, not manipulation or control from without.

- Respect yourself and don't be afraid to request that others do so also.

- Respect others. Release judgment and live with compassion, but always be willing to express your own needs.

- Be truthful without being cruel. Be encouraging and compassionate when the opportunity to genuinely support another comes up.

- Release prejudice and judgment based on differences in race, faith, or culture. Choose to see the sacred equality of each soul.

- Take the actions in your daily life that support the environment and the future of the planet.

- Muster up the courage to live with dignity and self-actualization—no blame, no excuses, just the determination to live according to your soul's intentions.

When you're engaged in right action, you know it. Value sings in your heart and broadcasts your own beautiful melody in echoes of attraction. It triggers harmony and brings Universal right action back to you; it's the path of a genuinely loving intention.

LOVING INTENTION

The primary intention behind right action is the creation of value and the expansion of love and peace. In fact, love is the energetic catalyst to all successful creative manifestation. When we align our own thoughts with this vibrating force, we connect our frequency with the higher consciousness that creates all things, and there's no greater power that we can enlist in the pursuit of our dreams.

The intention of love causes us to behave in ways that increase the value in our lives and the lives of others. When we talk about doing the "right" thing, we're making choices of reverence, value, and caring. In this way, we have the option to raise every vibration in every interaction and experience. We have the choice to accept instead of condemn, to support instead of discourage, to prioritize instead of dismiss, and to empower instead of control. Every day, we're faced with dozens of these kinds of choices—whether in the form of a passing compliment or a judgmental observation directed to ourselves or to someone else. The way you interact with others is a large part of what defines you—almost as much as the way you interact with yourself. When you choose to engage in respectful and honoring treatment, your energies vibrate with right action. And, believe it or not, being too passive or aggressive can carry equally dishonoring and resistant vibrations.

We're all special. Each of us, no matter what evidence we use to deny it, plays an extremely important part in the eternal scheme of things. So many people believe that our specialness is determined by grandiose acts, the accumulation of wealth, or the demonstration of extraordinary beauty or talent. But the workings of the Universe are like the workings of a huge, elaborate clock: there may be grand bells, beautiful moving characters, and gilded hands, but there are also countless pieces that have no outward appearance of importance. Yet even down to the smallest, seemingly most inconsequential part, each piece is important, purposeful, and special in its own way.

Our human structure is also a complicated network of many different functions, yet all are connected in a significant way. And whether we know it or not, each of us is a special part in the intricate mechanism of our Universe, bringing our unique energy to the grand experience.

Right action is not limited to our attitude and treatment of other individuals; it extends to groups, communities, and cultures. No matter what we may have been taught or how different our beliefs may be, each individual within any group is a soul entity who has been taught and influenced by his or her own group. We must bring a higher consciousness to our group perceptions and to the situations going on around us. Instead of judgment, we can at least bring prayers for calm clarity, patience, and peaceful resolution.

But if we choose to deny each soul's specialness, if we persist in deprecating our own value or that of others, then we create a resistance in the smooth workings of the clock of our global purpose. If we learn to honor ourselves as special and to perceive all others—no matter what their circumstances—as valuable mechanisms in the Divine clockwork, then we're able to see the Universe as a whole, and our own reverence expands right action in all directions.

Right action isn't about morality; it's about energetic cause and effect. In fact, some people would call this the Law of Cause and Effect. Either way, the energetic truth is undeniable: you *will* get back the same energy that you put out toward others. If you're hateful and manipulative, eventually you'll see that same treatment in your life. If you're deceitful and dishonest, beware. People will return that treatment to you in time. And if you're too passive and submissive, the Universe will send more people who will try to use you.

The Law of Magnetism says that your honoring should be focused on the treatment of yourself, while the Law of Right Action states that it should be focused on others and on the world. This may seem like a contradiction, but if you live in balance, you can prioritize others without sacrificing yourself, and you can make honoring—or right action—a part of your daily life.

The question of honoring is a subjective one, but the intention to do so is grounded in love. Your choice to engage in it will promote your sense of dignity and give you authentic—not fraudulent—power. You'll no longer need to gain your authority through the poisonous energies of arrogance or hostility—or even fear. Your ability to weigh the energetic consequences of your actions will go a long way in helping you do this, so when in doubt, reflect on the loving and honoring option. This is what right action is all about, and it's the choice that will always bring the right results.

Affirmations for Right Action

+ In all that I do and all that I think, I choose to honor myself and others.

+ It is safe for me to express myself, make reasonable requests, and follow the honoring path. I am strong.

+ I understand that my own action comes back to me. I can choose right action in any situation and with any person. All is well.

+ I release competition and choose to see people in a different light. I remain centered and balanced, and I know that everyone can be a blessing to me.

+ I am beginning to be more conscious of the energy of others. From now on I choose greater understanding, patience, and tolerance in my approach toward others. We are one.

✦ ✦ ✦

Chapter 7

The Law of Expanding Influence

The Seventh Universal Law of Success

*There is a thinking stuff from which all things are made,
and which, in its original state, permeates, penetrates,
and fills the interspaces of the universe.*

— W. D. WATTLES

The seventh law reveals how your resonance influences others—and how theirs has an effect you. All of life is an exchange of energy that's always moving everywhere around us. An ongoing process of accumulation creates the vibrational and emotional undercurrent to all our lives.

Of course, quantum-physical phenomena can demonstrate how this process works. The first influence is called *phase entanglement*. In the natural world, particles converge and separate, but often when two of them come together, each takes an energetic portion of the other with them when they part. This is the essence of phase entanglement: when two entities meet, each one's energy becomes attached to the other; each leaves something behind when it moves on.

The emotional experiences of humans can become phase entangled, too. In fact, it happens every day to each one of us. We engage with another person, and we take their vibration away with us—just as they take ours with them. For example, when we argue with a moody teenager, we can become irritable ourselves. When we spend time with a depressed person, we may notice ourselves feeling down, even long after we've left them. And being around someone who's jubilant leaves us carrying that joy with us. Emotions are contagious, and each person's energy is influential.

This is a critically important principle in our pursuit of success. Because of the intricacies of energetic influence, we must be acutely aware of the relationships we forge in not only our personal lives but also our social and professional lives. The resonance of others influences our thoughts, moods, and sense of well-being, and it shapes our choices.

You can see how this pattern would be an important consideration in owning or managing a business—the phenomenon makes it especially important to hire people of stability and integrity. Since energetic influences expand in the world, you wouldn't want someone of negative vibrations spreading the energies of neglect and deceit in your workplace. For the same reason, it's also important for *you* to have integrity in your business dealings.

There's an old adage that says, "As the king goes, so goes the country." This means that the resonant attitudes and actions of the leader are picked up by his people and spread far and wide. It's a truth that we can still see working in the world today. This is the case for countries as well as communities, companies, and families.

The **Law of Expanding Influence** shows that your own energy expands in the world and has influence in your personal life and in the world at large. You can—and do—have an impact on everything from the productivity of your company and the harmony of your family all the way to the peace of the world! The power of your own personal vibration becomes global by virtue of this law. When you choose to live with reverence in your heart and direct it toward those around you, that positive energy spreads to all your circles of influence . . . and eventually, your intention for harmony expands in the consciousness of every human being.

If you want your family life to be more peaceful, *you* must create that intention within yourself first. If you want your workers to be more industrious, *you* must begin to project that energy in your own life. Everyone needs to understand the influence and extent of their own power. In the pursuit of success, the requirements are honesty, enthusiasm, encouragement, and support. Whether we're talking about a well-oiled business or a happy and loving relationship, these are the personal wavelengths that are necessary to produce the most desirable results.

EXPANDING ACTION

As we saw earlier, Bell's theorem of nonlocality reveals that what happens in one location can have a significant influence in a far-off place. This is true for your personal energy and actions, too. In this amazing Universe of ours, anything can happen anyplace, anytime. Because of the quantum connections we all share, our actions and intentions can bring immediate results from surprising people and unexpected places. From the tiniest particle to the greatest mass, the Universe is a vibrating realm of potential, an abundant field of all possibilities. Because of these vast opportunities and our nonlocal power, we should remain encouraged to always continue to take action in the direction of our goals. The results may not come in the manner we expect, but with the right energy, the results will come just the same.

A friend of mine experienced this phenomenon when she was attempting to adopt a baby. Megan was seeking a domestic adoption in the U.S. through an agency, but after nearly a year of trying, she was ready to give up. Each prospective birth parent had their choice of multiple hopeful couples and families, and Megan was never picked. Her lawyer suggested that she send letters to the obstetricians and gynecologists in the area, in case any had interested patients. She sent out hundreds of letters and attended many meetings, yet still had no luck.

During this time, she often called me to express her frustration, and I advised her to keep taking action in every direction. Whenever you plant your seeds of intention, you never know when or where they're going to bloom. She continued in every way she could, and several months later, she got a call from the original agency that she'd long ago given up on. They had a birth mother who was due the following January and had picked out Megan and her husband, Sam, as one of three prospective adoptive families.

Megan was going to give up on sending the letters and making other contacts, but I advised her not to. I told her that continuing to work on the situation in many different ways would help her reach her goal. Expanded actions—that is, looking in every direction—helps reduce urgency and impatience, keeping away the negative influences of paradoxical intent. Megan experienced this because the more she kept working on her other options, the less desperate she felt about being chosen. She'd already had several potential adoptions fall through, and she needed to surrender her attachment to this outcome in order to attract the ultimate results. All her activity helped her to remember that what she wanted was a baby—and she was open to receiving it in the way the Universe directed. By continuing to see options in all sorts of different directions, she was able to let go of the urgency and maintain a hopeful heart.

In addition to reducing urgency, continued action greatly expands intention. The more you undertake, the more energy you send out regarding your intention. Each and every act is like placing another order with the Universe, and you never know how or when it's going to respond. You may plant the seeds in one area but end up seeing wonderful results somewhere else entirely.

Megan had given up on the original adoption agency, but all her other actions brought that plan back to her. Then, while she was going through the interviews with the birth parents, she continued joyously working in the other directions. This not only kept her calm but also reaffirmed her intention to make this dream a reality.

In the long run, all her efforts paid off. Slowly but surely, the other potential couples were weeded out, and Megan and Sam were chosen to be the adoptive parents of a little boy to come. Her dream became a reality—all because she refused to stop taking action in all sorts of directions.

The energetic power of our nonlocal nature is profoundly effective. *Every thought and every deed plants a new seed in the garden of our destiny.* We may not be immediately aware of the effects, but it's important to know that the process of intention and influence has no end. It always brings results in one way or another, so we might as well intend the best and take positive action in every direction. In this way, we open ourselves to all the options that the Universe may have in store—even the unexpected ones.

JOURNAL FOR SUCCESS

Use your journal to explore how you can expand your personal intentions in even more directions, all the while remembering to release any desperation. Considering each specific goal or desire, investigate different—or perhaps even unorthodox—ways to work on making them a reality. If necessary, do research or ask friends to help you brainstorm ideas. Jot them down and add new ones whenever they may come up. Once you have fresh approaches in mind, don't be afraid to implement them. Sometimes the best results can come from the most unusual concepts.

Taking lots of action does not have to lead to striving, obsession, or desperation. If you find yourself moving into those energies, it may be time to pull back a bit. Your expanding action should be a playful adventure, giving you new ideas and bringing unexpected inspiration. You may even find yourself shifting your goals and redirecting your plans. If so, let yourself be flexible and open to your intuition and your options. A brand-new, totally unexpected desire may end up bringing the exact solution you'd been hoping for, all because you allowed yourself to expand your focus in wider, brighter directions!

EXPANDING WORLDWIDE

The ripples of our influence aren't limited to the pursuit of our own personal goals. In fact, this is just a small part of consciousness creation. Whether we realize it or not, our impact expands outward to reach even the farthest corners of the world. The seventh Universal Law shows that your own energy moves out to bond with other energies that are similar. These clouds of bonded vibrations become fields of consciousness that exude immeasurable influence on the experience of our species.

These worldwide fields of consciousness are called *morphogenetic fields*, or M-fields for short. Like the electromagnetic and gravitational fields, M-fields are forces that are capable of swaying the very nature of our lives. Emotion and information are the energies that build in these fields, affecting the significant transitions of our species. These great storehouses of shared consciousness are fed by each individual's energy—including yours—and then that accumulated power billows out and touches the hearts and minds of others.

There are two major fields of emotional consciousness, that of love and that of fear or hate. As individuals, all our thoughts, beliefs, choices, and behaviors contribute to the expansion of one or the other of these. Every time that we make a loving choice, whether it's for ourselves or someone else, we feed the field of love. But every time we engage in hate or judgment—whether it's a passing self-criticism in the mirror or an angry condemnation of another—we're feeding the field of fear.

As the accumulated energy builds in each of these realms, the resonance of that particular energy increases in the Universe. Eventually a critical magnitude is reached, and the consciousness of love or hate moves out to influence the choices and experiences of others. Those that are hateful and considering doing harm could be pushed in that direction by the accumulating waves of violence and hostility. Those that are longing to achieve greater peace of mind could be influenced by the increasing intentions of the loving people around them. Whatever field is fed the most will have the greatest power in our world.

This is our individual responsibility: to choose love in our own minds and lives, thereby accelerating the energy of caring in the world. If we don't, then hate and fear will accelerate instead. This isn't a function of the fields having any specific intention; they're actually completely impartial. Just as gravity has no emotional investment in the literal ups and downs of our activities, the fields of love and hate are indifferent to how we feed and deal with their influence in the world.

Each person's intention determines the course of humanity; every individual's emotions and actions feed the energy and power that you see all around. If you want love—rather than hate—to expand in your life and in the world, then you must choose to engage in more caring energy toward yourself and others. As you'll see in the next section, the power of love is always at your disposal. Bring it to your consciousness, energy, and intention, and you'll not only bring blessings to your own life, your expanding influence will bring them to the entire world.

Affirmations for My Expanding Influence

✦ I know that my intentions expand in the world. The more focused action I take toward my goals, the more my plans are supported by the Universe.

✦ I walk and move at a comfortable pace. I do everything in a leisurely way. I choose to relax and carry that calm and tranquil energy with me.

✦ I know that my own energy and actions expand in my life and in the world. I choose unconflicted energy and peaceful actions. My life resonates with peace and purpose.

✦ I look for the joy I can bring to my life and to the world. I intend to bring greater happiness to all.

✦ I see the value in everyone around me. Together we share the energy of the world.

✦ ✦ ✦

PART II

The Six Personal Powers of Success

The Universal Laws place the responsibility of personal happiness and success upon your own shoulders. To make your dreams a reality, you'll have to investigate how you can align with those powerful forces. The demands of the laws may involve changing the way that you do things—and how you think about them—not because of mere idealism but because of the fundamental nature of your own vibrating essence.

People often long for change but do very little to actively bring it about. They look at it as a future occurrence, thinking such things as, *When my prospects or finances change, then everything will be okay.* But this is a *passive* approach to an *active* expectation, and it's not likely to yield very beneficial results. Instead of waiting, you need to take the inner and outer action to make it happen!

Transformation isn't a future event; it's the ongoing present activity that stimulates what's to come. Change is not the goal, it's the consistent *process* that leads to your desire. The emotional quality of your life is up to you, and if you're not happy with what's going on now, then you need to make new choices in the present in order to ensure a better tomorrow. In this way, you absolutely *do* have the ability to magnetize success!

In fact, all the resources you'll ever need already exist within you. Six truly dynamic personal powers are a part of your nature and always available. You can utilize them in a conscious way to change everything you attract to your life because ultimately, success comes from taking control. When you start to shift your energy and use your innate and often-neglected gifts, your life will move in an entirely new direction.

Each of your powers is a real force in the world, and each requires an awareness on your part. Some may even demand significant changes, but don't resist. Remember the old adage: *if you change nothing, nothing will change.* But if you activate these powerful forces, you'll find *everything* in your life changing!

Chapter 8

The Power of Letting Go

The First Personal Power of Success

*Progress is impossible without change, and those who cannot
change their minds cannot change anything.*

— GEORGE BERNARD SHAW

Letting go is the first personal power because it's the necessary
first step to change. Creating a wonderful destiny is like creating
a garden. It's pointless to plant the seeds of beautiful blossoms on
ground that is overgrown with weeds. You must remove those old,
unwanted plants, or they'll choke out the new flowers before they
even bloom. The same is true for the seeds of your success: in order
to produce the creative consciousness and magnetic energies that
will harvest the results you desire, it's important to dig up—and
let go of—the unhealthy patterns of the past. This is a key requirement for changing your energy and shifting your consciousness.
If you want real success, it's very likely that some of your old patterns won't work for you any longer.

There are several levels of letting go, with the first and most
obvious being physical. In this chapter, you'll also learn about
mental, emotional, and behavioral release, as well as how to let go
of attachments.

PHYSICAL RELEASE

Engaging in exercise or other movement on a regular basis is important for clearing out old, dense energy and creating a new, lighter, and more attractive vibration. This is helpful for many reasons. First, it releases past emotional trauma or unhappy memories that may be trapped in your cells and body. Physical activity and deep breathing help shift that stuck energy and move it out of your personal resonance, creating a more receptive state.

In addition, regular exercise assists you in releasing the chronic tension in your daily life. Stress is a very unhealthy and unattractive energy, and over time, it will draw even more tense situations and uptight people to you. The most attractive vibration you can project is that of a relaxed, peaceful, and confident spirit.

To relax your body, make sure that you breathe deeply and get regular muscle movement. Stretching and massage will also help, but you'll need to relax your mind and emotions, too. The process of mental release starts with letting go of your old negative thoughts, but it also has a significant impact on your physical and emotional vibrations since these elements of your life are energetically interconnected.

MENTAL RELEASE

Our minds generate energy constantly, sending out signals that convey our deepest beliefs and most commonly repeated thoughts. Everything we do and think has an immediate energetic consequence, although it may take a while to manifest in the physical world. *Your persistent thoughts—whether they're good or bad—create the greatest consequences of your life, whether you want them to or not.*

So many people go through their days—even their entire lives—simply reacting, without any conscious awareness of what their thoughts are or what effects they may be having. But to change your energy and your consciousness, you need to be aware of the clues of negative thinking.

The biggest hint is in your emotions. Whenever you're having an uncomfortable feeling, there's almost always a negative thought behind it. When you catch yourself feeling fear, depression, guilt, anger, embarrassment, or even just nervousness, ask yourself, *What am I thinking?* Look deep inside to find the negative conclusion that's making you so upset. You do have the power to change your energy by letting go of your old thought patterns, but to do so, you need information.

There are seven major negative thought patterns that people tend to unknowingly live in much of the time. They're important to know because without identifying the source of your negative energy, it will be next to impossible to change it. Your thoughts are powerful unseen forces, so to direct their energy beneficially, you need to identify and release the toxic beliefs that plague you the most. Only then can you consciously change those patterns and move your life in a more positive direction.

COGNITIVE CONTROL:
The Option Is Always Yours

It's time to grab your notebook and investigate exactly *what* you're thinking. For the next several days, record each negative or self-critical thought that you have. Even if your negative assumptions aren't that numerous, jot them down. Soon, you'll find the same issues arising over and over again. This information will be the foundation for your most important change, both in your thoughts and in the emotions they create.

Now look at the following list of the seven toxic thought patterns and identify which show up most commonly in your habits. Be honest, and don't be discouraged if you engage in a lot of them, because it doesn't have to be that way. You always have the power to choose what you think.

7 Toxic Thought Patterns

1. Devaluing

Devaluing is the practice of dismissing the value in yourself, in your life, in an experience, or in another person. For example, the thought *I'm not good enough—I'm a loser* devalues yourself, while *They're such losers* devalues others. And if you consider your job to be boring, you're devaluing your life.

Devaluing is one of the surest ways to rob yourself of your present happiness, creating a constant nagging discontent about what's wrong with you and your life, which only magnetizes more misery for you. Choosing to find and acknowledge the value—in yourself and in your world—is your only option.

You *are* inestimably valuable just as you are, and your life is a precious gift filled with opportunities for change and joy. You *can* choose to fill your *perception* with appreciation—and absolutely refuse to minimize or devalue yourself or your life in any way. When you decide to look for the good in yourself and your everyday experiences, value becomes your reality. *And when value is what you live, value will be what you attract!*

2. Catastrophic Thinking

Catastrophic thinking is the practice of anticipating negative outcomes for future events. It can be a mundane worry like *It's going to be a lousy day,* or as significant as, *What if my marriage fails?* This thinking can take many forms, both verbal and visual, including the unbridled imaginings of future disasters.

Worries, great or small, carry with them intense emotional consequences and a pervasive energy of fear. Fear is very agitating to your resonance, creating a repulsive charge. If fear is your dominant emotional energy, it will be impossible to relax. And without the peace of relaxation, there can be little positive attraction.

Even if you're convinced your concerns are valid, you must work on striking your worry patterns from your cognitive repertoire.

The only option is to choose trust instead of fear. "Brooding" and "what-if"-ing must be dispelled at every opportunity. Change your negative what-ifs to positive ones, such as *What if it turns out great? What if my dreams* do *come true?* Remember your power to breathe and choose trust. Never give that power away!

3. Urgency

This form of negativity isn't limited to your thoughts—it can become an entire lifestyle. Urgent thinkers tend to make long lists of things to do, hurrying to and through activities, feeling they just can't rest until everything is done. Unfortunately, the list never ends, and this attitude creates a constant state of emotional and physical unrest!

Urgency can also apply to major issues, such as relationships and careers. Urgent thinkers tend to analyze everything that's going on around them in terms of how it will affect their own agenda. Much of their urgency comes from the *need* to be certain about how and when things will turn out. This chronic analysis causes even more worry and agitated energy.

Perfectionism, control, fear, and lack are all vibrations that fragment your energy and block your results. So, *force yourself to slow down*—both mentally and physically. Start to speak more calmly, drive more slowly, and eat more leisurely. Choose to *enjoy* the moment instead of racing through it. The Universe loves a peaceful energy and is much more willing to send wonderful outcomes to peace than to panic.

4. Comparing and Competing

In this highly competitive world, it has become very common for people to compare themselves with others, usually in a negative way. They see people at work and think, *He makes more money than I do.* They see people on social media and think, *She's so much prettier than I am.* This "win-lose mentality" makes life a never-ending contest and a source of constant pressure. But when that's your mentality, everyone can become a potential threat, a measure of how much you don't have—and perhaps will never get.

This kind of approach eats away at your joy, making it impossible to relax because you have to worry about measuring up. Loving yourself unconditionally is extremely difficult when you're always under pressure to do, be, or get more.

Real happiness comes from a self-acceptance that doesn't depend on competing. When you let go of the constant comparisons, you'll find that the world is a far less hostile place and that the Universe is far more responsive to your desires. Instead of endless striving, you'll be able to take action with confidence and peace of mind, two essential elements in the achievement of your goals.

5. Victimization and Blame

Victimization is usually born out of past trauma, but it often grows into the perception of being wronged by virtually everyone. You blame others or your history for the problems in your life and consequently end up spending much of your time brooding about the past, complaining about the present, and making excuses for why things won't change in the future.

This mentality is totally disempowering. It works on the assumption that others have more power and are more capable of directing your life than you are. Your insistence that you have been—or are being—victimized will only bring more evidence of that from the Universe. This energetic paralysis simply can't create any happiness! Whether the offense happened long ago or is an ongoing concern, *you must be determined to get your power back!* Stop giving others power over your life. If you have unfinished anger, go ahead and get it out—write or talk about it or get therapy if necessary. But you need to get it out without letting it define you. If it's a present concern, you'll absolutely need to deal with it.

Ask yourself, *What can I do now to take action in my own behalf?* Reclaim your power and begin to take responsibility for your present happiness *now.* With courage, action, and a growing understanding of the true power within you can stand up for yourself and become the director of your own destiny. Your renewed strength and responsibility will finally get the results you've been longing for.

6. Absolutes and All-or-Nothings

This type of thinking looks at things in the extreme, rarely considering the middle ground. Signal words are *always, never, everybody, nobody, too, enough.* The sentiments are often both devaluing and catastrophic—for example, *I'm too old to ever get married* or *I'll always have a weight problem* or *Everybody* thinks I'm a jerk. No one will ever want to hire me.

All-or-nothing statements are filled with fear and self-condemnation, which are the repulsive energies in your life force. There's no room for self-limitation in the effort to magnetize joy. Remember, a truly attractive frequency never condemns itself!

And don't set yourself up for failure due to serious expectations of limitation. If you tell yourself such things as, *All the good men are already taken* or *I'll never be able to leave this dead-end job,* your beliefs will energize that into reality for you. *Always* and *never* are very long times. Strike the negative use of all these signal words out of your vocabulary. Abundance is everywhere. *Anything is possible—at any time!* Open your heart and your life to the never-ending possibilities!

7. Time Warping

This thought pattern is like catastrophic thinking but includes the past as well as the future. Time Warpers tend to rehash old experiences, reliving old shame, replaying yesterday's mistakes, and reviewing last year's embarrassments. Their self-talk usually includes thoughts such as, *How could I have done that?* Or *If only I'd said something different.*

If you find yourself brooding about the past, it's time to vent it, forgive yourself, and let it go. Write a compassionate letter to yourself—understand and affirm that you've always done the best that you could do given the circumstances you were in. Affirm that you're releasing the past along with any conclusions you may have made about it. Consciously choose to stay in the present, and let this choice free you from future expectations as well.

Time Warpers also tend to "run" anticipated events and conversations through their minds. They're often filled with dread and anxiety about what to do and say, thinking that a constant mental rehearsal will protect them in some way—perhaps even ensure a positive outcome. Unfortunately, this only makes them even more anxious, sabotaging both their comfort in the present as well as their success in the future.

Instead of jumping from past to future, choose to breathe in the peace of the present. Let go of past ruminations and trust in your own resourcefulness to deal with whatever the future may hold. In fact, this present, peaceful choice is the most dynamic action you can take to create the future destiny you desire.

Thought Restructuring: Releasing and Rewriting Toxic Thoughts

These are the most common toxic thought patterns that all of us engage in. It's important to know them, but it's also important to be flexible in our process. Humans tend to have a "negative bias" in their spontaneous thoughts. This means that an unexpected and unwanted negative thought could just pop up out of nowhere. Do not blame yourself when this happens!

This normal and all-too-common occurrence may be a natural response, but *you do not have to stay in that negative loop.* Your recognition of a present negative or critical thought is your point of real power, so make a choice and make a change! Every time you choose a new positive thought response, you create a new neural pathway in the brain. With enough repetition, the continued positive responses could become your spontaneous thought pattern, replacing the old ways with wonderful new energy.

So if you see yourself engaging in these toxic thoughts, do *not* panic. Anything learned can be unlearned. Any habit and any energy can be turned around when you reclaim your power and tap the brilliant unseen forces within and all around you!

JOURNAL FOR SUCCESS

As a thinking adult, you have the option and the power to follow a new path and choose a new belief system. In fact, it's your soul's directive to finally let go of the old lies and limitations. Working on these cognitive patterns is not just busy work; it's an absolute energetic necessity. Don't condemn yourself for any negative thinking. Simply forgive yourself and reaffirm your intention to move on. Make it a gentle, peaceful determination. In time, your strong new attitude will become a way of life.

Here's how the process of thought restructuring works: Divide your paper into two columns as shown in the following example. On the left side, place the negative thoughts, concerns, fears, and self-criticisms that arise throughout your day. Also identify the *toxic thought patterns* they represent:

1. Devaluing

2. Catastrophic thinking

3. Urgency

4. Comparing and competing

5. Victimization and blame

6. Absolutes and all-or-nothings

7. Time warping

Place the appropriate pattern numbers next to each negative thought. Then on the right, replace each thought with different, *more supportive and self-valuing options.* Whether you believe them or not, these are your truths. You *must* write them down and be open to them as real options for you. In time, you'll know that this is the *only healthy way* to think. These new thoughts are going to create a higher, brighter magnetism in your personal energy field, one that will bring you real happiness in the present and far greater success in the future.

A client named Robert did this process regarding his doubts about a possible promotion at work. Take a look at a list of some of the thoughts that were at the basis of his negative reactions— along with the responses that he chose to replace them. See if you can identify how your thinking might follow similar patterns. Using the following thought restructuring sheet as a sample, create your own that focuses on your specific issues.

Thought Restructuring Sheet

Thoughts and Concerns	Positive Options
What if I apply and don't make it? People will think I'm a loser. (Patterns 2 and 7)	It doesn't matter what people think. I'm never a loser. I am whole and complete just as I am. I am all that I need. Whatever happens, I can still create happiness.
If someone else gets picked, there must be something wrong with me. (Patterns 1 and 6)	I'm just as worthy as anyone else. I choose to believe in myself. I can relax and accept myself just as I am.
What if I embarrass myself at the interview? I never know the right thing to say. (Patterns 2 and 6)	I'll be fine. I don't have to be perfect; I just have to be myself and accept myself. I don't have to make it mean so much. I can trust myself and be happy.
If I don't get this, I'll have to quit, but no one else will ever want me. I'm worthless. (Patterns 1, 2, 4, 6, and 7)	If I don't get this, I can choose to stay or leave. If I want, I can always find the right place at the right time. I always value myself and know that I'm worthy.

Will the Person on the Right Please Stand Up?

Notice the difference between the energies of each column. If you go back and read *only* the column on the left, you'll clearly sense the energy of self-doubt and despair. But if you go back and read *only* the column on the right, you'll have an entirely different energetic reaction. Take a moment to do this now—it has a startling effect.

When Robert read the two columns separately, he was amazed at the difference in energy, and he understood what a negative vibration his attitudes were projecting. He made an unwavering determination to become the "person on the right," taking the time to write and reverse *all* his toxic patterns, especially the thoughts of limitation and self-doubt.

Robert especially recognized his tendency to make everything mean too much. He'd become addicted to all-or-nothing thinking that devalued him and created the potential for a lifetime of misery.

It seemed like a daunting task, but Robert intervened on all the old thoughts that projected a negative frequency. He *inundated* himself with new, optimistic responses until they were so familiar, they actually became his spontaneous reaction. It took a while, but in time, Robert noticed a big difference in how he was feeling. His personal energy was changing to a happier, lighter, more fluid, peaceful experience, and his happy, confident state attracted far greater results to him.

The New You Is Waiting

Every time you change your thinking, you shift away from old ugly, dark energies to brighter, more attractive ones. By changing the thoughts that you generate, you'll be changing your very life force as well as changing *all the consequences* that you set in motion for your future.

Like Robert, you can liberate yourself from that old sense of hopelessness that's so devastatingly disempowering. When you do, you'll sense a greater power and control growing within, but you must keep at it. Whenever you catch yourself catastrophizing about the future or devaluing yourself in any way, *you must force yourself to stop*—no matter how strong the compulsion to continue may be. No matter what, this is not an option! It's an absolute energetic necessity. *You must stop polluting the resonant signals you send out about yourself.*

Let yourself investigate the thoughts behind your uncomfortable experiences. Even if it's just at the end of the day, try to remember what you were thinking that may have made the experience so difficult. *Remember, it's not the situation, but your perception of it, that determines the energy you generate. You can always choose to be completely in charge of your responses.*

Replace each thought with a more supportive, self-loving assertion. If you can't come up with a *positive* alternative to the toxic thought, *at least release the negative.* Say, *I don't have to think this way any longer* or *This thought doesn't serve me. I'm releasing it now* or *I can think better of myself, and as I let this thought go, I can change my energy and my future.*

Everything you think moves outward from you in invisible— but unmistakable—waves of energetic information. The Laws and unseen forces will always respectfully send your own self-respect back to you. Since that self-respect is the most basic part of what you want to project, you should use the intention of self-valuing as an inner compass to move you in a new direction. *Any time you find yourself feeling bad about yourself, write down your false thoughts, along with the corresponding healthy and loving options.*

Changing your negative thoughts will shift your emotions and project a brilliant, receptive resonance to the world. You may have to work on it, but you are certainly worth your own time, effort, and loving priority!

EMOTIONAL RELEASE: The Incredibly Liberating Energy of Venting Letters

Feelings represent a palpable vibration, and they carry very clear messages with them. Whether you realize it or not, if you haven't ventilated your feelings, you could still be sending out old—even very old—signals of grief, anger, rejection, and other negative emotional vibrations still lingering in your energy field.

Many people have a difficult time expressing or even identifying their feelings. They have often experienced trauma and disappointment without ever giving voice to the real emotions involved. This only accumulates in clouds of negative energy that broadcast abrasive resonance in every direction. You carry these with you whether you're thinking about it or not, and people and situations can pick up on that dark energy.

To get rid of that black fog, you need to let go of unexpressed feelings from the past. In fact, it may be necessary to purge your old feelings even if the difficult events happened quite a while ago. If you've never had the opportunity to release them, the emotions from distant experiences may be creating powerful signals in your energy field, blocking new achievements and sending out painful vibrations without your even knowing it.

Denying or dismissing difficult experiences of the past is like leaving a garden hose out in the yard for years. It becomes filled with bugs, dirt, roots, and mold. Then when you turn on the water, either nothing comes out or it spits out a mess of disgusting detritus. And that will be the nature of what you project if your difficult past remains unexpressed.

You don't have to go back and relive every trauma or difficult passage. You know which difficulties still may be haunting you, so get out your journal and start writing about it. Use the process below to express all the feelings that you still need to release; don't obsess about it, just ventilate it.

Be especially conscious of the assumptions that you made about your upsetting experiences. As you recount an old experience, ask yourself, *What conclusions did I draw from this experience that I may want to change now? What did I make this mean about myself, my value, or my power in the world?* Write down any of those false beliefs, then choose to replace them with new truths.

For example, if you got fired and experienced emotions such as anger, fear, and rejection, you may have concluded, *I'll never be accepted. I'll never be a success.* Turn that thought around by ventilating the feelings and then writing down a healthy belief, such as *I'm still capable of succeeding. I deserve to believe in myself, and*

I choose to do so now. Continue letting go of both the negative thoughts and difficult emotions from the past in this way, always affirming your present capabilities and your expectations of a bright and happy future.

In addition to releasing the feelings of days gone by, it's also important to let go of them as they come up. While it doesn't have to be done as a daily activity, if you get a chance to vent in response to present problems, you'll find that it's easier to change your thinking and your vibrations as well. Holding on to negative emotions such as resentment, anger, or fear majorly blocks your energy and significantly impacts your results. Relinquish them, and your energy will be clear, open, and ready to receive!

JOURNAL FOR SUCCESS

Let's assume that everyone has something in their history that was emotionally difficult. From mild dismissal to harsh mistreatment and even mental, verbal, or physical abuse, a wide array of past pains are often a part of our emotional makeup. We may not like it, but these experiences need to be acknowledged and released so that we can get that agitated energy out of our life-force projection—and, in fact, out of our very definition!

This is not an exercise in blame, though on the surface it may seem that way. It is commonly understood that parents generally just give what they got, unaware that their behavior is reaching back through generations of ancesral distortion and gets projected into future generations that will need to seek healing.

But there is a simple process that can help us in our quest for clearing this jagged, dark energy from our minds and hearts. It's the easy technique of *Venting Letters*. This process is designed to dispel the anger, hurt, rejection, and resentment that we could be unknowingly carrying with us throughout our lives. Such unexpressed yet deeply painful experiences become a very active part in our energy projection. They are, in fact, one of the most significant generators of our own personal life-force vibration.

Here is how the process works:

- In unedited entries in your journal, write short notes to the person who has hurt or upset you. This can be from long ago or about an infraction that happened yesterday.

- Once you vent in this directed way, follow it up with a releasing and an empowering statement. This is designed to reverse the false beliefs that were formed out of the difficult experience.

  For example, you might follow up a venting entry with releasing statements like: *I'm letting go of all the negative energy from that experience.* Or, *I'm releasing your negative energy and all its influence over me.* Or, *I'm releasing any toxic attachment to you. I am free.*

- Finaly, be sure to close with an empowering statement, such as, *I am reclaiming my power. I am strong and self-directed.* Or, *I am reclaiming my ability to define and love myself—and to direct my life in the way that I desire.*

There are a few important things to keep in mind as you write. First, even though you direct your notes to a person, do *not* intend to send or show them this material. If you think you're going to reveal it, you'll unconsciously edit it in some way, and you want this to release the unedited, raw feelings that are still vibrating within you.

Take your time with this; it usually takes many small entries or little notes rather than a single attempt. Once you start to recount and recall old hurts and griefs, you are likely to remember more and more. In fact, you may have moments of regret that you let this particular cat out of the bag. But the truth is, if there's more old pain bubbling up to the surface, it's just an indicator of how deeply embedded this jagged energy pattern is! And it needs to come out in order to redirect your vibration to higher mental and emotional fields.

Start the entry directing it to the person involved. It could say anything from "Damn it, Mom! How could you treat me that way?" Never be afraid to vent, even if it means a little coarse language. They'll never see it anyway, and the more powerful the approach, the more energy you get out.

I think it's most effective to write it out by hand. Others do it on their computer. Still others keep the approach in their heads. The problem with this last attempt is that the memory then often plays out as an endless loop tape over and over again, repeating but never *releasing* the energy.

Now, you may have heard that if you want to attract good things, you should never let yourself express anger or even have a negative thought at all. This is not only unrealistic, it's entirely unhealthy. Denial of your old hurts does not make them go away. They still reverberate in your resonant field, and not only that, the deeply covered-up trauma can often lead to physical and emotional problems, imbalance, and disorientation.

It's ridiculous to admonish people to never have negative feelings and thoughts. The human experience takes us through countless difficult times in our lives. It's what we do with the experience, how we express our reactions, honor our intentions, and deal with the fallout that counts. We must love ourselves through the troubled events of our lives, knowing that the lessons we learn and the power we reclaim are our soul's true intention for the experience. Don't hesitate to get it all out, unedited and unrestricted. You have the right to get angry and get free of it!

It's important not to skip the releasing and empowering statements. Think about the important soul forces that were rightfully yours but were stripped away—and remember to reclaim those as well. These powerful true parts of your nature may seem to have been missing for a long time but they are still there for you. Reclaim a deeper sense of your true value and awakening self-esteem. Affirm that you know you are truly worthy, deserving of all the value the world has to offer. Acknowledge that you do have the power to live in and speak your truth. And reclaim your courage and willingness to take action in your own behalf, knowing that you always have the right to do so!

This process can be so liberating. It lifts the heaviness of old hurts from your heart and from your energy. When I was going through my second divorce, I filled a five-subject notebook with these little entries, venting my hurt and anger. The funny thing was I hadn't even felt that angry at first. It just seemed like a logical ending, but I was in denial. I had to let go of the loss of the marriage, but on top of that, I had to release the pain of losing what I had envisioned my life to be, the idealistic expectations of having a life together, including all its joys and adventures. It took me a year to fill up that notebook, but by the time I was done, I had no emotional reaction at all. I was free and clear and all the dark energy was dispelled, opening me up to the ability to attract the man that I was really supposed to create my future with!

So give these little venting letters a try. Many people resist because it seems easier to ignore the pain, but energetically this denial can create a lifetime of difficult attraction. Have the courage to get started. You may have a lot to unpack, but be willing to get it all out. The resulting self-empowerment and clarity of energy can completely change the trajectory of your life!

BEHAVIORAL RELEASE

Letting go of unhealthy and harmful behaviors, especially indulgences and addictions, is also important in creating an attractive energy and productive consciousness. People indulge in all sorts of unhealthy or self-sabotaging things, including too much alcohol, drugs, cigarettes, food, television, exercise, gossip, sex, work, relationships, and drama. We turn to such activities to provide us with a sense of distraction or escape, to numb our emotions and make us feel better, at least for a little while. When we turn on the television, we zone out; when we eat the chips or cookies, we feel we're comforting ourselves in some way.

Even more subtle habits such as manipulation, deceit, or meanness are compelling because they can make us feel better at the time—but this is false power. Eventually, our harmful behaviors cause a greater disconnect from others and from the flow of the Universe, fragmenting our energy and throwing up more blocks to our authentic happiness and success.

When you engage in any of these actions, you should peel back the layers of your motivation to find out what you're running away from. Whether it's boredom or pain, it's time to face what's wrong. Break through to the self-love you may have been missing. Clear out the old misinformation, then go directly to the source.

The light of your Divine identity is always within, and the power and value that you seek from outside are already alive within. No matter what you've been told, your worthiness is a shining vibration that's always intrinsic to your being, right down to your very cells. Whatever difficult experience or painful treatment may have compelled you to escape into unhealthy patterns, it's now time to own your truth, to deal with the patterns, and express your feelings. Release negative conclusions including any self-judgment about being stuck in this pattern. No matter how long you've been engaged in escapism or distraction, you have the power to move on to new, healthier, and more self-nurturing choices.

It's time to fill the old emptiness with the light of your own sacred identity. This is all the refuge you'll ever need—and the real solution to all that you seek. Behaviors of escapism, indulgence, addiction, and power-mongering only create an even bigger hole, taking you further away from your real source of comfort and power. Moreover, they destroy your energy with vibrations of need, fear, and overindulgence, driving you deeper into a desperation that attracts unpleasant results that continue to feed your need to escape.

While it may be difficult to rid yourself of these habits, you can start by intervening on the behaviors for just a few minutes at a time. Create a system of replacement activities and write them in your journal. Enlist the support of someone you trust; even get professional help if you need it because this is too important to dismiss.

When you engage in an indulgent or harmful action, remind yourself of the energetic truth that *all* your choices create your life-force energy. Do you really want the vibrations of imbalance and escapism to be what you project to the world? If the answer is no, then consistently make the choice to let the old habits go.

Again, be careful not to judge yourself for falling into unhealthy patterns because doing so only adds fuel to the negative fire, increasing your need to escape. So, as you're letting go of everything else, let yourself release any judgment for missing an opportunity to let go.

Learning to release can be a lifelong process. Every day, renew your determination to let go of the past and relinquish the worry. This will clear the way for your new, healthy choices that are certain to bring clarity and make your life sparkle. When you give up the thoughts, emotions, and behaviors that have been holding you back, you'll activate your vital energy and resonate a brilliant and beautiful vibration for all the world to see—and to respond to.

When you wake up in the morning, you can take a few minutes to meditate on the day ahead. Consider your common behaviors and your thought and emotional reactions and choose just one that you can focus a higher intention on. See yourself being strong and resisting the usual temptations of the day. Visualize yourself being more conscious of your thoughts and choosing optimism and honoring in situations that may have been a challenge before. Then, as the opportunity arises, you can recall that intention and consciously choose a healthier behavior, a more optimistic thought, or a peaceful emotion.

I've included a very helpful meditation audio in the bonus download called "Clearing the Road Ahead." In this process, you can place your thought and emotional patterns and your unhealthy addictions and distractions on the road in front of you.

You can even see the people that you have unfinished business with—anything you want to let go of—before you. Then you visualize yourself stretching out your arm and swishing it all into the ditch on the side of the road, where the problems and people gently fall away, clearing the road ahead. You are then free to move forward on your path. You easily go down your cleared road till you find yourself at your Sacred Temple, where you can receive all the guidance and information you will ever need!

Affirmations for Letting Go

✦ I am becoming more and more comfortable with letting go. I release past patterns of fear and worry. I am free.

✦ I let go of any negative thought that may come up. I take a deep breath and choose conclusions of trust and present peace.

✦ It's safe and comfortable for me to face and release any painful memories and feelings from the past. I deserve to speak my truth.

✦ I let go of unhealthy and dishonoring habits. I always remember my options to empower myself and create healthy, new choices in all I do.

✦ I embrace a peaceful approach to life. I let go of worry, hurry, and the need for control.

✦ ✦ ✦

Chapter 9

The Power of Consciousness

The Second Personal Power of Success

Consciousness is the creative element in the universe.
Without it, nothing would appear.

— FRED ALAN WOLF, PH.D.

Physics is the science of possibilities, and consciousness is the source. The theory of consciousness-created reality is widely accepted, but what is the process of manifestation? How do things come into being? More important, how are our personal destinies shaped by our own consciousness?

Through quantum physics, we know that reality isn't separate from the observation of it, and the same is true for our own lives. What we experience in the real world can't be separated from our perception of it. In fact, the study of biomechanics reveals that the brain isn't even capable of distinguishing the difference between reality and memory. Whether we see something or merely remember it, the same neurons are sparked.

The key to your consciousness creation is found in your perception—what you perceive about yourself and your reality and how it makes you feel. In fact, this creates many of the chemical and emotional responses of your body and your mind. It's an ongoing process of cause and effect: perception stimulates reaction; reaction reinforces perception. Your consciousness is so powerful that it not only determines the emotional quality of your life but also evokes significant physiological responses.

The process begins when a single emotion or thought triggers the brain to release certain neurotransmitters or neuropeptides. This process creates a chemical reaction that matches and perpetuates the original emotional state. Whether positive or negative, similar thoughts and experiences will produce similar transmitters or peptides and similar emotions.

The greater the repetition of this pattern, the more your perception becomes fixed, repeatedly setting off a biochemical chain of events that perpetuates the same old feelings. This is how emotional habits—and even addictions—can take shape. It may sound complicated, but it's a relatively simple and very spontaneous process. And it has a huge impact on your consciousness and energy production because of the extensive cognitive, emotional, and biochemical involvement.

Let's look at an example of how the process might work.

You meet a new, attractive person at work. They flirt with you and make you laugh. You start dating, and the happy, excited feelings increase your levels of oxytocin, which make you feel even happier and connected. This causes you to long to be together, and eventually the two of you get married.

You and your partner slowly grow more and more accustomed to each other. Over time, something seems to be missing. You feel a longing to escape and so you turn to eating more snacks, especially sweets, to cover it up. This releases dopamine, making you feel much better, but compelling you to eat more to get that good feeling back.

Your spouse turns to alcohol to feel better. This releases the neuropeptide galanin, a chemical that causes them to want even more alcohol. This is called a positive feedback loop, not because the process lends to positive results, but because the pattern keeps increasing. Unfortunately, both of you will continue to engage in these patterns until you choose to make healthier choices, which will reduce these biochemical reactions and create more genuine forms of happiness in your lives.

It's important to know that your emotions stimulate the chemistry, which tends to keep you stuck in your mental, emotional, and behavioral patterns. It takes a focused, conscious intention to turn your conclusions and choices around in order to get out of this emotional and biochemical labyrinth.

Changing your thoughts is one way to change your emotions and the chemistry that perpetuates your energetic projection. There are many things you can do, but your consciousness is the key to all of your inner forces—and to your external life consequences.

CHANGE YOUR BIOCHEMISTRY FOR IRRESISTIBLE ATTRACTION

There are very specific processes and actions that you can take to change your patterns of negative perception and the resulting biochemical involvement.

1. Neurotransmitter Affirmations

When you feel a negative emotion welling up within, stop and take a deep breath. Repeat the following affirmations: *My body is releasing more and more <u>neurotransmitters of peace and well-being</u>, bringing me great feelings of <u>tranquility</u> and <u>happiness</u> now.* You can be even more specific by saying something like: *My body is releasing <u>serotonin</u> and <u>oxytocin</u>, creating great feelings of <u>joy</u> and <u>vitality</u>.*

You can switch out the two emotional states at the end of each statement with other intentions, including the following:

Courage	Balance
Purpose	Creativity
Vitality	Clarity
Excitement	Hope
Joy	Understanding
Confidence	Equanimity
Peace of mind	Satisfaction
Trust	
Calm	. . . or any other positive emotional state you'd like to achieve
Comfort	
Contentment	

If you are prone to depression, you can use the technique of *affirmation saturation* to repeat this neurotransmitter instruction many times a day. (You'll find more detailed instructions for affirmation saturation in Chapter 15.) I've had clients who repeated variations of this statement 10 to 20 times in the morning and 10 to 20 times in the afternoon, switching the emotional states in the underlined positions. They consistently report significant shifts in their daily moods when they remember to use this tool.

2. Happy Memory Imagery

Studies show that just reliving a happy or loving memory can release beneficial and mood-enhancing neurotransmitters. Take a deep breath and immerse yourself in an image that recalls happiness, enjoyment, or love. Place pictures around you to stimulate the fond memory. Breathe in the deep feelings, let all other thoughts go, and allow your body to produce the chemicals that will lift you up.

3. Muscle Movement and Massage

Vigorous exercise releases endorphins, but many other muscle movements can also help. Stretching, yoga, and massage—along with some deep breathing—are likely to increase beneficial bio-chemicals. A walk in nature would provide both the positive imagery and movement that stimulates greater happiness.

4. Time with Beloved Friends and Family

Studies show that supportive and meaningful conversations between friends can generate feelings of comfort and security. Even having meals together creates a spike in oxytocin. If you add hugs and laughter, that's guaranteed to increase the chemistry of good feelings for all.

You can choose to engage in all these positive experiences that produce the biochemicals that promote hope, excitement, and happiness. Even spending time with pets, meditating, singing or listening to music are known to have this beneficial biological effect. But it's not just the activities that are important, it's what you focus on while doing them that really makes the difference. In this way, your own consciousness can be the strongest force of your destiny creation.

CONSCIOUSNESS PIE

Three main ingredients activate your power of consciousness: perception, imagination, and expectation, or what I refer to as consciousness PIE. A positive experience in these mental and emotional elements of your life is the most vital accelerant in your pursuit of success. In fact, for good or for bad, these are the three key pieces of consciousness creation. They're energetically linked in a dynamic process that can give you an amazing amount of control over the consequences of your life. Let's take a deeper look at how each piece works.

The Power of Perception

It's clear that your perception stimulates the production of biochemicals that perpetuate emotional experiences. When you see something as being negative, it produces a biochemical reaction that reinforces the unfavorable emotional state, and the opposite is true as well. This alone should be motivation enough to keep working on consciously creating a positive outlook, but let's also examine how perception affects energy.

The way you see things is filtered through your history, yet it's powerful enough to create your future. In very real ways, this is what defines you, right down to your physiological reality. How you perceive yourself, your world, and your future is the cognitive foundation underlying all your moods. Studies show that self-perception and self-talk can increase (or decrease) serotonin levels that, when present, can perpetuate ongoing feelings of joy and satisfaction.

But this piece of the consciousness PIE is so powerful that its influence doesn't stop there. There are documented cases where people with dissociative identity disorder (formerly called multiple personality disorder) manifest varying diagnosable physical conditions when a different personality is "in control." Conditions such as diabetes and vision problems become real physiological issues when a particular identity takes over. But the same physical body showed no signs of these problems when other personalities (with other perceptions) were in charge.

This isn't the only case where consciousness changes physiology. People are able to walk on burning hot coals without injury by shifting their perception, and I myself experienced this phenomenon many years ago. I took a fire-walking class in which nearly 100 people were taught how to change their state of mind by completely shifting their focus from the experience of stepping on hot coals to the memory of something that evoked thrilling and happy sensations.

I envisioned myself skiing down my favorite slope in Colorado, visually and emotionally putting myself on that ski run in the crisp, cold, beautiful mountains. This changed the experience and my physiology, and I was able to walk over 15 feet of burning hot coals that were at a temperature of several hundred degrees.

While I was completely uninjured, some people burned themselves. They perceived the burning coals as dangerous, and as a result, they experienced them that way. But those of us who changed our perception were able to completely transform our physical reality.

You, too, have the power to alter your perception. No matter what has happened to you, you don't have to perceive yourself or the world in any of the old, negative ways. Instead, you can use your power of letting go to release your old, limited outlooks and open your heart and mind to a healthy new one. *No matter what you may be experiencing, remember that you always have the option to choose a new perception!*

This is the key to consciousness-created reality: what you observe to be true frames your awareness. Choose to empower yourself and change your observations. See things differently, and imagine everything in your life in new, beneficial, and optimistic ways. In fact, this is the next important piece of your consciousness PIE.

Imagery Is Everything

As you make positive shifts in your perceptions, you'll find it easier and easier to fire up your imagination. I'm not just speaking about your ability to daydream and fantasize about your future; I'm referring to your ability to create mental images—living pictures of what you want your present and your future to look like. This is a powerful skill when pursuing specific scenarios of success.

Where processing mental imagery is concerned, the brain can't distinguish between present events and memories. Nor can it tell the difference between what's vividly imagined and what's real. In fact, several physicists don't even believe that a single reality exists. The Many-Worlds Interpretation (MWI) suggests that several realities are going on all at the same time, and some scientists believe that you can choose the one you want. This may sound like science fiction, but it only goes to show the unlimited possibilities of your life. You need to imagine all that you can experience! Remember, to create it, you must see it.

> You have the ability to imagine vivid pictures of happiness and success throughout your life. If the pictures floating in your imagination right now don't correspond with what you truly want to experience in your future, you need to develop some new ones. To create success, you must create successful and happy feelings and images.

Consciousness-created imaging happens on two levels. Perform the following steps often to establish a powerful new perception of success.

- **Successful imaging of yourself and your present life:** You need to paint the pictures of how you want yourself to be, to look, to feel, and to act in your daily life. You don't have to look perfect, but it's important to see and sense yourself as vital, energetic, and happy, which are energies that are beautiful in and of themselves. Create vivid images of happy experiences throughout your day, and then move within this happy view of yourself. Live it, feel it, and intend it. Let yourself envision joy many times a day, and before long, you'll create it!

- **Successful imaging of your specific goals:** Create clear, bright pictures of exactly what it is you want to achieve. Make the imagery so vivid that you feel as if you're already there in the center of it. Imagine the joyous outcome of each goal, and then put the mental photograph of that *future* event into your *memory*. See it as a favorite moment already captured in a photo album, one that you turn to over and over. And if you keep a treasure map or vision board, be sure to put some pictures of your present happy moments along with your future goal images. In this way, you're informing your brain that that images of the future have already happened; that reality exists.

Some people have a difficult time visualizing a success that has continually eluded them. If this is hard for you, you can create mental images of your family and friends congratulating you on your achievement. Whether it's successful weight loss or a happy engagement, imaging their congratulations can be just as powerful a catalyst to achieving your desired results!

Once you've established your successful pictures clearly, notice and let go of any thoughts that negate them in any way. When you visualize each one, enlarge it. See it clearly, not off in the distance or moving left or right, since that could change the power of its reality as well as its energetic timing. Hold the image with peace in the center of your heart without becoming attached or desperate. Make it real and tranquil in your mind.

The more you experience your images of joyous outcomes, the more your brain and consciousness will accept them as reality. As you continue to reproduce each picture—clear, heartfelt, and centered in your thinking—you'll create more and more of the positive emotions that charge a highly creative consciousness and magnetic energy. This will help fine-tune your expectation, the final piece of your consciousness PIE.

Expect the Best

There's a big difference between what you desire and what you expect, and the Universe can sense the difference. It's important to consistently expect the best—and trust yourself to create it. To facilitate that, you need to find out what your hidden expectations may be.

Whether you realize it or not, you tend to look at each day with certain assumptions about how it's going to go. This projects your daily energy patterns into the future. The problem is that if you're often dissatisfied with the present, it's pretty hard to create positive expectations about the future.

Underneath it all, how do you look at your daily life? Do you feel enthusiastic about the day ahead, or do you drag yourself through it with little happiness and fun? Do you hope for peace and acceptance, yet expect stress and rejection? Do you long for success, yet anticipate failure? Do you wish for happiness, yet resign yourself to boredom, drudgery, or disappointment? If you expect today to be difficult, then whatever your goal may be, you're likely to find only more of the same. But you always have the option to create new expectations and beliefs about what you're capable of achieving—today, tomorrow, and always.

The battle between desire and expectation is an emotional one. Your desires are where your *wishes* are; your expectations are where your experiences, emotions, and *beliefs* are. In the formula of destiny creation, not much wields more power than your emotions and beliefs.

Your convictions must support a positive expectation—the fundamental assumption of a valuable outcome, whether it's about the day ahead or the next year. You can no longer desire the best yet expect the worst; the Universe simply can't reconcile such a split of consciousness. You must begin to look for the best in both your day-to-day life and in the fulfillment of your dreams, knowing that you're capable of bringing your highest and happiest awareness to *all* that you experience. Take your power back and create a conscious perception of your ideal day and your ideal future. Know that you're capable of making it happen—and expect it.

Your daily expectations accelerate your energetic momentum, so stop dismissing the value of your everyday life. Choose to take a grander view of your present experiences and of your goals to come. This is a big part of the recipe for successful consciousness creation:

- Positive perceptions of yourself and your present life
- Vivid and creative images of your future experiences
- Excitedly optimistic expectations for the days, months, and years to come

Just a small shift in any one of these attitudes can create a major change in your consciousness and in your reality. It's the steadfast choice to live in an awakened state in the here and now, one in which you freely *choose* to find or create some genuine happiness every day. In this choice, you give yourself the power to create a positive new perception, a valuable view, and great expectations of what already is—and what can be—real for you. Choose that now!

Affirmations for a Power Consciousness

- ✦ I choose a strong, successful perception of myself. I am capable, energetic, and truly deserving.

- ✦ I visualize a peaceful life for myself. I choose to see myself as a bright and beautiful soul—confident, vibrant, and happy—now and always.

- ✦ I expect the best. In my daily life and in my future, I always anticipate and create happy and fulfilling experiences.

- ✦ My body is releasing biochemicals of peace and well-being. I consciously choose the thoughts, images, and activities that create increasing contentment and happiness in my life.

- ✦ I visualize my goals with excitement and belief. I receive many wonderful, joyful experiences in my life.

✦ ✦ ✦

Chapter 10

The Power of Energy

The Third Personal Power of Success

*The world is a looking glass and gives back to
every man the reflection of his own face.*

— WILLIAM MAKEPEACE THACKERAY

The Universe is alive with energy; nothing exists without it. Everything that you see—and most of what you don't—is full of waves and vibrations. No matter where you go or what you do, you're constantly sending and receiving energy, and you live in a confluence of unseen frequencies all the time.

You pick up signals from other individuals and project ones of your own. You broadcast the energy that largely determines your consequences. You're wired for this, and whether you realize it or not, your results reflect the vibrations of your resonant personal energy field. The beautiful thing about this is that if you don't like what's coming in, you're always free to change what you're sending out.

Energy is one of your primary powers. It combines with consciousness to form the greatest generator of your destiny. By consciously choosing what kind of energy you want to project, you direct the greatest part of your destiny. It's a process of energetic exchange that goes on all the time.

In the physical world, the matching of frequencies is a phenomenon known as entrainment. When similar signals come together, they tend to vibrate as the same resonance; this creates a sense of attraction. It's not chemistry—it's matching energy. The principles apply across the board. Whether it's social, romantic, professional, or personal, your energy is returned. In order to change your present experience and your future manifestation, you need to find out how you're creating your personal energy field right now.

OUR BIG, FAT ENERGY PRODUCERS

Your electromagnetic vibrations are the resonance of your light energy, the frequency of your mind, heart, and soul. As we saw earlier, the biggest part of this can be found in your mind and feelings. But where do your thoughts and emotions come from? Do they just appear out of nowhere? What makes this part of your personal energy engine run?

The foundation of your emotional and cognitive power is formulated in your core conclusions. In fact, much of what you manifest can be traced back to them. Simply put, your belief system is a network of fundamental assumptions that you've embraced as a result of your upbringing and personal experience.

Similar to the way they deal with their thoughts, most people don't examine what they hold to be true. We live with our belief system the same way we live with our language: we've been given it from birth, so it's all that we know. It's quite literally the framework for all the emotions that we experience, and we're so accustomed to it that it doesn't even occur to us to try something different. But when we live without a conscious awareness of our beliefs, we willingly give up our power to change.

No matter what we've been taught or how we've been treated in the past, our beliefs are now a *present* choice. As thinking adults, we always have the option to change what we believe. We can choose for ourselves what represents our own truth—consciously releasing whatever perpetuates fear and negativity and choosing empowering beliefs instead. In terms of energy and consciousness creation, a healthier, happier, more honest, and honoring belief system is the bottom line of greater success in every arena.

Although the positive or negative nature of our vibrational energy is most powerfully expressed in our thoughts and emotions, underneath those are our fundamental beliefs. Obviously, judgmental, fatalistic, or otherwise negative convictions can create only negative emotions and thoughts. Positive ones—those that nurture the self and provide hope for the future—produce correspondingly uplifting feelings and ideas. This is, of course, the most desirable frequency to project because this is what gets the wonderful results we're looking for.

Let's take a look at how these energy producers are connected. Our beliefs are the underlying conclusions from which all assumptions and free-floating thoughts derive. We develop these beliefs either directly (through what we've been taught) or indirectly (through how we've been treated by our parents and other authority figures). It doesn't matter that these teachings may be untrue, unhealthy, or even downright destructive; the source of their influence makes them true in our minds. Each belief creates related thoughts that elicit emotional reactions, all combining to create the predominant energetic vibration that you unknowingly broadcast throughout your life.

For example, you may have been given the tenet that money proves your worth. This is a core belief, resulting in a lot of corresponding thoughts and conclusions, such as *I'll never be able to approve of myself until I make lots more money*, or *I'm just a failure now*. Such toxic thoughts create devastating emotions, such as fear, desperation, and self-loathing. The energetic and real consequences of this process are significant and can be seen in the following chart.

Core Belief: It's really hard to make it in this world.		
Thought	**Emotions**	**Energy**
I don't have what it takes.	Shame, fear	Repulsive, resistant
There's never enough to go around.	Hopelessness, despair	Heavy, dark
Why does everyone else get the breaks?	Anger, envy	Abrasive, agitated

This is just one guiding belief, but when you look at this process, it becomes clear how powerful your fundamental assumptions about life can be. Through them, you create the emotional energy that sets the tone of your world. Such powerful conclusions can set you up for success or failure, happiness or grief—and it's up to you to recognize these self-sabotaging patterns and switch to the beliefs that honor and nurture you from now on.

PLACE YOUR BETS

Some people resist creating new, positive beliefs. They think that doing so would be deluding themselves, denying a difficult reality in order to create a fantasy view of life. An even more skewed reason for not changing beliefs is the pretense of motivation. Many people assume that they're driven by their urgent and desperate convictions, and if they give up these negative precepts, they'll no longer be motivated to do what it takes to achieve their goals—but exactly the opposite is true. For example, many people think they're more likely to lose weight if they negatively judge their present appearance and health status. But studies have consistently shown that those who felt that way had far less success in reaching their goals than those with positive motivations, especially for health reasons.

When you change your belief system, you also change both your perception and the resulting emotions and thoughts. This is the triple connection of energy production. A more positive belief system stimulates far greater enthusiasm, increasing creativity and projecting much brighter energy.

But when your BETs (**beliefs, emotions, and thoughts**) are negative, you're actually wagering your life on faulty conclusions of failure and difficulty. Where's that likely to lead? You might as well stake your energy on more positive beliefs because at least then you have a chance to make them true. If you BET on the negative, you can't be truly happy, and your miserable mentality creates the expectation (and believe it or not, on a strange level, even an energy of hope) that the unfavorable outcome will appear. This is why it's so important to find out how your beliefs can be keeping you stuck.

JOURNAL FOR SUCCESS

We've already examined the seven types of toxic thought patterns in Chapter 8, all of which are based in our belief system, the foundation of our energy production. Let's take this one step further. In order to become the master of your beliefs, answer the following questions in your journal. Give yourself time to think things through and make clear decisions about the optional, honoring beliefs that you could use to replace the old, negative ones.

- What are some of the things you've been taught to *believe* about yourself, your value, your power, and your worthiness?

- How do these conclusions make you feel?

- What beliefs can you choose that would honor your true value and produce happier emotions now and healthier, more attractive energy in the future?

- What are some of the things that you've been taught about the power and value of other people and your own value and power relating to them?

- How do such conclusions make you feel?

- What healthier, more honoring conclusions can you now embrace about others and your equality to them?

- What are some of the things that you've been taught about money and success? How is this reflected in your life?

Don't skip this exercise. Think honestly about your responses and come up with some creative options because this is the only way to experience the kind of peace in the present that causes good things to come in the future. If you're going to stake your life on something, place your BET on honoring beliefs, happier emotions, and optimistic thoughts. When you do, the Universe will be glad to pay up!

TEST YOUR AQ

Your personal energy field is made up of your mental and emotional patterns, your beliefs and attitudes, and even the way you move and speak. This is the magnetic force behind your life experiences. You may think that getting ahead depends on things such as your looks, how much money you make, or even your IQ. But ultimately it's your *AQ*—your *Attraction Quotient*—that indicates whether you have the energy it takes to achieve in both the personal and professional realms.

To get an indication of your own leanings, take the following quiz. Your AQ indicates your positive energy production and the resonant patterns of your magnetic attraction. Retake this test periodically to see how your vibration may be changing.

Attraction Quotient Quiz

Assess yourself based on the following questions on a scale of 1 to 10, with 1 being never/none and 10 being all the time/abundantly. Write your rating on the line on the left—and be honest!

On a scale of 1 to 10 . . .

_____ how much confidence do you have in the things you do?

_____ how much do you respect yourself and see yourself as equal to others?

_____ how fully do you accept yourself (including your looks) right now?

_____ how often do you look for happy experiences in your present circumstances?

_____ do you generally feel optimistic about the day ahead and about the future to come?

_____ how often do you make your own goals and happiness a priority?

_____ how often are you willing to take risks and express yourself?

_____ how often do you find yourself thinking positively when faced with difficult situations?

_____ how often do you notice and stop to appreciate the good things already in your life?

_____ how much do you respect your body by eating healthfully and getting regular exercise?

_____% (Add your total score here to get your AQ.)

The total of your Attraction Quotient reveals, at its most basic level, how generally happy you are—the percentage of time and energy that you spend experiencing life in an enjoyable, fulfilling, and self-actualized way. It also represents the percentage of optimistic and peaceful energy that you tend to project in the world as well as your potential for attracting successful experiences back into your life, including professional success and healthy relationships.

Don't be discouraged if your number is low—even if it's very low. I have noticed my own score changing depending on the amount of stress or demands in my life. Here is how the scoring works:

- **80 to 100% AQ:** You're pretty happy, and your personal energy will reflect that. You're relatively comfortable with yourself, and your personal energy is pretty attractive. But if there's still something you're working on, pay attention to the specific items on the quiz that may be a problem. There may be only one or two issues that you need to work on, so make these a priority. Even a little change in your habits can make a very big difference in your personal energy field.

- **60 to 80% AQ:** If this is your score, you aren't alone. The majority of people fit into the 60 to 70 percent range. You're doing okay, but there's still room for improvement. You may need to work on being more spontaneous and self-honoring. And if you find that you often put yourself second, investigate your patterns. Use the energy-changing techniques described later in this chapter to create the peaceful resonance that attracts more happy outcomes.

- **40 to 60% AQ:** This is a common score as well. You may often feel like you're just getting by. You can increase your happiness by striving less and being more loving and forgiving of yourself. Balance is key.

It will be *very* important to use the tools in this book to prioritize yourself, release judgment, and create a stronger, more magnetic and self-directed personal energy. Don't blow it off! *All* your efforts will increase your energy of attraction. Life will surely change when you finally put yourself first!

- **20 to 40% AQ:** Don't give up! You may have been greatly discouraged lately, feeling self-doubt, uncertainty, and fear. But you can still build a positive personal energy field by making healthy self-love and positive self-talk a *top priority*. Keep at it. Structure *all* these techniques into your daily life, and it *will* pay off!

- **Less than 20% AQ:** You're probably very unhappy, feeling like you're fighting your way through life. A profound insecurity may have been part of your history—but it does *not* have to remain your reality. You need to accept yourself in an entirely new way. Set aside time each day to work on these issues. By consistently making changes in your thinking, you *will* change your energy *and* your reality. It's never too late!

Change Your Energy, Change Your Results

Whatever your score may be, you can use this test as an opportunity to become aware of the energetic changes you need to make in order to alter your life results.

To create a specific focus for a more positive resonance, change all the AQ quiz questions that received less than an 8 rating into positive intentions and affirmations. Use these on a daily basis to change the momentum in your energy production. For example, for the third question, you could affirm: *I am learning to accept myself just as I am. The beauty of my soul shines brightly for all to see.* For the fifth question, affirm: *I am feeling more and more optimistic about my future and about the day ahead. I have the power to make my life better in every way.*

For each answer with a low score, write relevant positive statements on index cards to carry with you and read often. *Each day, use one of these statements as a personal intention.* Practice making these new choices in your daily life, and those intentions will become more true for you.

Don't look at this as just busywork. It opens you up to more magnetic approaches that could totally turn your life around. You are—and always will be—the generator of your own happiness and success. Choose to broadcast a brighter vibration, and you're bound to tune in to brilliant results.

Affirmations for Attractive Energy

✦ Only I choose what is true for me. From now on, I release any belief that is toxic or dishonoring in any way.

✦ I am choosing a new, honoring, and optimistic belief system for myself. It is my right, my present choice, and my future reality.

✦ As I choose to think more positively, I send out more receptive energy and attract better and better results.

✦ The emotional quality of my life is up to me. I am strong enough to create a more loving and peaceful view of myself and of my world.

✦ I accept myself, my value, my worthiness, and my appearance. I deserve my own high regard in every way.

✦ ✦ ✦

Chapter 11

The Power of Intention

The Fourth Personal Power of Success

Keep your thoughts on what you intend to create. Stay consistently matched up with the field of intention, and then watch for the clues that what you're summoning from the all-creative Source is arriving in your life.

— DR. WAYNE W. DYER

Your intentions are key catalysts for the laws of desire and intent. Nothing you do is without purpose, whether you're aware of it or not. When you have clear and honoring intentions in both your daily life and the pursuit of your goals, you tap into the natural forces of the Law of Pure Desire—and once again, consciousness is key. You must become aware of (and take control of) your intentions.

Any action, decision, or behavior that you choose to engage in could have several different objectives behind it. Although the deed may not change, a different intention can transform its energy completely, and therefore modify the consequences that you draw back into your life.

As an example, let's look at a common workplace situation that may seem positive on the surface but depends on intention.

Let's say that you give your supervisor a compliment. If you're expressing how you genuinely feel and you want to share something supportive and affirmative, then both the intention and the act are positive. This creates a genuinely honoring resonance, and only beneficial results will come back to you.

Let's say, however, you don't honestly feel that way. Maybe you even dislike them, yet you're trying to use the compliment to ingratiate yourself, perhaps hoping to get a raise or a good evaluation. In this case, your intention is manipulative, and your energy resonates with a dense and deceitful vibration. Of course, you may still get the raise or the good review, but eventually you're bound to magnetize something deceptive and controlling from someone else.

If your motivation to be kind or even submissive in any situation is an attempt to gain approval, you're essentially sacrificing your self-esteem for a longed-for acceptance that you'll never really get. Such a dishonoring purpose can only negate the energy you send out, broadcasting a very clear message that you don't believe you deserve to be valued for yourself. Your compliment (or any other caring act) may seem to be kind, but if it's made out of desperation, it completely reverses the energy involved. Such is the power of your intentions—to radically change your vibration and therefore the consequences of your life.

This happened to a client of mine who longed for the approval and acceptance of her in-laws. She made herself available for everything they needed, from babysitting to baking. She felt this would guarantee their kindness and inclusion in their family events, but she was wrong. No matter how much she did for them, they were still dismissive and even hurtful to her. When I talked to her about the energy of it, she realized she had to stop striving and start self-prioritizing. She set new boundaries, and while her in-laws were surprised at the change in her, in time they came to respect her more. Then she was able to connect with them in more meaningful ways.

Everything you do is driven by intention. Whether you're eating breakfast, driving to work, writing a check, or doing your job, you're engaging in these activities with energetic meaning. Even the most tedious task has intention underneath it. Of course there's the obvious purpose, but there's also an underlying resonance that you may not be aware of. You may think that your goal for driving to work is simply to get there, but what is your intention for the *emotional experience* of it? What kind of energy do you *intend to feel* during this activity? It may be just a morning commute, but the way you go through it is important. Your obvious purpose for writing a check is to pay for something, but what is the energetic force behind that? It's not just the surface reasons that you have to consider; it's also the *intention of your feelings during the experience.*

When you're driving to work, you can listen to your favorite music and decide to enjoy the ride, or you can spend your time worrying about what you have to get done that day. While purchasing something, you can choose to appreciate what you're paying for, or you can worry about the amount of money it costs. While doing your job, you can be grateful for the work you have and intend to enjoy it as you do your best, or you can drag yourself through the day, resenting having to be there at all.

In performing these activities, which of these options do you think will garner the best energetic results? Your mental intentions are a powerful force because they strongly direct your consciousness creation. Think of how many experiences you go through each day without ever considering how you want to *feel* about them. You may think that it's no big deal to have negative emotions about minor daily activities, but ongoing resentful and judgmental emotions can create a pervasive depression that increases the energies of unhappiness and even hopelessness. But you always have the option to choose higher emotional intentions at any time and in any situation.

INTEND TO BE HAPPY!

It's time to experience the activities of your life with more positive intentions, to see each part of your reality with gratitude and trust instead of constant dissatisfaction or worry. When fear and anxiety become your dominant emotions, their energy darkens your intentions. That's what happens when you're always thinking things like *What if I can't pay the bills? What if I don't make the sale? I hate my job! It's such a drag!* Over time, these and other negative thoughts will become your expectations.

You've probably heard of self-fulfilling prophecies. Well, believe it or not, this concept is scientifically sound. The focus of your emotional energy can transform the fear of future problems into a subconscious plan to make those problems a reality. You may think your goal is wealth, but if you live in terror of poverty, that ongoing resonance of fear becomes your driving intention! The more you fear being poor, the more your negative vibration pushes abundance away. This is the energy dynamic of paradoxical intent; you must shift from desperation to determination.

You can work on your goals and intend to trust, planning to live in happiness now. Whether you're weeding the garden or doing the laundry, get out of your doldrums or negativity and aim to see the potential for joy in every task.

This is especially important in the pursuit of your dreams. Your intention for wealth—or any other good thing—must *not* be driven by constant dissatisfaction in the present. People often ask me how to maintain a strong focus on their desires without falling into this paradoxical emotional pit. Think of the energetic difference between desperation and determination. The former is a fear-based need for your desired results. The latter, on the other hand, is the intention to take peaceful but persistent action in the direction of your dreams, all the while aiming to create happiness even now, without them.

These experiences are poles apart. You can feel different vibrations even when you just say the words *desperation* and *determination*. When you become desperate, you give way too much power to the unknown, ignoring your ability to create a beautiful vibration now. But you can take back control of your energy by returning to a present, valuing intention.

Shift to a Determined, Pure Intention

Surrendering fearful, emotional attachments to your goals is a crucial part of shifting to a pure intention that is more peaceful, receptive, and attractive. To figure out what kind of approach you're taking, look at the following statements of desperate intentions versus determined intentions. As you read the chart, you can feel the different energy that each set produces. Which group represents your energy the most? Which energy would you rather live in?

Desperate Intentions	Determined Intentions
My goal (job, money, relationship, etc.) is what really will make me happy.	I have the power to make myself happy.
Only this achievement will make me a success.	There are many forms of success, including being happy now. I can reach my goals later and still feel successful today.
I can finally accept myself when I make more money (lose weight, get a better job, etc.).	I can choose to accept myself now. I deserve my own high regard.
Only when I get ahead will I feel safe or secure.	I can choose to trust that I am safe and secure right now.
I have to hurry to make this goal happen. I can't relax. I can't stop working and striving until I get it done.	I can work on my goal and still create all the positive emotions I desire even now. I choose trust and peace throughout my process.

Choose to shift your negative intention and move to a more determined approach, all the while looking for present opportunities for joy. A positive consciousness and a trusting, optimistic purpose will create the magnetic resonance that draws your desires to you. Surrendering your need for your goal will magnetize it more quickly. This is more easily achieved when you embrace your present emotional intentions for happiness, satisfaction, and peace in your current activities.

Never assume there's only one way to achieve your emotional dreams; open yourself up to all the options that may be available to you to create those feelings right now. When you get anxious about a specific goal, visualize the outcome you desire with enthusiasm and optimism. Then affirm: *This or something better is coming to my life—in just the right way at just the right time.* This will awaken you to the abundant options in all your pursuits.

Surrender and trust in the open outcome of your desires. There's no more magnetic energy than trust, present peace, and flexibility—and no greater way to turn your intentions into reality.

JOURNAL FOR SUCCESS

In order to genuinely surrender, you must look inside for your real intentions. Ask yourself these questions both in meditation and in your journal:

- When I think of my desires, what are my emotions? Do I feel desperate, worried, and doubtful or optimistic, peaceful, and hopeful?

- What emotional (not financial) outcome do I intend this goal to bring to my life? What can I do, choose, or think right now to create this state of being today?

- Is my purpose fear-based or manipulative in any way? Does it increase or decrease my own sense of dignity and honor?

- Is my intention optimistic—not only for future outcomes but also for present activities? If not, what am I doubting or perhaps dreading? What other attitudes or approaches can I choose to shift this energy now?

- Are the intentions around my goal conflicting in any way? If so, what positive and pure motivation can I focus my energy on now?

OPEN, CLEAR, AND UNCONFLICTED

Since your intentions are your Universal order forms, you must be very specific, sure, and optimistic. Being unclear would be like going into a restaurant and just telling the server, "I'm hungry." You have to be aware of what you want and let the Universe know that you deserve it. Conflicting thoughts can derail even long-held desires. You must live with certain knowledge and strong belief, telling yourself: *I can do this. I am capable and I deserve it!* So let go of the questions, self-doubt, or contradictions, and choose only pure, straightforward intentions from now on.

Whether it's about your abilities or your worthiness, you can't muddy your Universal order with negativity and resistance. Consider what would happen if you went into a restaurant and told the server, "Well, I'd like the steak, but maybe I should just have a hamburger." She'd give up and walk away.

But let's say that she gives you a second chance. This time, you say, "I'd really like the lobster, but I don't deserve to spend that much money on myself. I guess I should just get a fish sandwich." Eventually the server won't even come back!

The Universe is the same way. If you're constantly shifting from one intention to another, from desire to undeserving, from belief to doubt, it just can't know what to serve—so it won't give you anything! You may think, *I want a new relationship,* but also think, *I've been hurt so many times; I don't want to be hurt again.* You may hope that you get a big promotion, but you may also fear that the other candidates are more qualified. Such conflicting approaches poison your energy and cloud your consciousness, turning away the Universal flow.

Releasing Conflicting Intentions

To avoid the trap of conflicting intentions, you must believe four things about yourself and your goal. If you don't believe these now, affirm that you're learning to embrace these truths. If you can't seem to arrive at these beliefs, switch your goal to one that resonates with *all* the following conditions:

- You believe you are capable of achieving it.

- You believe you deserve it.

- You believe that your goal is safe for you.

- You believe that the Universe can provide it for you.

Your intentions must be clear and unconflicted, and you must be open to receiving. Maintain a strong vision of your goal and send that vision out before you. Know that you deserve it and that you are capable of creating it! No matter what you've experienced in the past, love is safe and so is great wealth. And whatever it is you desire, the Universe is waiting and willing to bring it to you!

Create an ongoing consciousness about your intentions—not just about your long-term goals but also about your daily life. For example, when I consider the day ahead, my first intention is to create happiness and value in all that I do, and I work on sharing those energies with others. As I begin a new activity, I try to plan my emotional approach. Since every single thing you do has a focus that directs your energy production, you need to be fully aware of your real and emotional motivations. In this way you can magnetize many moments of happiness and success each day and increasingly greater joy and success in the future.

Tips for Powerful Intentions

You can have more control over your energy production by weaving these simple techniques for powerful intentions into your daily life.

- **Spend a few minutes each morning meditating on—or writing about—your emotional intentions for the day ahead.** See yourself going happily through your planned activities, bringing your consciousness to each activity, making positive, optimistic, and joyful intentions. By doing so, you're projecting a brighter consciousness out into the world each day, filling it with a happy, successful life-force energy.

- **Focus your intentions many times a day.** If you're experiencing a difficult time or are working on a challenging project, renew your conscious direction as often as possible. Take a break midmorning, at lunch, or after work to breathe in a peaceful attitude and create a positive intention for the next few hours.

- **Try to engage in more positive intentions during the more mundane activities of your life.** Be aware of your mental direction as you're doing such things as eating, driving, and performing household chores. Find a positive, heartfelt, and grateful purpose in the experience of every single task, and it will change the nature of your energy completely.

- **In the evening, consciously create an intention for your nighttime energy.** Affirm: *I sleep peacefully through the night, waking up relaxed, refreshed, and enthusiastic about the day ahead.*

- **Reevaluate your specific goal intentions periodically.** Make sure you're not creating conflict around your desires by clouding them with fear and feelings of unworthiness. Stay focused, open, determined, and optimistic in order to keep your desires on track.

Your present intentions lay the groundwork for your future success, so don't let them get tangled up in doubt and confusion. Never negate your abilities or dismiss your worthiness—and never, ever minimize the great abundance of Universal possibilities. A pure desire knows that your goal is available and achievable. You deserve it, so intend it!

Affirmations for Pure and Powerful Intentions

+ I am beginning to take a closer look at why I do the things I do. I understand that my choices about how I want to feel are powerful forces in my life.

+ I have the power to make myself happy. This is my responsibility and my present intention.

+ I am open to all the abundant options the Universe has to offer. There are plenty of ways to make myself happy and to make my dreams come true.

+ Every day I am becoming more aware of my present and future intentions. I choose to live in trust, self-love, and a peaceful approach to life.

+ I bring joyful intentions to all that I do—even the little tasks of life. I find many moments of happiness and gratitude each day.

+ + +

Chapter 12

The Power of Choice

The Fifth Personal Power of Success

You are free to choose, but the choices you make today
will determine what you will have, be, and do
in the tomorrow of your life.

— ZIG ZIGLAR

The dynamic personal power that links all the others is *choice*. Unfortunately, we're often so stuck in our habits that we may be completely unaware that our options *always* remain open. This is true from our seemingly insignificant and mundane picks to our most monumental, life-altering decisions.

A lot of times we resist change due to the circumstances of our lives. We think, *I can't leave my job because I have to pay the mortgage,* yet we are free to look for a new job while retaining the old. Sometimes stay stuck in a present career because of an old decision to pursue it. We're often compelled to keep sticking with the same thing over and over simply because we've done so in the past.

We're also inclined to limit our choices according to the patterns we've been taught. We think that we don't have the option to stand up for ourselves because we were never given the chance to do so in the past. We continue to *choose* to be people pleasers because that priority was forced on us by others. We rely on past ways of doing things, and long-held manners of speaking, eating, learning, communicating, and prioritizing. Day after day, we make thousands of choices, but it rarely occurs to us that we have the ability to do everything differently—if we so desire.

I once heard a funny story about a woman who made delicious roasts and gravies. The meat was so tender that it would almost melt in your mouth. She'd learned the recipe from her mother, and she passed the tradition down to her daughter, saying that one of the keys to a juicy roast was to cut the ends off before putting it in the roaster. Her daughter obediently did this and followed her directions to the letter, and she, too, was able to make a delicious dinner.

One day when she was visiting her grandmother—the woman who'd come up with the recipe to begin with—she said, "I'm so glad that mom told me your secret. Everybody thinks I make the juiciest roasts in town."

Her grandmother asked, "What secret is that?"

"Cutting the ends off the roast, of course!" the girl answered. "Mom's been doing it since she started cooking. She does it because you did it that way, and your roasts were always delicious, too."

Upon hearing that, the old grandmother laughed and laughed. When she finally composed herself, she told her granddaughter, "Honey, I didn't cut the ends off the roast because it made it juicier. I did it because my oven was so small that I couldn't fit the whole thing in at one time!"

This is a funny but very revealing illustration of why we often continue to make the same choices throughout our lives: they become habits that we maintain without consciousness. There may have been good reasons for them originally, but do we get any benefit from continuing to pick the same things now? This is an important question because so many of the decisions we've become locked into have the power to affect the energy—and even the very quality—of our lives.

In every single moment, we face an energetic choice of some kind. Not only do we decide what to do, we also determine what to think, believe, feel, and perceive about the situations we're in. In the long run, it's our daily choices that come together to create the tapestry of our existence. Our moment-to-moment decisions weave the picture of who we are and what we become. These are our *defining moments*, the ongoing little decisions that determine the energy and direction of our lives.

Where our patterns are concerned, we have to understand that we don't just make a decision once; we do so over and over again. You may have decided to smoke when you were a teenager, but every time you light up, you're making that monumental agreement with yourself all over again. Every single time it's a new choice, even when you're not at all conscious of it. Unfortunately, your lack of awareness doesn't diminish its power in your life.

Our days are filled with countless unconscious choices and hundreds of conscious ones, and our unconsidered actions have just as much power as the decisions we spend a long time thinking about. In fact, these choices can be so habitual that they're likely to have an even greater impact! But when we take control of all our possibilities, we begin to redirect the energetic momentum of our lives. This power, this ability to choose, allows us to orchestrate the success of our desires in two fundamental ways—in our choices of attitude and action.

ATTITUDE AND ACTION

The choices you make always revolve around one of two things, attitude or action. The former is inherently linked to your perception and beliefs, the two fundamental pieces of consciousness and energy. In this way, your attitude is a primary catalyst both to what you magnetize and what you manifest; it's the subtle combination of thought and emotion focused on everything from particular issues to profound experiences.

We may say that we have a good attitude (or a bad one), but we have to look more closely at what this really means. In most cases, the good is based on positive convictions and uplifting emotions; the bad arises from pessimistic conclusions combined with fearful or hostile feelings.

You may have had horrible attitudes about yourself and your life experiences in the past, but you don't have to embrace them any longer. Your mentality creates your reality, and where the forces of success are concerned, attitude *is* everything. This is energetically true because your outlook is the propellant of your consciousness creation. It may not have occurred to you before, but you choose how you approach every day—in fact, every moment. And you choose how you *react* to every experience. Equanimity, the ability to respond with calm focus no matter what's going on around you, is one of the most steady and persistently magnetic energies you can engage in. It's important to know that you have the power to choose that and other empowering and positive attitudes at any time.

It's also a good idea to investigate the decisions you make concerning your actions. There are three main courses of action you pursue all the time, and those are your consistent behaviors concerning yourself, others, and your goals. These actions can include anything from what you choose to eat for lunch to whom you spend your time with and how often you make yourself a priority in your daily life. All these choices—and countless others—have the power to enhance your movement forward or derail it, so if you're not pursuing behavioral options that are honoring and healthy, it's time to start making new choices now.

JOURNAL FOR SUCCESS

Think about the attitudes and actions that you engage in concerning the following issues. Write your answers in your journal, then determine to apply more positive choices to your daily life.

Attitude Choices

1. What's your attitude about your present work situation?

- What are your thoughts about it? Do they tend to be positive or negative?

- How do you feel about your job? Do you generally feel comfortable and purposeful or unhappy and even resentful during your work experience?

- What can you change about your thoughts, beliefs, or perceptions that can make your feelings and attitude about work more positive? Remember this: even if you want to find another job, you can still look for something in the present one to be positive about— or even enjoy. This energetic choice will make it more likely to find a job you do enjoy in the future.

2. What's your attitude about money?

- What are the thoughts and emotions you have concerning money?

- Do these make you feel satisfied and happy or urgent and needy?

- How can you redefine your beliefs about money to create better feelings about it? Affirm yourself and your resourcefulness. Know that you are capable of making all the money you need and affirm that greater wealth is coming to you in wonderful and unexpected ways.

3. What's your attitude about pursuing your goals?

- List a few of your most dominant thoughts related to each goal.

- How do you *feel* about your goals? Do you tend to be hopeful and resolute or doubtful and hesitant?

- Write down positive intentions to reverse the negative feelings you may have about your plans. If you're convinced that something you've chosen isn't going to work or doesn't quite fit with you, it may be time to look at other options where your goals are concerned.

Create the intention to engage in beliefs and emotions that will broadcast a healthier resonance and more attractive energy concerning all these issues. Remind yourself that these options are your choices every day. Read your new conclusions; breathe deeply and affirm your new positive attitudes often. You always have a choice, and you deserve to make a conscious one!

Action Choices

1. Self-action

- What behaviors do you engage in on a daily basis that might be considered dishonoring to you? (Include what you ingest, how you talk to yourself, and how you spend your time.)

- Make a list of alternative choices that would create a more positive lifestyle and higher energetic vibrations to attract better results. Read your list each morning. What can you do to implement your new empowering behaviors on a regular basis? Pick some things from your list to write on index cards and use them as reminders throughout the day.

- What are the behaviors and actions that you engage in on a regular basis that tend to honor you and your way of living?

- Make a list to remind yourself about these options and make these choices more often.

2. Actions toward others

- Which of the following adjectives generally describe your attitude, feelings, and actions toward others? Circle one from each column.

Passive	Assertive
Kind	Disinterested or Abrasive
Trusting	Fearful
Equal	Inferior or Superior
Flexible	Controlling
Peaceful	Uncomfortable
Communicative	Shut down

- Where do you think these responses came from? Look at your history and consider the source of these patterns. Remember that you no longer have to hold on to the beliefs that crated these patterns.

- What kind of energy do these choices create? Make a conscious decision about whether you want to continue engaging in these energetic choices.

- If you circled any item from the right-hand column, how can you change both your beliefs and behaviors to create a more harmonic resonance? It may feel very risky at first, but you must see yourself as equal and deserving. Slowly start to take steps in more honoring and self-empowered directions.

3. Goal actions

- How often do you take action toward your goals?

- When making the choice between acting on your dreams or doing another task, what usually takes precedence?

- How enthusiastic are you when you engage in goal-oriented actions?

- What can you do to take more frequent and more positive energetic action toward these desires?

To succeed at your goals, you must often choose them over other things, and this is where the power of choice connects with the power of letting go. You may have to release a habit or even personal gratification in order to make your goal a higher priority. In fact, no matter what the issue is, if you're conscious about your life, you'll find that time and time again you have the option to positively apply both these principles. This is one of the most liberating and empowering decisions you can make: *the choice to let go of an old unhealthy response and to choose a new approach.*

How many times a day are you given the chance to either hold on or relax your grip on your old responses? Whether it's a spontaneous habit, a negative thought pattern, or a difficult emotion such as fear or anger, you always have the option to either clutch it to you or cast it aside. Yet so many people feel compelled to hang on because they think that doing so is what gives them their power. They hold on to their habits, other people, their titles, their comfort zones, and even their self-sabotaging routines. But setting these things free gives you your ultimate power—the power to completely change your life.

When you *choose* to let go, you free yourself of attachment, fear, and the need for control—and with each of these decisions, you gain *more* strength. Especially be determined to let go of your old negative patterns, attitudes, and habits. If they haven't gotten you where you want to be so far, they obviously aren't working. It's time to choose new, healthy habits and empowering patterns now.

There's an old story about a village in northern Alaska that is 40 miles north of the closest town. The road leading out of that town going up to that village is a dirt road that is mostly mud from the months of May to September. The rest of the year, it becomes frozen in the deep ruts that had been cut into the mud during the warmer months. As one leaves the paved road of the town and enters that frozen dirt road, there's a sign that says, "Be careful which rut you enter. You'll be in it for the next 40 miles."

Our lives can be much the same way. We can fall into ruts of habits at a very young age and, if we remain unconscious, we can stay in those ruts for 40 years or more. But our power of choice is always available to us, and no matter how deep the rut is, we can change it now.

CHOICE OR CONSEQUENCE

In the rhythm of your life, every moment is a choice—and every single one of them has a consequence. In fact, each choice has two kinds of consequence: actual and energetic. Sometimes the actual results are easy to see. For example, if you keep over-eating, you'll gain weight. That's the actual, physical result. But what's the energetic outcome? The resonance of the decision to overindulge is dishonoring, sending out messages of self-dismissal and even self-loathing, a resonance that's bound to attract people and situations who'll promote even more of those feelings.

Many times, however, the consequences aren't so clear. Whether you're making a phone call, ordering a meal, or hiring a vice president, it's important to consider both the actual and energetic consequences of your choice. You may not always be able to predict the outcome, but you need to weigh the options and look at the energy involved before you decide. Your choices should ring true for you, and to achieve that end, they must resonate with dignity, integrity, and self-honoring. But if you fall into old, unwanted patterns, don't be too hard on yourself. Self-forgiveness and renewed higher intentions are both honoring choices as well. Whatever happens, always remember to love yourself through it. That is one of the most powerful choices you can make.

Whenever you're choosing a course of action—big or small—there are two questions that will help reveal the energetic nature of the consequences. Ask yourself: *Does this choice honor me? Does it enhance my sense of dignity and maintain my integrity?*

If you can answer yes to these questions, then whatever that decision may be, you'll know that you're going with the highest option possible. The Universe longs to support your honoring energy, so you can rest assured that every choice you make with this intention will bring genuine power and ever-increasing blessings!

Affirmations for Healthy, Happy, and Powerful Choices

✦ I know that I have countless choices every day.
I bring my consciousness to each and every one.

✦ All my daily decisions define me and determine
my energy. I make loving and honoring choices in
thought, word, and deed each day.

✦ I release unhealthy habits and choose more honoring
actions and behaviors. More and more I am conscious
and in control!

✦ I always choose to engage in a more empowering and
loving perception of myself.

✦ I choose to live free of fear, worry, envy, or judgment.
I breathe and let go of concerns. I choose to live in
heartfelt peace and trust.

✦ ✦ ✦

Chapter 13

The Power of Love

The Sixth Personal Power of Success

*Love is an essential ingredient for success. Without it,
your life suffers in emptiness. With it, your life
vibrates with warmth and satisfaction.*

— GLENN VAN EKEREN

When I talk about the power of love to my business clients, they often balk. One man in management said, "You had me right up to this point. The science of it all makes sense, but when you talk about love, you lose me."

This is a common reaction. When people understand the human application of quantum physics, they can see that their consciousness, energy, and intention carry great power in the consequences of their lives. But when it comes to success, most people want to know, "What's love got to do with it?"

Love is a very powerful force within both the Universe and individuals. It's an energy that can be deeply felt, not just romantically but in every way. Its strong, vibrating, creative resonance moves freely and fluidly throughout the world. When we align our own personal energy of love with this Universal current, there's nothing that we can't achieve.

This vibration is the absence of hate and fear. The choice to experience, perceive, and promote love causes you to see the real value in yourself, in your life, and in the world. This choice draws amazing value back to you. The energy not only accelerates the achievement of your goals, it creates a profoundly happy resonance that permeates your entire life. Every time you choose to approach anything with a loving attitude, you stimulate the action of all the laws and forces of success, so let's look at how you can use this power to harness the force of each law.

LOVE AND THE 7 LAWS OF SUCCESS

1. The Law of Manifestation. To establish a loving consciousness, step back and choose a persistently peaceful and caring perception of yourself and others. This stimulates the creation of a personal reality filled with joy. In addition, when you understand the principle of observer-created reality, you know that your observation of all the forms of love in your life increases tender responses from the Universe, manifesting abundantly wonderful experiences.

2. The Law of Magnetism. Love—including self-love—is the single most magnetic energy that you can project. Unfortunately, fear and hate can also be pretty attractive—in all the wrong ways. Remember, the Universe returns your own self-regard and treatment back to you. So take a deep breath, let go of self-judgment, and affirm: *I choose to love and accept myself as I am.* Your personal energy will have an irresistible vibration.

3. The Law of Pure Desire. A loving heart is full of hope and excitement. Genuine belief in yourself increases your hope for the future and for your goals. And when you choose to embrace your life right now, you're much more able to surrender your attachment, which purifies your desire and greatly accelerates your results.

4. The Law of Paradoxical Intent. Loving intentions are free from fear. Instead of worry, trust becomes your way of life—and your predominant energy. You can bring peaceful intentions to all that you do, whether you're working, playing, eating, talking, thinking, or even just breathing. To do so, affirm: *I can consciously choose peace in this moment.*

5. The Law of Harmony. The key to harmony—and the magic of synchronicity—is to live with an honoring attitude. Choose to release judgment and hostility, both toward yourself and others. Open yourself to tolerance, forgiveness, and compassion, too. All these will harmonize you with the mystical forces of synchronicity and a Universe of opportunity.

6. The Law of Right Action. Bringing loving treatment to the world is the ultimate right action. The world responds and brings this back to you in the form of assistance, support, and blessings. When you're in a situation where you don't know what to do, ask yourself, *How do I bring love to this experience?* (Remember, bringing love does not mean being passive and always putting others first. You must ask what choice brings balance to you and to the situation, then express yourself in a clear, compassionate way.)

7. The Law of Expanding Influence. Your intention to spread loving energy expands your positive and peaceful life experience—and that of everyone around you. In your family, business dealings, social life, and community, your choice to engage in caring thoughts and actions expands the peace in the world. It also brings greater serenity and prosperity back to you.

LOVE AT THE CENTER

No matter what Universal Law you're working with, you simply can't go wrong when you make the choice to spread love throughout your life. As always, the best place to start is with the self. Without the power of self-love, you can only live in fear and trepidation, and nothing positive can be promoted in that state of mind.

This is a central energetic point: self-love is not arrogant or conceited; it's the starting point of your ability to value everything and everyone around you. To stimulate this personal source of power, look in the mirror and affirm that you love, value, and appreciate yourself. Stop looking for the faults, and start acknowledging your eternal truth and qualities.

Love is a strong, pulsating vibration. But if you refuse to cherish yourself, your abrasive inner energy causes others to refuse to care for you, too. Make no mistake about this—you simply can't engage in self-loathing and still expect to succeed.

In addition to affirming yourself, it's also a good idea to do nice things for yourself. Create an atmosphere at home and work that inspires you. Periodically throughout your day, take a few minutes to relax and regroup; give yourself the encouragement to keep going and say congratulations for a job well done. Choose to love the little moments of your life. Treasure the day, the sights around you, and the tasks and activities you're engaged in. Your self-encouragement and life appreciation will attract the same wonderful vibrations from other people and from the world.

Once you've established your own self-loving energy, you can extend it by channeling it into the hearts of those around you. Smile sincerely and send affection through your gaze as you make eye contact with a friend; feel it moving out your fingers as you shake someone's hand. Intend it in your voice and your heart in every activity, great or small. Visualize a bright, caring light and energy flowing from your heart to those of others.

Sometimes, if you're just feeling too frustrated or tired—or if you encounter people who stimulate lower emotions, you may find it difficult to visualize sending your own caring energy to them. In this case, you can choose to be a channel of the Universal vibration that's always present. Encircle these people with Divine light and Love, and then let any concerns or even thoughts of them go. Choose peace in the present.

ENERGY-SOFTENING TECHNIQUE:
Freezing Names

Projecting the energy of love to others may seem silly even with people we care about, but it can feel downright impossible with people who are critical or even hostile toward us. When this happens, I recommend a technique that I call *Freezing Names*. While truly strange-sounding, this is a very simple, effective energy process that is designed to soften the energy between you and a person who may be creating a problem or conflict in your life.

Start with a small piece of paper and write the person's full name at the top. Circle that name in yellow, using either a highlighter or yellow crayon. Below that circle, write the person's full name again followed by the phrase "is sealed in the Light." Then fold the paper into a small square and place it in a paper cup that you fill with water and place in the freezer. The paper will float, but a thin layer of ice will freeze over it. If you prefer, you can use a lemon and put a small slit in one side, then place the folded paper into the opening and throw the lemon in the freezer.

This technique is not for ill-wishing or intending to send negative energy to a person. It's actually sealing them in the Light of Divine Consciousness, surrounding them with that perfect love. When a person is surrounded with this wonderful energy, they feel far less inclined to seek power through anger or hostility. It may take a while, but just do the process and let it go. If the person persists in negative action, you can throw the original lemon away and redo the process until the energy gets better or the situation is resolved.

This might seem absurd to some, but I have taught this technique to countless people who have had incredible results. Some have seen immediate changes, while others have had to wait a while and repeat it several times. As I said in the introduction, some of these techniques may seem strange, but when done together, they can create great energetic shifts. When you combine this process with the Venting Letters process described in Chapter 8, it becomes a powerful tool!

LOVE: The Power of a Single Word

What's in a word? If the word is *love*, quite a bit. The amazing work done by Dr. Masaru Emoto examines the consciousness of water and shows that molecules of water are affected by single words, phrases, thoughts, and even feelings. He did several experiments where he examined both the effects of human consciousness on water as well as the effects of water (especially that which was "treated" with his specific experiments) on human experiences, including physical healing. His findings can be found in his book, *The Hidden Messages in Water*.

His experiments used high-speed microscopic photography to record the type of crystal formed during the melting of frozen water that had been exposed to specific words, thoughts, and even music. One of his approaches was to write words on paper and then place those papers (facing the water) on the bottle or petri dish. He was careful to use water from the same source when comparing the results. (He consistently found that natural spring water created far more beautiful crystals—even when untreated— than tap water.)

In one of his experiments, he labeled one bottle with the words, "Thank you." On another bottle of the same water, he wrote, "You fool." The results were astounding. The crystal formation in the "Thank you" bottle resembled a perfectly formed snowflake with beautiful lacey points. But the "You fool" crystal—the same water exposed to those words for the same amount of time—didn't even form a crystal, it was more of shapeless mass with random fragmented, irregular points.

Similar results were found when experimenters talked to the water and when different music was played. It's no surprise that the kinder statements formed more beautiful crystals while the harsh ones formed unrecognizable forms that had no beauty at all. And the classical, more peaceful music had much more striking results than the heavy metal. The difference in these pictures is visible in the photographs in Emoto's books, and they are striking reminders of the power of consciousness. Emoto's conclusions included the concept that water has a consciousness that is able to pick up and be influenced by verbal and emotional information. And, as an extension, the same positively "charged" water is able to convey that beneficial energy to the people who drink it.

So what do you think were the most positively charged words creating the most beautiful results in the crystals? The first was *love* and the next was *gratitude*. These words were by far the most beneficially influential individually, but a surprising increase in the size, perfection, and beauty was seen when they were used together. And another single word that created positive results was *hope*.

The message here is clear. If words can change the quality of water, what can they do to and for us? It may seem simplistic to say and send the word *love* to ourselves and others, but is it really? If we bring our consciousness to this simple process, it can have great meaning and powerful results, even physically. Emoto concludes that the energy and vibrations we send out and are exposed to can impact everything from the subatomic level up to entire organs in the body, causing either better or worsening health, depending on the types of words, phrases, or emotions. And it goes even further, reaching out to the people and experiences of our lives. After all, if drops of water have consciousness and we are made up of 55 to 60 percent water—and if Earth, this blue planet of ours, is largely covered by water, where does the influence end?

I highly recommend Masaru Emoto's books to get the full effect of this incredible work. I also recommend putting the words *love* and *gratitude* on your own water bottles and in your affirmations and prayers. Say them in the mirror and bring these energies to the people and situations in your life. It may seem like a silly and simplistic exercise, but as Emoto proves, it is a strong energetic cause. The use of words like *love, gratitude, hope,* and *thank you* may sound like a simple process, but that doesn't make it superficial or meaningless. It is certainly worth what little energy it takes to shift consciousness in a truly significant way. I also want to recommend Sharon Anne Klingler's book, *Power Words*, which contains many extremely simple techniques to shift your energy rapidly with just a word or two.

Love as a Directed Energetic Intention

It's interesting that just using the word *love* as an energetic intention directed toward certain people or situations can bring a more harmonious resonance that brings resolution. I have seen this process work in both my personal life and in professional situations in my counseling practice. In one case, I was doing marriage counseling with two people who were getting on each other's nerves. He was a penny-pincher, and she was a spendthrift. I told them that they were each making the issue of money mean too much, but each wanted to be right and each was absolutely determined to get their way. They were so resistant that nothing I said could get them to stop arguing, and I was getting ready to tell them I couldn't help them when I finally decided to try sending the situation and the couple love. In the morning on the drive to work before our sessions, and whenever I thought about them, I would simply say the word *love* and think about that energy.

It took a few weeks, but one day they came in with an entirely different attitude. They said they realized I had been right when I told them that they needed to meet in the middle and make their relationship more important than the money. After months of headbutting, they picked up on the energy and intention of love, and they finally decided to give it to each other.

Love brings peace to animosity and resolution to difficulty. It's one of the most powerful intentions you can make and one of the most beneficial actions you take. Say it, feel it, and allow it to be your own gentle attitude toward yourself, toward others, and toward the situations you find yourself in. Make love a real presence in your energy and your life, and you'll soon be more conscious of a wonderfully loving reality.

Meditation: Surround It with Love

Try this for yourself. The next time something comes up that you can't find an answer for, meditate on your intention to surround it with love. When a problem arises with someone in your life, repeatedly and gently direct the energy of love and then completely let it go. And even when nothing in particular is going on, just stop, close your eyes, and breathe in the word and its peaceful energy.

This isn't just some fluffy, feel-good farce; it's *real* energetic power. Love changes your consciousness, your frequency, and even your physiology. It activates your heart center like nothing else, fueling your emotional receptivity. When you bring your heart and your head together in a loving purpose, the Universe's tender intention will direct the river of abundance right to your own empowered heart.

Affirmations for Living in Love

+ I live with a consciousness of love. I see myself and my life with loving, accepting eyes.

+ In my attitude toward myself and my life, I choose love and gratitude.

+ I release judgment, striving, and conflict. I quiet my mind and rest my consciousness in the peace of my heart.

+ I send my love to all that I see. Many times a day, I think, feel, and say the word *love* with a grateful and heartfelt intention.

+ I happily look for the opportunity to help others and be of service in little and big ways. I balance my own self-love with compassion for others.

+ + +

PART III

The Five Magnetic Energies of Success

Success isn't just a random occurrence that happens to a lucky few; it's a consciousness creation that comes from your personal alignment with the unseen forces and Universal Laws. What seems like chance is energetic synchronicity, a process of entraining—or matching—your own vibration with that of the Universal flow. A constant stream of blessings is always available from that mighty river, and the biggest influence that determines its direction is your own personal resonance.

That power of personal resonance is within you always, and no matter what you've attracted so far, you can still connect your own life force with that wonderfully abundant realm of all possibilities. When you choose to bring the magnetic forces into your heart and mind on a daily basis, you'll create a major shift in consciousness and an entirely different resonance. Your images and vibrations will change. Your view of yourself and your life will take on a higher, grander understanding, and you'll find that you can live a successful and happy life every day, opening yourself to receiving truly awe-inspiring results.

Chapter 14

The Energy of Confidence

The First Magnetic Energy of Success

We can change our whole life and the attitude of people around us simply by changing ourselves.

— RUDOLF DREIKURS

When you're talking about success, the first and foremost magnetic energy is that of self-confidence. In fact, lack of it is one of the biggest reasons people don't succeed—not because they can't but because they don't believe in their own worth and abilities. How do you feel about yourself? Do you believe that you're worthy and able? This is what confident energy is all about!

Even if you're the kind of person who's never felt that way, you can still change things. No matter what you've felt like or how you've performed in the past, you do have the power to create the confidence you need now. *There is no energy pattern that you can't change.* If you're willing to give it a little time and effort, you can use all the powers discussed in Part II to completely transform your view of yourself!

Sometimes confidence can be selective. For example, we may feel good about participating in a sport but lack security in the business world; we may be sure of ourselves at work yet feel totally incapable when it comes to romance. Generally speaking, though, we tend to know whether we have the kind of confidence it takes to be a success.

What do you feel about yourself regarding this issue? Are you sure about your capability to succeed, or do you struggle with hesitation and self-doubt? Confidence seems to be an elusive commodity that few people understand and even fewer know how to consciously create. But when you look at the quantum mechanics of it, you'll realize that it's doable and it's necessary.

> The source of your confidence comes largely from your self-image—and image is a key ingredient in consciousness creation. How you see yourself is intrinsically connected to what you expect of yourself. If you have a negative picture, you'll assume that you're going to perform poorly, and it's likely your reality will meet those assumptions. But if you have a positive, healthy self-image, you'll expect the best of yourself, and your consciousness will create that reality. In terms of consciousness creation, your self-perception moves outward to create your personal results.

Here's an example of how this works. Let's say that you had difficulty speaking in public when you were younger. In a high school speech class, you suffered through a few disastrous experiences where you had anxiety and stuttered all through your presentation. That caused you to perceive yourself as a failure in this area, and now you expect that "truth" to continue throughout your life.

Many years later, if someone were to ask you to give a speech at work, you'd have a spontaneous image of your past defeats, and even though you weren't in the process of stuttering in front of a group at that time, you'd immediately produce the biochemical reaction that matched the unpleasant, fearful emotions from the past. This would further cement your poor self-image concerning this issue.

Sounds like an impossible cycle, doesn't it? Failure leads to negative images and feelings that result in further failure. But don't despair; there's good news. Once again, the quantum mechanics of energy and physiology gives us the power to change things from the inside out. No matter what's happened in the past, you always have the option to access a new neural network, create a brand-new image, and redefine any personal issue.

How can this be? Remember that the brain can't distinguish between an image of experience and one of vivid imagination. The visual cortex relies only partially on what is being seen. The bulk of our visual experience is made up of both the memories of past images and personal information forming specific expectations. If you change the scenes in your expectations, you can change your observable reality, as well as your consciousness creation!

I utilized this imagery and awareness shift while working with a client who was dealing with his own phobia of public speaking. Tom had come to see me at age 35, when he was faced with a dilemma at work. He'd moved up the corporate ladder rather rapidly and was now up for a promotion on a national level. There was only one problem: he was going to have to give presentations to large auditoriums filled with people, the mere thought of which paralyzed him with panic.

He'd always had a fear of public speaking but had reached a tolerable level of comfort in conducting small meetings in groups of five or ten people held in conference rooms. Even that had been difficult at first, but he took medication and somehow managed to get through it. Now he'd have to speak to groups of hundreds— eventually even a few thousand—and just the idea of it threw him into horrendous panic attacks that the medication couldn't even touch.

When he came to see me, he told me about his past experiences with an attitude of hopeless resignation. He thought it was ludicrous when I told him, "Tom, we're going to change your history." When he asked me how, I answered, "Simple—by changing your imagery."

I began by teaching him relaxation techniques, along with affirmations releasing his attachment to his past conclusions and images, which he used whenever the old thoughts came to mind. Then we started the process of creating new visuals—as well as fresh emotions to go along with them.

We did this through a series of hypnosis sessions, starting with a relaxing induction, followed by the visualization of a new, successful image. We used a process called mental desensitization, where the picture would change somewhat with each consecutive session, expanding on the previous one and adding new elements of success and emotion each time.

In the first session, we created a scene where Tom was standing on a stage in a small auditorium. He was totally alone; there was no one in the audience or with him onstage. Since the room was empty, he saw himself speaking with complete confidence, comfort, and even enjoyment.

In the next session, he pictured only one person in the audience. I told him to choose someone who was supportive and encouraging, and he picked his wife. Again, he saw himself speaking with ease and enthusiasm. In his mind, his wife smiled up at him, laughed at all his jokes, and applauded at the end of his imaginary speech.

Over time, we switched to other individuals, such as a good friend from work or a buddy on his golf team. Then we changed the locations. For example, instead of standing onstage, Tom saw himself stepping off into the wings, where the person from the audience excitedly congratulated him and praised the great job he had done.

We slowly added more people to the picture. First came his children, then his other friends and family members, and then a few supportive co-workers from his office. Slowly, we brought more and more people into the auditorium, giving him more confidence with bigger and bigger audiences. With each visualization, he saw himself as a powerful speaker, relaxed and engaging. Each time, we practiced deep breathing and attached feelings of enjoyment, comfort, and relaxation. It took several sessions, but eventually Tom imagined himself speaking to an entire audience filled with people—and he saw himself having fun while he was doing it!

He did these systematic desensitization visualizations in my office, and we made recordings for him to listen to every night at home. After about six months, it was time for the real thing. Tom was scheduled to address a group of around 700 people—at least 50 times larger than any other meeting he'd ever conducted. He was nervous, but excited, too. He continued smiling, relaxing, breathing deeply, affirming himself, and reliving the revised images, complete with the new emotions of enjoyment, comfort, and success. He never realized it, but he was now accessing a fresh neural network, producing different neurotransmitters, new neural pathways, and entirely altered feelings.

His presentation was a great success; he was relaxed and funny, and he didn't even need the medication he'd been using in the little conference-room meetings. Tom got the promotion, along with a big raise and stock options to go with it—and since then, he moved up even further! Now he conducts seminars in front of thousands without even thinking twice. His modified images and emotions created a new consciousness, biochemistry, and reality.

Whatever problems you may be facing, and whatever negative self-images may be haunting you, they *can* be turned around. The images that you now embrace about yourself only represent a certain part of your history, not your truth—or your future. They may seem accurate because they're familiar, and they may even feel irresistible because of their strong emotional charge. But don't be deterred by these false assumptions.

Use your power of letting go to release the old limitations, and then employ your powers of choice and consciousness to create new, strong self-images that rewire your neuropathways. The following investigation will help you identify and release your negative self-images. Continue the process until you've created fresh pictures that will be the source of your new, exciting, and successful reality.

SHIFT YOUR SELF-IMAGE: Creating New Neural Pathways of Self-Confidence

You can change your brain chemistry and shift old, negative images and thoughts of yourself into powerful positive views and beliefs.

Begin by listing some of the images that you now have of yourself, then identify each one as either negative or positive according to the way it makes you feel. (For example, you might write: a good golfer—positive; unattractive—negative; a kind person—positive; an alcoholic—negative.) Add and identify more images as you think of them, then follow these steps for each one:

- **For every negative image that you listed, write down the corresponding pessimistic conclusion or belief.** (For example: I'm too fat, and I'll never be able to lose weight. People don't like overweight people, so I'll never succeed.)

- **Write releasing affirmations related to each conclusion.** (For example: I release any image or judgment about my weight. I deserve to be accepted as I am. My new picture of myself is healthy, strong, and attractive.)

- **You can use variations of the neurotransmitter affirmations discussed in Chapter 9 to facilitate this change.** Start with the basic sentence, "My body is releasing more and more neurotransmitters of peace and well-being, bringing me greater _____." Then fill in the end with emotional qualities such as *self-acceptance, confidence, strength, courage, belief in myself, acceptance of my appearance,* or *peace and power in any situation.* If confidence is a significant issue for you, remember to repeat these statements many, many times for an affirmation saturation. Your repetition forges new neural pathways and helps your brain to create these reactions!

- **Write down a vivid description of each new positive image, filling it with colorful and happy details.** (For example: I see myself dressed stylishly and looking better than ever. I'm wearing an attractive outfit, and I notice that I'm looking more energetic and vibrant. I see myself smiling and happy, and I radiate confidence and joyous energy to others.

- **Visualize your new images.** First, do some deep breathing to relax; then picture all the details of your new scene with joy. See the entire thing as brightly and clearly as possible. Make it colorful; continue to relax and breathe deeply as you see the details more clearly. Smile and bring uplifting emotional words to this view, such as *fun, attractive, strong,* and *enjoyable.*

- **Let yourself relax and re-experience this positive image for a few minutes once or twice a day.** Hold it close and feel it becoming more and more familiar to you. Repeat it often and know that this represents your *true* reality. The new pictures and loving emotions will create a new biochemical response and bring greater confidence and happiness, along with increasingly successful results in every area of your life.

Only *you* can decide how to perceive, define, and imagine yourself. Your old negative memories and conclusions were formed out of past experiences, but you can create new ones now. This is a different time, a fresh opportunity to reinvent yourself from the inside out. Since the Law of Magnetism shows that the world can only regard you in the same way that you see yourself, it's time to let go of the old limited images and self-judgments and choose to regard yourself more highly *now.*

Repeat your positive changes in perception and self-image, and your shift in consciousness will be complete. You'll create a sparkling new reality when you consciously determine to see yourself as valuable, capable, and deserving. In every single moment, you have the option to paint another picture of yourself, to embrace a new image, and to broadcast a vibrant and magnetic personal energy—so choose confidence now and always. Honor yourself in every thought, and you can confidently move toward a magnificent future.

Affirmations for Charismatic Confidence

✦ I am choosing to think more highly of myself. I know that I deserve to believe in myself no matter what the situation may be.

✦ I affirm myself with a gentle and loving voice. I feel my worth and deserving energy growing each day.

✦ I choose to accept myself. I know that I am worthy of great success.

✦ I love my life and my self-loving energy. I am valuable and special just as I am, and I see the truth of this more and more each day.

✦ I choose to believe only the best about myself. I am learning to love and accept myself without reservation. I have all that I need to create all that I want to feel and experience.

✦ ✦ ✦

Chapter 15

The Energy of Optimism

The Second Magnetic Energy of Success

. . . see it [the thing you want] as an existent fact—
and anything you can rightly wish for is yours.

— ROBERT COLLIER

The second important magnetic energy is optimism, an attitude of positive assumption and the overall expectation that everything's going to be okay. It's closely connected to confidence, because it's easier for an optimistic person to be self-confident, and it's an absolutely natural progression for a confident person to be optimistic. Your decision to work on either of these energies is bound to greatly enhance the other one as well.

There's a special kind of charge to optimism, a peaceful assurance that no matter what may be going on now, good things will generally come your way. It comes with an undercurrent of self-trust, a knowledge that even if something difficult happens, you know you have the resourcefulness to handle it and bring it to a beneficial resolution. This hopeful and self-trusting expectation projects a dynamic and productive awareness. An optimistic outlook turns hope into reality and produces a vibrant and beautiful energy that aligns with the Universal flow of abundance.

PLODDING IN FEAR VERSUS PROSPERING IN FLOW

Pessimists fill their consciousness with worry—although they may not even be aware of it. They often become so consumed with fear and negative expectations that they even forget that they have the option to look at things differently.

An optimist develops an ongoing awareness of any worry patterns. He notices when they're getting out of control, and he tries to make the conscious choice to intervene on them. An optimist thinks, *What if everything turns out great?* But a pessimist wonders, *What if everything falls apart?*

This becomes a self-fulfilling prophecy that's perpetuated by the pessimist's own energy. As is true of all mental and emotional patterns, your own resonance magnetizes corresponding vibrations from the Universe. A pessimist thinks catastrophically, assuming the worst, grinding out energies of fear and doubt, and inevitably attracting the very results that he feared. It's alarmingly easy to get caught up in this cycle. Worry begets loss, which perpetuates even more anxiety. In this way, fear is a major deterrent to the energies of solution and success.

Optimism produces positive results, perpetuating even more hopeful expectations. An upbeat attitude creates the kind of happiness that carries you through life, even if the results may be a little slow in coming. No matter what's going on, real optimism—the attitude of hope and positive expectation—puts you in the state of flow, that magical confluence of personal intention and Universal solution.

Which of these attitudes do you tend to embrace most? Are you living in fear or in flow? Check the following list to determine whether you tend to be more pessimistic or optimistic.

Pessimist	Optimist
Tends to be fearful and worrisome much of the time	Feels generally relaxed in the present and trusting in the future
Sees a negative event as potentially life altering and even irreversible	Isolates individual problems and sees them as temporary
Feels powerless, as if he can't handle things	Looks for manageable solutions and takes action
Tends to be more nervous, jittery, and uncomfortable	Tends to be more spontaneous and have more fun
Tends to be less active and more habitual or addictive	Tends to be more balanced, active, and social
Is easily depressed by outside circumstances, and with each new problem the depression gets worse	May be depressed temporarily, but is more likely to work through it and move on; determines to let go of the past

You can easily see how the patterns in the optimist column would create a more peaceful and receptive psychology, but there are many other reasons to choose to embrace this attitude. Studies show that optimistic people are less likely to catch infectious diseases and more likely to recover from them quickly. They also live longer and develop fewer catastrophic illnesses. A recent study of octogenarians showed that the single greatest factor in healthy longevity is the ability to bounce back from loss or defeat and still look forward to the future.

Over and above all the physiological and psychological inducements, there's another—perhaps even more compelling—motivation to become an optimist; that's the energetic and consciousness changes it brings to your life. You not only become a happier person but also draw more positive people to you! Assistance from the Universe also manifests in remarkable and surprising ways.

From finding a convenient parking spot to getting that dream job, you're far, far more likely to attract the good stuff when you're in the optimistic state of Divine flow.

GETTING PAST THE PESSIMIST

The choice to become an optimist may not be easy, but it's worth it. Like most important decisions, you don't just make it once, you do so every single day. However, it's important enough—and valuable enough—to see that daily action through. No matter how compelled you are to engage in negative thinking, you must use every opportunity to choose a new approach, a fresh attitude that frees you from that old mental prison.

If you're lucky, your gloomy outlook is merely a fleeting fear concerning a specific issue that's sensitive for you. But if you're like most pessimists, you can be absolutely addicted to the process of negative anticipation. A lot of people think that if they worry enough, it will help them deal with whatever problem may come up. But being prepared requires planning—not worry. It's energetically true that *no amount of negative focus can ensure a positive outcome*. Prepare what you need to, but always take aggressive action to cancel any negative mentality while you're doing it.

JOURNAL FOR SUCCESS

Whenever worry takes over, remind yourself of the consequences by asking yourself the following questions. Do this often in your journal until it becomes your spontaneous mental reaction to your pessimistic thinking.

- What is this negative thought creating for me emotionally?

- Is engaging in this thought really solving any problem?

- Does this approach honor me, increase my sense of self-empowerment, or make me feel better in any way? If not, why am I still choosing it?

- What kind of energy is this pessimism creating? Do I really want to perpetuate that vibration in my life?

- What kind of results will the resonance of this old pattern produce? What new conclusions of peace, trust, and optimism can I choose to shift to a more empowering response?

Worrying doesn't protect you in any way. It only makes you miserable in your present and ensures that you'll attract more heartache in the future. Therefore, you must aggressively attack your negative tendencies. You may not be able to control your negative spontaneous thought, but you do have the option to change your response to it. When a cynical conclusion comes up, write it out and always know that you are in control of what you do next.

You can use the thought restructuring sheets process from Chapter 8 in which you write your thoughts and concerns in a left-hand column then a positive option for each in a right-hand column. Or simply list the things that you're worried about, and then write some optimistic conclusions to counter those assumptions. At the very least, affirm: *I don't have to make this mean so much. I can let this worry go.* Better yet, affirm: *I am powerful. I believe in my ability to handle anything that may come up. Everything is going to turn out fine.*

THE POWER OF RECEPTIVE AFFIRMATIONS — OPEN UP TO THE TRUTH!

Some people tend to dismiss the use of affirmations as being too simplistic, but when you understand their conscious and subconscious resonance, they can be a powerful tool in creating both a shift in energy and in results. They're especially helpful in projecting a strong magnetic resonance because they perpetuate the conscious intention to establish more optimistic mental conclusions, counteracting the negative bias that has become a way of life for so many. In fact, chances are high that if you're not purposely engaged in affirmation, you're likely to be unconsciously engaged in negation.

This is why it's so vital for you to live a more affirmative way of life. It gives you options, shifts both your mental and physical energy, and even creates new neural pathways that can make joy and optimism more spontaneous reactions for you.

Affirmations have an intrinsic power to redirect your energy and open your willingness to believe, but to have that affect, you need to be receptive to their truth. This is an important point that most people never consider. In fact, this is one of the reasons so many people don't do affirmations—or don't stay with them.

There's a funny story I like to tell about a client who experienced this firsthand. Rob had fallen on hard times. He was living in his father's basement after having lost his job. He sold his fancy car that he could no longer pay for, and instead used his dad's 30-year-old rusted-out Gremlin. One day, while driving that beaten-up old car, Rob was listening to a tape by someone discussing the use of affirmations. The speaker explained that they needed to be present, powerful, and spoken loudly. On the tape, this person stated, "Repeat after me, I *am* a millionaire. I *am* a millionaire." He repeated the line several times, continuously raising his voice.

As he was sitting at a red light, Rob complied, repeating the statements strongly and loudly. In fact, Rob got so revved up, he stomped his foot a little too hard, breaking right through the rusty floor of that car! After carefully driving home with his foot elevated above the hole in the floor, he called me. Sadly, he said, "Sandy, I'm not a millionaire. I'm nowhere near being a millionaire." He said he couldn't keep saying affirmations that weren't true because he felt that he was just lying to himself.

Affirmations like this are rejected by the subconscious mind, making them *resistant* affirmations because they cause us to dismiss the new belief and totally resist doing affirmations all together. I told Rob he didn't have to stop doing affirmations, he just had to change them to something that his subconscious mind could be receptive to. So, I gave him an alternative to what he now called "the rusty millionaire debacle." I told him to start with something like, "I am attracting more and more money in wonderful and unexpected ways. I open my life to the increasing income I deserve."

I asked Rob if these statements were easier to believe, and he said they were. We started with them and slowly made his statements more expansive. In time he was able to get a good job, get a new car, and get out of his dad's basement. He had shifted to using *receptive* affirmations, and it paid off. *Receptive* affirmations are statements that your subconscious mind will be more willing to accept. They are still positive sentiments, but they are worded in a way that your mind can recognize as true or potentially true for you, making you more receptive and therefore more likely to repeat.

These types of affirmations are especially important when focusing the thoughts on yourself. For instance, if you were taught that you were powerless or undeserving or lacking in value, your subconscious mind might refuse even simple statements like, "I love myself. I believe in myself. I prioritize myself. I know that I am worthy." In fact, your teaching and treatment may be so contrary to these statements, that your subconscious mind may be saying, "Who are you trying to kid? You don't feel that way at all!"

Fortunately, there's an easy fix to this seemingly impossible problem. Like Rob, all you have to do is adjust the statement by opening each affirmation with a qualifying phrase. For example: *I am learning to love myself more and more each day. I am beginning to believe in myself and know I deserve to respect myself. I am open to seeing my value and starting to feel a deeper sense of my own deserving.* These approaches are much more comfortable to say, and they also give your subconscious mind the freedom to be open to their truth. These and other receptive affirmations can be used daily to brighten your energy and shift your resonance on an ongoing basis. But remember to write your affirmations in a receptive way even when you're dealing with an issue that may be more challenging.

THE ENERGETIC VORTEX OF MIRROR AFFIRMATIONS

Understanding the energy of receptivity is especially important in doing *mirror affirmations, in which you repeat positive statements while looking at yourself in the mirror.* People often resist doing this process partially because they don't like to look at themselves and because they don't like the sound of their own voices. But there are three important energetic reasons why mirror affirmations can be extremely powerful:

1. The thought itself is electromagnetic in nature, sending out a specific impulse.

2. If you speak your affirmations out loud, their energy is amplified by the acoustic resonance of your voice.

3. A vortex of expanding vibration is created by the energy circling from your personal self to your image in the mirror. This vortex builds up momentum and moves out into the Universe. You can even visualize that vortex projecting your affirmations as beautiful signals about you.

   This is why it's so important to use receptive rather than resistant statements in mirror work. If you look into the mirror and say such things as, "I love myself; I believe in myself," and your history of hurt and trauma won't let you believe that, you're resistant vibration will fragment the energy and make you feel off center. It will also splinter the resonance of your life force because it is essentially sending out two opposing messages about you.

So, if you sense a resistance to your mirror work, use qualifying phrases and soften the words to statements that will open your heart. Look in the mirror and affirm: *I choose to value myself. I am learning to love myself and expect the best. I am beginning to believe in myself and understand that I deserve the best today and always. The Universe supports me.*

It is always good to switch to the second person and use the word "you" in your mirror affirmations. For example: *I am learning to love you and believe in you more and more each day.* Eventually you will want to arrive at the absolute, unqualified statements of self-love and deserving. When you feel ready, look at yourself and say: *I love you. I believe in you. I'm making you a priority. You deserve to be happy.* In fact, if you want to hear such things from others, this triple resonance approach is one of the best energetic ways to make it happen.

AFFIRMATION SATURATION

If you're dealing with a difficult issue or an especially destructive belief, use receptive sentiments to practice the technique of affirmation saturation. Shower yourself with positive conclusions of release and reversal. Keep repeating your affirmations—dozens or even hundreds of times a day—until you feel a shift in attitude. No matter what's going on, you can intend to perceive things in a different way.

Affirmation saturation isn't just the simpleminded repetition of positive but somewhat meaningless statements. Real affirmation is a way of life, a flow of positive intentions and observations that carry you through your day in an optimistic frame of mind. This attitude can help you live with honoring and appreciation, engaging in all the magnetic energy changes at once.

> Affirmative thinking is the beginning of change, the foundation of destiny creation. The Power of Consciousness decrees: in the beginning—of all things—is the word. Make it a positive one!

You can learn and remember to use new optimistic tricks. Do whatever it takes to silence the voice of your inner enemy, that "evil twin" that is pessimistic and critical. Stop and distract yourself; intervene, let go, and affirm. *Force* yourself to release your pessimistic thoughts and make them more appealing to your subconscious mind. Eventually, you can make them completely optimistic. Even resistant affirmations can seep into your subconscious mind with excessive repetitions. However you affirm yourself and your life, whatever words you use, repeatedly choose positive assumptions that will bring increasingly positive results.

When adversity rears its ugly head, deal with it but never, ever let it define you. Living in pessimism makes *you* your biggest obstacle, creating conflicted thought and contradictory intentions. If you desire your goal, yet you're pessimistic about the outcome, you're definitely sending the Universe mixed signals. An attitude of optimism allows you to move toward your dreams with determination instead of desperation. It's the state of unconflicted thought, single-mindedness, and pure intention, and as such, it's a compelling force that the Universe is bound to respond to. When you live with optimism, you achieve optimal results.

Affirmations for Overwhelming Optimism

- ✦ No matter what may be going on, I'm learning to let go, trust, and choose optimism from now on.

- ✦ I am relaxed and resourceful. I can trust in myself and in my future.

- ✦ Every day, I am learning to be more spontaneous, fun loving, happy, active, and hopeful.

- ✦ I continue to let go of fear and worry. I look forward to good feelings each day. Optimism is my new approach to everything.

- ✦ I live an affirmative and optimistic life in all that I do, think, and choose. I affirm and acknowledge myself, my value, and my life every day.

✦ ✦ ✦

Chapter 16

The Energy of Purpose

The Third Magnetic Energy of Success

*Go forward in life with a twinkle in your eye
and a smile on your face, but with a great and
strong purpose in your heart.*

— GORDON B. HINCKLEY

Are you living on purpose? Do you have a guiding principle or a central goal that directs your choices and carries you forward? If not, you could be spinning your wheels, spending a lot of time and energy moving in different directions and never ending up at the destination of your choice.

The difference between being *off* purpose and being *on* is like the difference between a game of pinball and one of bowling. Off purpose, you're bounced around from one event to another, blindsided by unexpected occurrences, getting sidetracked into dead-end destinations. Your life, like a game of pinball, is filled with scattered energy, bringing results that are largely influenced by luck.

Living on purpose, however, makes you more centered and focused and puts you on more of a direct path. Like the game of bowling, your energy and your life are on the straight and narrow, following a more direct course to your goals. Of course, you can always throw gutter balls as you're fine-tuning your energy game, but eventually a purposeful resonance will score a perfect strike.

What would you say your primary purpose is? Take a moment to think about it now, and if your answer has something to do with work, think again—that's your *professional* purpose. If you believe that it has something to do with your family, you also need to try once more because that's your *personal* purpose.

Your primary purpose has nothing to do with anything outside of you; it's about your inner life. In your movement from birth to death, there's something greater that must be done—more than acquiring a big house or belonging to a country club, beyond fortune or even fame. It's the only thing that you'll take with you when you leave this life; it's your own personal and spiritual growth.

Primary means "first" or "most important," and both meanings apply to our spiritual purpose. It's our first motivation for coming to this reality, and it's the most important reason for staying. Clarity of understanding, self-mastery, and deepening love are all part of the process of the spiritual self, the central meaning of our human experience. The wonderful thing is that when these qualities are at the core of your life, it creates a dramatic shift in energy and consciousness, and all your other goals seem to fall into place.

Only *you* can determine what your spiritual purpose is, although for most, it's about love. Whether it's learning to care for yourself or others, or learning to find a greater passion in your relationship with God and the Universe, love is our greatest education. And once we learn about it, we have to consciously choose it. That's where the Law of Expanding Influence comes in.

The more we release hate and embrace love, the more that positive energy expands in our world—not just for us, but for everyone. Sometimes I go through my day simply repeating this intention as my mantra: *Choose love; choose love; choose love.* If

I'm looking critically at myself in the mirror, I let it go and say, "Choose love." If someone cuts me off on my way to work, I release the anger, take a deep breath, and remind myself: *Choose love.* If I'm frustrated with someone at work, I look in that person's direction and simply repeat the word *love,* and breathe it into my heart.

> Choosing love as a spiritual purpose isn't just meaningless New Age claptrap. It's a powerful energetic choice, a process of switching from a heavy, dense, earthbound vibration to a light, fluid, and beautifully attractive one. As a result, your spiritual purpose can't be entirely separated from your personal or professional ones. The more you work this priority into your life, the more your resonance will sparkle in every arena.

I feel exceedingly fortunate to be able to tie all my purposes together and make my life's work what I love to do. I feel that my primary—or spiritual—reason for being here is to experience Divine Love to the fullest extent possible and then to expand that into the world. As an author, lecturer, and counselor, this has become a big part of my professional purpose as well. And, of course, it's a top priority in my personal life as wife and mother.

Many people are striving to find their purpose—whether spiritual, personal, or professional. Part of the problem is a confusion between purpose and motivation. You may be motivated to pay the rent each month, but is this your purpose in life? If you're like most individuals, you're often so driven by your immediate needs, that they—rather than purpose—become the most compelling forces of your life.

But in order to align your energies with the Universal Laws, it's important to determine what your purposes are and then choose to honor them. The most compelling and magnetic meaning that you can bring to your life is one that sparks your passion.

PASSION + PURPOSE = POWER

It always surprises me to see how many people fantasize about success without knowing what specific goal or activity they want to succeed at! So many people tell me that they want to make a lot of money or become famous, yet when I ask them how they're going to do that, they have either absolutely no idea or have a dozen options floating in their heads. But it's impossible to achieve if you haven't clearly identified your purpose and defined your goal. Without this as your starting point, you won't be focused enough to turn your hopes into realities.

There's a big difference between a dreamer and a doer. The former pictures himself driving a fancy car or flying off to exotic locations, but he has no clue about how he's going to make it happen. Unfortunately, big dreams with no purpose only create a vacuum of activity and energy, one where nothing gets done, no real success is achieved, and a sense of lack or even depression seeps in.

This is the case for countless people who drift through life resenting their ho-hum jobs yet hoping to win the lottery or inherit a windfall. They envy those who have what they want, and this feeling, combined with their own purposelessness, only leads to more depressing energy, which repulses the very things they're envious of.

The doer understands this pitfall. Unlike the dreamer, he determines for himself what kind of pursuit he's going to engage in. He still has a dream, but he knows what it entails, and he's willing to take all the action necessary to make it come true. Like his aimless counterpart, a doer may also picture himself in that expensive car or jetting around the world, but he builds those images on a steady foundation of personal purpose, planning, activity, and real passion—and that's the energy accelerator. The more ardent the pursuit, the more likely the success, and that passion is not just focused on the result, but carries the momentum of the daily activity as well.

So how do you find a purpose with passion? Some individuals are fortunate to realize at an early age what kind of path they want to pursue. They're driven by an inner knowing, or perhaps a natural talent. And if they persist, they may find a career where this can be both personally and financially rewarding.

A surprising number of people don't consciously choose their professions, however. Serendipity or circumstance nudges them into their career. I've known many who, having accepted what they thought would be a temporary job at age 18, found themselves in the same career 30 years later. It may not be what they chose, but if they're really lucky, that path brought them joy and fulfillment.

Yet many others aren't that fortunate when they "fall into" a profession merely by chance. They may think that they're just checking it out, yet they're still there years later, whether they're truly happy or not. They choose to stay due to familiarity and seeming security, preferring to let go of their dreams in order to maintain the status quo. But this apparent comfort is seductive. It can keep you stuck, even if you're not happy—and it may be especially enticing if you're making enough money to feel somewhat comfortable. Unfortunately, this combination of income and habit can be a trap.

That trap is fear, and it snaps down around your hopes and imagination like a steel jaw. It slams shut when you find yourself making enough money at something you don't enjoy, yet fearing that you won't be able to equal that sum if you move on to a career you love. *The irony is that you're willing to give up happiness in order to make the money that you think will bring you happiness!* This financial catch-22 can keep people stuck for years, decades, or even their entire lives. They think, *I'll never make it if I try something new. I've been doing this for so long that it's too late to start over now.*

It's never too late to find a purpose that sparks your passion and pursue something that you enjoy. In fact, it's virtually impossible to achieve genuine success in a field you resent or in a job that you loathe. The resonant frequencies around those kinds of emotions are just too abrasive to attract something joyous to your life.

Passion, on the other hand, is a catalyst for success because it adds the element of excitement, a prime energizer of the Law of

Pure Desire. Without that fervor, you can't hope to create the level of excitement necessary to activate the Universal Laws. But with it, your energy of excitement will move you to continued action and spark the energetic fields into wonderful response.

JOURNAL FOR SUCCESS

The following will help you determine your purpose and pinpoint those goals and activities that are most likely to ignite your own personal passion. Take the time to do the following exercise in your journal, and make sure that you consider each item seriously. Remember that your personal and professional purposes are expressions of your individuality—and of your soul's longing. They should speak to your heart and resonate with your interests, reflecting what you enjoy.

- List the things that make you uniquely *you*. Include your personal interests as well as the activities you like to engage in. (For example: interested in politics or enjoy baseball, horseback riding, or watercolors.) Make sure you include all the activities that give you pleasure or pique your interest. You can even look back at your childhood to open up to things you used to love even though you haven't done them in a while.

- Now scan that list and write down any work activities, hobbies, or goals that can be connected with those interests. If you're unsure, do some research.

- Consider the answers you just gave. Which of these related pursuits do you think can become a professional purpose for you? Which would excite your passions the most?

For any real satisfaction, your purpose should reflect your own personal values. If it's at odds with your core beliefs, you'll constantly feel off balance—and you may even feel as if you're living a lie. This is absolute poison to your energy, and you can never be truly happy in this state. Keeping that in mind, move on to the following steps.

- List what you value most. It's fine to include money, but don't limit your list to that. Some of these items may have already been included in your earlier list. (For example: time with family and friends, outdoor activities, your religion or spiritual pursuits.)

- What purpose—either personal or professional—will help you prioritize these values?

- What will it take to make this purpose a part of your everyday life?

These are important—even life-changing—questions, and they need to be answered honestly if you want to create a *genuine* experience of success in your life. It's also a good idea to meditate on your options. Relax and be open to the voice of your eternal self. Having a heart-centered motivation is one of the most magnetic vibrations because aligning with your own personal purpose projects a very dynamic and attractive resonance. In fact, purpose (driven by optimism) is the major component of creating a life of passion. This combination is not only a primary source of personal satisfaction but also a driving force behind the process of manifestation.

When your purpose aligns with your life work, you get the sensation: *This is who I am. This is what I should be doing.* When you can look at your career path and think in that way, you'll know that in an important sense, you are already a success.

Affirmations for a Powerful Purpose

✦ A happy and hopeful life is my purpose.

✦ Every day I look for all the joy, understanding, and self-mastery that I can achieve. Personal growth is an important purpose for me.

✦ I live with passion and personal power. I act on my own behalf each day.

✦ I live with alignment. I stay centered and focused, prioritizing my own goals and purposes.

✦ It's safe for me to follow my bliss. I make choices that honor my spirit.

✦ ✦ ✦

Chapter 17

The Energy of Presence

The Fourth Magnetic Energy of Success

For eternally and always there is only now, one and the same now; the present is the only thing that has no end.

— ERWIN SCHRÖDINGER

There's an old adage that goes, "Today is a gift; that's why they call it the present." This may sound like just a cute little saying, but it's important to look at the energetic truth of it: *energetically, we create our reality every moment that we live.* In fact, in terms of our consciousness creation, we never have any other opportunity to do so. That's what makes each second so precious, so much of a gift. The present is our window of opportunity. It opens us to our options of choosing a new approach that will make a difference in our lives. *This is the wonderfully magnetic energy of presence: the power to change our future.* Every single second is a Universal gift.

But there are so many moments that we just throw away. We're given the blessing of a beautiful sunset, but we're too busy to notice. The Universe offers us another present—perhaps an opportunity to relax—but maybe we're too worried to do so, so we trash that as well. One moment may bring an opportunity to have fun with friends, but we're too distracted by work or other obligations, so we just toss that out, too. What would you do if you kept sending presents to someone who repeatedly threw them away? Of course, you'd stop giving them!

Every moment that we discard is an act of rejection, a brutal dismissal of our own life, and if this becomes a way of life, the Universe will respond by dismissing our desires. But if we acknowledge the value of each instant, if we see the beauty, grace, opportunity, and abundance that's offered there, we'll dramatically change our energy right now and alter the results that will appear in our future.

So many of us spend our time elsewhere, worrying about future events and brooding about past difficulties. But what happens when we're continually ruminating about the past or anticipating the future? We lose the potential power of the present. We simply can't take the right kind of mental and emotional energetic action if our minds keep jumping back and forth.

NOW VOYAGER

Oftentimes, we don't have any desire to stay in the present because we simply don't think that it's special enough to be worth our full attention. This approach is just biding time while waiting for something better to come along. We see our lives as an endless series of mediocre and mundane activities sprinkled with only a few truly happy or special events. And while we're waiting for those red-letter days to come along, we live with boredom and disinterest in what's going on around us—or perhaps even resentment and disgust.

This "layover" mentality sparks the energy of Paradoxical Intent, implying that since we are not presently at our destination, we can't be happy now. Whether consciously or unconsciously, we are telling ourselves—and the Universe—that our everyday life doesn't warrant enthusiasm or happiness. We're merely on a layover, waiting for a special but all-too-fleeting event to lift us temporarily out of our doldrums. Some people never even consider being happy while they're immersed in their daily routine. In the meantime, they'll stay irritable, frustrated, angry, or bored.

Unfortunately, this is how too many individuals look at their world. They're just biding their time (or even dragging themselves through their days) until something better comes along. This can become such an ingrained lifestyle pattern that it's possible to go through long stretches—even decades—only seeing life as a burden.

What kind of miserable consciousness does this create, and what kind of reality will come from it? If you're constantly dismissing and devaluing significant periods of your life, you'll only get disregarded and be unappreciated in return. Dismissal of your present is literally creating a consciousness of lack about your very existence!

You must ask yourself: *How often do I feel like I'm just biding my time, just going through the motions?* Whatever activity you're engaged in, you do have the option to value your present and create a positive energy there. Even if you have a job that makes you miserable, you can try to create some joy in it while you're actively looking for another. This choice is where the two magnetic vibrations of appreciation and presence come together to create a brilliant vortex of energy that changes everything from this point forward. This moment isn't just a meaningless layover on the way to something else, this moment is your life! It's an actual destination in and of itself—an energetic powerhouse waiting for you to light it up!

Every present moment that you arrive at a new perception, a new way of looking at things, you're making a shift in your energy production. And if you choose an honoring, loving, and joyous point of view in the present, you're igniting it with all your powers at once. No matter what you're doing, you can choose to see value in this instant—even if you're just engaged in a mundane activity, such as driving to work or doing a household chore. This moment is truly special. It's the doorway to the energetic realm and the only time that you'll have this precise opportunity.

Long ago, I heard a wonderful affirmation by Louise Hay: *My point of power is in the present moment.* When you study the science of energy and consciousness creation, you can see the absolute truth of these words. There's no solution in the past and no certainty in the future. The only time that you can take any real or energetic action is right now—and filling your minutes with brooding about the past or worry about the future is not the kind of action you want to take.

Even if you have a very difficult situation going on in the present, you can still empower yourself by going inward, seeking solutions that honor you and taking action with self-trust, all the while continuing to look for and create moments of peace and joy.

Choose to empower yourself in the present instead of choosing fear or doubt. Energize each moment with value, optimism, and appreciation, the rest will take care of itself—unfolding in seemingly magical ways. Time is the energetic source of your strength, so it's time to take it seriously.

The Universal Laws respond directly to your attitude about your present life. If you can quit worrying about tomorrow and engage in the happiness you seek right now, this will ensure the future you're looking for. Stop waiting for a "special" occurrence to enjoy yourself. The quality of your days doesn't come from extraordinary activities, pleasure-seeking excursions, or wish fulfillment. It bubbles up from deep within, from both your attitude and your intention. You not only need to stay conscious of what you're experiencing, but you also need to *value* it.

Remember that your power of choice puts you in charge of your attitude toward life—whether it's about the present or any other thing. If you find yourself feeling fearful about the future, affirm that you can let it go and choose trust instead. If you're brooding about the past, release that, too, and take back your power in this instant. *Staying present is the ultimate expression of trust; finding joy in the here and now is the divining rod to the endless spring of future joy.*

The fact is that anything short of choosing to value this moment ends up destroying the worth of what's to come. So, don't spend your life playing the waiting game, thinking that someday soon you'll be happy but dismissing the chance to choose that now. Take control of your intentions, take action on your own behalf, and intend to appreciate the present. Bring real value to the center of your mind and your life. Don't postpone your potential for peace and happiness even one moment longer.

JOURNAL FOR SUCCESS

In order to get a handle on your present energy, answer the following questions in your journal. Do this exercise often, especially when you feel as if things are getting out of control.

- How am I spending most of my present moments?
- What kind of thoughts and emotions do I find myself repeating?
- Do I tend to acknowledge the value of my present activities or see them as tedious or a burden?
- What are the energetic consequences this could be creating?
- What kind of conclusions can I make or actions can I take to create more positive attitudes and emotions on a regular basis?
- What can I affirm or appreciate about myself or my experience *right now*? What can I do to maintain my power in the present moment?

Are you willing to do whatever it takes to experience real appreciation and happiness today and stop waiting for your life to begin later—maybe much later? *You may not realize it, but this— right now—is the greatest moment of your life.* Now is the moment of creation and opportunity, the energetic seed of all future happiness. You can't go back and make it happen in the past, and you can't leap forward and take action in the future. In fact, the best way to ensure the happy emotions you want to experience then is to engage in them now.

It's not the big choices of your life that define you, though of course they influence your life immensely. But in reality, the accumulation of all the little present moments—the thoughts, emotions, choices, and ongoing perceptions you engage in—are what truly defines you. Use each moment to change your consciousness, energy, intention, action, and attitude, and you'll be doing all that you can to create a brilliant tomorrow. The power of self is found in the simplest moments—every single one of which defines you. You must ask yourself, *What do I choose now? And now? And now?* This is the perfect—and only—time to take control. Don't deceive yourself; you absolutely *can* do it. You already have the power, so give yourself the present!

Affirmations for a Powerful Presence

+ I release the need to worry about the future or relive the past. I focus only on the present from now on.

+ This very moment creates the energetic momentum of my life. I choose to see real value and energetic opportunity in every present activity.

+ I look for the joy in my life right now and take action to create it in all that I do.

+ This is a new day—a new opportunity. I can embrace a new attitude right now. I am in control of my thoughts and choices.

+ I enjoy the present and trust in the future. I see my life as an adventure that I create every day.

✦ ✦ ✦

Chapter 18

The Energy of Appreciation

The Fifth Magnetic Energy of Success

*There is an inherent law of mind that we increase
whatever we praise. The whole of creation
responds to praise and thankfulness.*

— CHARLES FILLMORE

The fourth dynamically magnetic energy is one of the most valuable vibrations in your personal field: appreciation. It's the intention to live with gratitude, the conscious acknowledgment of the value within and around you, the willingness to notice all the good things you already have, and the desire to experience all of life with this attitude. But to create this vibration, your daily life has to resonate with an awareness of the potential for gratitude in the here and now. This isn't just an idealistic fantasy; it's an energetic necessity, for appreciation is where real happiness comes from.

The fact is that you can't experience joy without gratitude. Think about the times that you've been happy; recall where you were, what you were doing, and whom you were with. Stop for a moment and let yourself dwell upon those good times now, letting a smile come to your lips and feeling the delight resurface in your heart. As you remember these episodes, ask yourself, "In each situation, what was I feeling grateful for?"

> Whether you realize it or not, every single time that you feel happy, underneath it all you're in the state of appreciation. No matter what it is you're excited about, that joyous feeling means that you're thankful for something. The more you feel that resonance, the more you create a happy life, and according to the laws and forces of success, your energy of gratitude will only attract more to appreciate in the future.

This is a truly empowering and liberating realization because you don't have to wait for happiness to come at a vague point in the distant future. You don't have to rely on such things as more money, a new love, a bigger house, or a better job to experience that state of well-being. You can consciously choose to engage in appreciation right now. And when you decide to *really feel* it, you will bring bliss to your everyday life.

This is a pivotal point in your energy and consciousness production. You may pursue your goals because you think that they'll make you happy later, but with that attitude, it's impossible to be joyous now. However, when you live by filtering everything through a genuine sense of appreciation, you not only create what you seek right now, you also magnetize increasingly cheerful results in the time to come.

WHAT STATE DO YOU COME FROM?

When we look at our emotional lives, we can see that we tend to bounce around from one state of being to another: happy one day, unhappy the next; excited one moment, worried the next. Our moods are easily shaped by outside circumstances, and most of us are much more sensitive to negative influences than to positive ones. We're often easily frightened, and sometimes the littlest thing annoys us. But what lies beneath these variations?

As you've seen, underneath every emotion of happiness is the mentality of appreciation. The opposite is true for negative feelings: beneath most of them is worry or dissatisfaction. Which of these mental activities do you engage in most: Do you consciously seek to enjoy yourself in the present and acknowledge what you already have? Or do you look at your life and see everything that's missing? If it's the latter, you need to know that your attitude affects both your consciousness and your energy, and it only perpetuates the dejection you're already feeling.

Some people live in a constant state of dissatisfaction. They grumble their way through life, complaining about what's wrong and focusing on what they lack. It seems that nothing ever pleases them, and unfortunately, their energy makes this sad fact true. *The Universal Laws are clear: That which you focus on will expand in your life. And if you're constantly dwelling on what you lack, then the deficiencies in your life will become overwhelming.*

Your choice to concentrate on what's missing is opting to obsess about the problem instead of the solution. This makes it impossible to establish a consciousness of success; instead you're filtering everything through an awareness of deprivation. Just think of the pieces of your consciousness PIE from Chapter 9.

Perception is the first slice. Identifying lack produces the biochemical responses that match and perpetuate the emotion of hopelessness, creating increasing cycles of negative consciousness creation.

Imagery is the next piece. The picture of lack is that of a void, a vision of dark emptiness that encourages you to become needy, urgent, and fearful, engaging the difficult forces of the Law of Paradoxical Intent.

For the final piece, examine the quality of your expectation when you tend to see everything through the sensation of scarcity. If that's what you experience, then it's also what you expect—and, of course, it's what you will get.

Some people filter their general dissatisfaction through certain issues. For example, I have numerous clients who have never been satisfied with their looks, often fixating on their weight. One woman revealed to me that everything in her life—every experience, relationship, and endeavor—has been interpreted through the lens of this issue. At age 40, she said, "I remember being on perfectly wonderful tropical vacations but never allowing myself to be happy because I felt that I looked horrible in a bathing suit." She grieved over all the fun times that she'd lost due to worry and self-consciousness. She believed that she'd wasted most of her life filtering her experiences through this discontentment. She then vowed to never let her own judgment of her looks, and especially of her weight, stop her from experiencing the real happiness of her life.

The Law of Paradoxical Intent rang true. She consistently made this change of mental focus, no longer obsessing over her weight and choosing to have fun instead. She lost a few pounds with ease, although she did not magically become the "skinny" person she thought she'd longed to be. Instead, she finally found herself experiencing a joy that she'd never before allowed herself.

For other people, the focusing lens is money and acquisition. It seems that no matter how much they earn, there's never enough. They may drive a nice car, but it's not fancy enough; they may live in a nice home, but it's not big enough. Yet until they choose to be satisfied with what they have, they lose the opportunity for genuine happiness because they'll never feel they have enough.

Unfortunately, many people have an inflated sense of need: they get what they want and then still crave more. We've become a culture of great wealth, but instead of our riches increasing our compassion and appreciation, they seem only to perpetuate greater longing for acquisition. Even for the wealthiest people, the need for more becomes a driving force.

CAN'T GET NO SATISFACTION?

What is this phenomenon of having more and yet not engaging in true appreciation? In this wonderfully abundant society of ours, we have so much exposure to so many things that we've become desensitized to the real value in our lives, and we end up needing more to stimulate us. It's important for each person to find something to truly appreciate in one's life—and to acknowledge that.

Rich or poor, many people feel compelled to obsess about what they lack because they believe that their negative focus will force them to find a solution. They're always thinking and judging, trying to determine what would be more valuable to them. But this choice to judge creates a harshness in our energy, a readiness to be dissatisfied—or even annoyed, agitated, or angry. Jealousy can make us feel more competitive and even threatened. This is what results from the schism between the mind and heart.

Analysis and judgment are functions of the mind, which assigns value, while the heart experiences it. The former looks for problems, but the latter sees solutions. In fact, when we examine our state of dissatisfaction, we can see that *we* are the biggest obstacles to our own happiness. No matter what happens to us, it's often what occurs within us—in our minds and thoughts, in our seeking and striving—that causes our greatest misery.

It may seem simplistic, but what would happen if we just quit analyzing and worrying—if we *simply stopped being judgmental and focused on lack?* It would turn our need for competition into compassion and our obsession about acquisition into present appreciation. Our energy—and our universal connection—would shift from agitated resistance to willing receptivity.

The consciousness of living from the heart is the key to a spectacular destiny creation. Use your power of letting go to release your dissatisfaction, and harness your power of choice to cultivate your appreciation. Search for things to be grateful for throughout your life and deep within yourself. As you practice consistent and conscious appreciation, you'll see dramatic shifts in your daily happiness, and you'll see big changes in the long-term results of your life.

JOURNAL FOR SUCCESS

A long time ago, there was a movement suggesting people keep a gratitude journal. This may seem like just silly busywork, but it's far from that. Two important energetic causes are involved. That's why I still recommend keeping one, though I call it an appreciation journal. You can keep a separate notebook for this, or you can include it in your Success Journal, but wherever you do it, make it a priority.

Every night before you go to bed, jot down a few things that you appreciated that day. Include the big things you have to be grateful for, but also make note of all the little gifts of life, such as the scent of spring lilacs, the sound of birds on a summer morning, or the sparkle of freshly fallen snow in the moonlight. This isn't just a cliché admonishing you to "smell the roses." It's a part of your consciousness and energy production, and your willingness to acknowledge and delight in even the simple things will magnetize joy in great abundance.

Don't limit your appreciation to the outside world. Also write down a few items each day that you acknowledge and appreciate about yourself. Even if it's just saying *thank you* to yourself for going to the gym or acknowledging the courage it took to speak up for yourself, recognizing your healthy and strong choices will remind you to make even more of them! This process expands your energy of confidence and causes you to see *yourself* as deserving of encouragement. Not only that, it creates a resonance of increasing self-respect, a vibration that will draw back respect and appreciation from others.

SHARPEN YOUR APPRECIATION SKILLS

It's a good idea to take some of your favorite things from your appreciation journal and copy them on another list that you can refer to whenever you're down and need a lift or when you're stuck in your head and need to move your consciousness into your heart. So many things can bring gratitude, whether they're beautiful, funny, heartwarming, exciting, or deeply emotional. But when we get lost in the stress of everyday life, we forget all that we have to be thankful for and focus on the negative instead—and this is where the list comes in handy. Use it to remind yourself of your positive reality so you don't get stuck in the negative. They co-exist, and your focus on what you have to be grateful for is a valuable shift.

In fact, look at your list or your gratitude journal often. This creates the first energetic cause of *grateful intentions*—causing you to increase your focus of gratitude throughout the day.

I often refer to my own record of thanksgiving. When things get overwhelming, I review it to remind myself of all the wonderful things that I've experienced throughout my life. Some of them are funny little stories about my kids and nephew, and some are beautiful memories of distant travels, skiing, hiking, and white-water rafting.

I remember a time when I was having difficulty with a seriously depressed client. Our phase entanglement—or connecting energy—really got me down, and I knew that I had to release that energetic influence and move into a heart-centered consciousness. I pulled out my list of appreciation, and just scanning its contents automatically made me happier. But I still went on to look for something specific to give me a lift.

I found a little story that I'd written about my nephew when he was just three years old. I was visiting him one day while he was playing with toy tools at a little workbench. I asked, "Are you being a builder today?" He said, "Yes," and continued playing for a moment. Then he dropped his little toy hammer and came running over to me. He jumped into my lap, gave me a big hug, and exclaimed, "I love you more than *all* my tools!"

Rereading this anecdote made me laugh, and that touching memory completely shifted my focus from worrying about my distraught client to the feelings of happiness that were already present in my heart. It was a simple thing to do, but it brought such dramatic results, creating an immediate emotional and energetic change.

This is the second important energetic cause: *imaging, memory, and neurotransmitter production.* Studies show that imaging something happy or recalling a happy memory increases your production of beneficial biochemicals that raise your mood and increase feelings of happiness and well-being! So turn to your gratitude list and add to it a little bit every day. Your growing appreciation will continue to draw more value to you.

Stop, Drop, and Cop

You can fine-tune your appreciation skills by using a technique that I call Stop, Drop, and Cop.

- Whenever you're feeling down about something, *Stop* what you're doing.

- Take a moment to become aware of what you're thinking about, and then *drop* the negativity— whether it's worry, judgment, or dissatisfaction, say, "I can let this go," and just drop it!

- Then—wherever you are or whatever you're doing— *cop an attitude of gratitude* right away. Find something you can be thankful for either in your memory, in your list of appreciated people, things, and places, or in your environment right now. If you can't find anything in the present moment, think of something positive from your list, and if you need more help, do the heart-centered process below.

The more you practice it, the more easily you'll be able to make this amazing energy shift—even in challenging times.

Heart-Centered Shift

When you catch yourself worrying about something or when you're annoyed or dissatisfied, use your power of choice to shift your consciousness from the anxiety of your head to the peace of your heart. Take a deep breath, close your eyes, and relax your muscles. Visualize your problem lifting up and floating away like a cloud disappearing on the horizon. Take another deep breath, and as you inhale, sense the energy of your mind quieting down; feel your awareness slowly dropping down into your heart center. Just relax, keep letting go of all concerns, and focus your consciousness on your heart.

Then, as you continue to loosen up, let yourself think about something that makes you happy, something you appreciate. Whether it's a bright memory, a person you love, or a favorite sport or vacation spot, let yourself picture that now. Be in the moment and visualize all the details. Put yourself right in the situation, feeling the joy, then completely immerse yourself in that happy experience.

Feel a sense of elation and let yourself smile. You're so relaxed, happy, and peaceful. This is the state of appreciation, the warm feeling of grateful intention. Hold on to it. Know that its ultimate form is loving your life, and when you go back to your daily activities, choose to find gladness and peace in all that you do.

APPRECIATING THE FUTURE:
Power Up Your Visions of Success

Many people like to put images of what they want to achieve on display, such as on a poster board, so they can more easily visualize their results. These storyboards of future intention have had a lot of different names, such as *treasure maps* and *vision boards*. Whatever you want to call them, they can help rekindle your motivation and inspire more action.

There is an important variation on this process that most people don't know of, which I'm now sharing with you. Alongside the pictures of your desires, add pictures of things you have *already* achieved as well as happy photos that trigger joyous memories and appreciation.

This process connects the joyous memories of what has already happened to the images of what is desired to come. This creates the energy of a photo album, and as one scans the pictures, it renders the feeling that all of it has *already* happened. Also, the deep feelings of appreciation of past events then spreads to the pictures of future dreams, making them feel more real and more possible. Furthermore, the neurotransmitter production generates feelings of joy, confidence, excitement, and even courage, charging those desired outcomes with positive emotions, accelerating both intention and action in happy and hopeful directions.

The bonus download contains the meditation "Planting Your Destiny Garden" that can be used to activate the images on your vision board. You visualize the board as a packet of garden seeds, and just as the cover of a seed packet shows colorful flowers in full bloom, your Destiny Garden seed packet shows the blossoming of your dreams fulfilled. The meditation takes you through the process of planting the seeds then adds the assistance of Divine Consciousness planting the seeds of your desires all over the globe, nurturing them with Divine light. It has been a very powerful process for me and for many others. Use your vision board or make your own Destiny Garden seed packet with all your desires pictured there in bright and beautiful detail. (Check out the Download page for more information.)

Joyous appreciation is such an important energy that it can't be overemphasized. It brings serenity in the release of striving and allows you to rejoice in what you already have—opening your heart to receiving even more. Every moment spent in this resonance creates a highly attractive vibration and a powerfully creative consciousness. Along with self-honoring, it's one of the most life-changing things that you can do!

Remember the studies by Masaru Emoto discussed in Chapter 13, which showed that the word *gratitude* was second only to the word *love* in terms of the powerful results displayed in his experiments. And when used together, the influence was the most spectacular of all! In addition, their early experiments demonstrated the amazing power of the simple phrase *thank you.*

I try to use this phase often. Whether I'm thanking a family member for a kind little gesture, or thanking the sun for its warming rays and beautiful light, or thanking myself for taking a deep breath, or thanking God for the incredible scent of a lilac or a hyacinth, it becomes a meaningful moment of appreciation. And even if it's just a fleeting glimmer of gratitude that's immediately distracted by the activities of life, I know that I have noticed a blessing and I am so grateful.

I often tell my clients that there's more than one meaning to the word *appreciate.* Of course, the one that we've been talking about here is "to be grateful for." But when referring to commodities such as real estate, the term means "to increase in value," which is an absolute energetic truth. Your life will increase in value when you choose to appreciate it. And when you create a real intention to be aware of the many blessings of your days, you bring more value there, too. Choose to experience joy in the present, and you can be assured that your jubilant energy will magnetize much more to enjoy in the future.

Affirmations for Endless Appreciation

✦ I have so much to be grateful for! I look around and see my blessings, big and small, and I say, "Thank you."

✦ I live with joyous gratitude. As I appreciate my life, I attract more and more to appreciate.

✦ I'm learning to value my life and myself more and more each day. I deserve my own self-appreciation.

✦ I always take responsibility for my own happiness. I notice many wonderful things to be happy about each day, and I am grateful.

✦ I am choosing to increase my focus on appreciation and self-acknowledgment. I become more and more conscious of all that I have to be thankful for, and I take time to acknowledge it each day.

✦ ✦ ✦

PART IV

The Four Steps to Success

All the Universal Laws and forces of attraction are very real influences in your life, but you need to focus on more than just the energetic and consciousness aspects of your creativity. Serious planning and real action will be required if you want to achieve your desired goals. For many people, this is the part of the process that gets the most attention, and yet it's so often misunderstood. It's the technical side of pursuing success, and it takes a profound clarity of intention as well as unfaltering honesty and self-awareness.

The logistics of your process demand an objective approach; you must be able to think clearly about both your desired outcome and what it will take to reach it. While you can do many things to accelerate your progress and enhance the results, you must follow four basic steps to arrive at your successful destination. They speak to your planning, preparation, and commitment; and they're so intrinsic to the path of success that no real achievement can be attained without them. To become what you seek, your goal must be woven into the fabric of your daily life. It must become your purpose and priority, an ever-present passion that continues to propel you forward.

Chapter 19

Commit to Your Goal

The First Step to Success

*Nothing is as necessary for success as the
single-minded pursuit of an objective.*

— FRED SMITH, FOUNDER OF FEDEX CORPORATION

For success to be real, you must make it a part of your life. It's not enough to fantasize about your goal as a distant dream—a hoped-for future event that you may someday get around to. If your plan is to get ahead, you must consciously commit to that. Without paying enough attention, your *in*tention for it will be empty. In this state, it can't become enough of a force of consciousness to become a reality.

This is a requirement of the Law of Manifestation—for if you want to create something concrete in your life, it must take a real hold in your consciousness first. Your deliberate intention is the link to the creative energy of the Universe, the conduit from thought to reality. If you can't consistently and purposely focus on the pursuit of your goal, then your intentions will falter, wandering off in all sorts of directions, which makes it very difficult to achieve that which you desire most.

A highly focused creative consciousness must have the following three things in order to achieve successful manifestation:

- **A vivid image and emotional experience of the desired outcome.** You must be able to see the details of the end results clearly, and allow yourself to experience all the accompanying joyous emotions.

- **A clear understanding of the specific process required to pursue your goal.** You need to know exactly what action is necessary to get to your desired outcome, all the while investigating your options and adjusting your action if necessary.

- **A complete willingness to commit to both the process and the goal—whatever that may mean in terms of time, effort, focus, and priority.** This kind of commitment is the determination to prioritize your dream over habits, distractions, fears, addictions, and even immediate gratification.

DISMISSING THE DISTRACTIONS

Life has a way of taking over—often pushing our goals out of the picture entirely. We can easily become distracted by daily necessities and by our own habits and indulgences. Practically anything in our daily routine can become a rut, from the time we get up and what we eat for breakfast to what we do after work and in our free time. Eventually, these patterns begin to rule our lives, and many become so deeply indoctrinated that we never even think twice about them.

In this way, we can easily become stuck in a routine; and if it hasn't included our goal from the beginning, we may have difficulty fitting any action in. This can be true even when we have a lot of leisure time because we become accustomed to our patterns of pleasure. We think that we need them to be happy or just to get by, but we may be using them to bypass the demands of our goals and desires.

For example, I had a friend who wanted to start his own consulting business. He was stressed at his job, but he didn't want to quit until he got his new business up and running. He'd been in the habit of stopping for a few beers after work and then grabbing takeout, eating it in front of the television, and falling asleep on the couch.

Since he lived alone, this didn't seem to be a problem—until he had the desire to move on professionally. He knew that he should be using his free time in the evenings to lay the groundwork for his new company, but he was so stuck in his after-work pattern that he couldn't seem to get started. He kept telling himself, "I'll get on it tomorrow," but each day brought more of the same.

When he came to me to talk about it, I told him to investigate what really mattered to him and to write a detailed list of reasons for taking action toward his goal. We also created a schedule that slowly moved him out of his routine. He began by giving up the stop at the bar three days a week and instead used that time to start making his plans.

Slowly, his enthusiasm about the project increased, and that made it easier to cut out his trips to the bar almost entirely and to spend more and more time on his goal. He allowed himself one evening a week to follow the old routine, but in time, he didn't even want to do that. He started his own business, and now he loves what he does. He's very successful at it—but he had to give up a deeply ingrained habit to get there.

POWER OVER PATTERNS OF ESCAPISM AND ADDICTION

We often use our habits and addictions as vehicles of escape. Whether we're driven by boredom, stress, anger, or depression, we engage in activities such as eating, drinking, or watching television to distance ourselves from our moods and thoughts. Over time, we tend to assign very rigid patterns to these temporarily gratifying and distracting activities. We may eat in front of TV, drink after work, or smoke in the car, day after day and year after year, until the force of the habit itself becomes the motivation for perpetuating it.

I had a friend who turned an occasional bowl of ice cream before bed into a nightly addiction that he engaged in for years. He paid for it with the loss of productive time and the gain of about 30 pounds! People can become so deeply entrenched in their daily patterns that they find themselves feeling uncomfortable—or even downright anxious—if they have to give them up. Far from controlling their own lives, their habits control them, creating an inertia of energy and consciousness that's absolutely lethal to the process of real achievement.

Though these habits are often driven out of old behaviors that were established in our youth, they could also represent subconscious patterns of escapism. In fact, it's not uncommon to develop new habits of distraction when we start considering an important goal or plan on taking action. Self-doubt, fear, and anxiety about our ability to achieve our desires can drive us to the distractions that lead us away from them. For this reason, it's important to investigate our motives as well as change our actions. When we arrive at a true understanding of what's going on and why, it helps give us the courage we need to tackle very difficult and deeply held addictions. Ultimately, you need to prioritize your goals, yourself, and your own higher intentions. Only then will you be able to move on.

CONSCIOUS, EVERYDAY CHOICES

Your everyday actions are conscious choices that have very real consequences. It's easy to get into a rut and difficult to get out of it—especially where your habits and weaknesses are concerned. But remember, you do have the power of choice. Each day at every moment, you have absolute power over the decisions you make.

It may be easy to keep moving through life, letting your accustomed behaviors lead the way. But staying locked into your old patterns has significant energetic consequences, causing your energy to pool around you and blocking good things from getting in and moving your life in the same old directions. It's time to be honest about your patterns, to choose to let go, and to finally commit to your goals.

> More often than not, pursuing an important goal requires greater effort—and success demands even more! It takes extra time, a more dedicated focus, and a greater desire to make your purpose a priority. You must consciously engage your power of choice and make your goal a part of your daily habits. Then the action you take and the priorities you set will become spontaneous parts of both your life and your nature. This is what real commitment is all about.

Whether your goal is to improve your health, paint a masterpiece, own a business, write a novel, or become an architect, it will never happen if you don't consciously commit to making it a priority in your daily life. Do you get excited enough about this desire to make it an ongoing priority in your life? If not, are you willing to pay the price of time, attention, and effort and make the necessary changes to accommodate it?

JOURNAL FOR SUCCESS

Are you committed to success? Answer the following questions to determine if you have what it takes to achieve—which means a real commitment to your goal. Write your responses in your journal, and reevaluate them periodically to see if you're still on track.

- What is your goal, and what would it take to make it reality? What would you have to do on a regular basis?

- What might you have to give up—or at least change in some way—to remain committed to your dreams? List the habits that may be impediments, and consider the actions you would need to take in order to alter them.

- How can you balance this priority with the other important things in your life? Structure a plan that allocates the time you would need to spend on your goal in relation to all your other priorities, even if it's only a short time to begin with.

Your commitment is a promise to yourself and your future. The energetic consequences of dismissing this important part of your life can be severe because in essence, you're broadcasting the message that your own success isn't important to you. The Universe will receive that message and respond accordingly. But if you choose to make your goal a priority in your life and allow yourself to get excited about its ultimate fulfillment, your passion will muster up support from the world around you. Hold on to your commitment—every step of the way.

Affirmations for Real Commitment

✦ I am excited about my goal. I make it a priority in some way every day.

✦ I am to commit to my process and devote all the time and effort necessary to make it happen.

✦ I create balance in my life. I happily include my goals in my daily routine.

✦ I pursue my goal joyfully. I remain willing and focused for however long it may take.

✦ My goal is already taking shape in the energetic realm. It is an exciting part of my consciousness creation even now.

✦ ✦ ✦

Chapter 20

Set Up a Step-by-Step Plan

The Second Step to Success

To achieve the success of your dreams, you have to live it every day. Success can only happen in small, repeated steps—one step at a time, one day at a time.

— SHARON ANNE KLINGLER

Making a specific plan may seem like an obvious part of the process of achievement, but you'd be amazed at how many people leave this important step to chance. They may have a vague notion about how they might be able to approach their goal, they may even check things out on the Internet, but they often don't take it any further than that. This type of casual attitude only encourages procrastination and "future" thinking, both of which will slow you down—or even completely block your desired end results.

A specific plan of action moves you forward, gives you guidelines, and establishes the focus of your conscious energy. According to the **Law of Manifestation,** everything exists in consciousness first, so if you want the details of your desire to exist in reality, you *must* establish them firmly in your conscious *activity* before anything else can happen. Your action plan is your mental map to the destination of your desire, so follow it!

I once had a client named Roxanne who was feeling stifled at her secretarial job. She was very creative, but she didn't know what she wanted to do with her talents, so in her spare time, she tried different activities. One week, she'd focus on writing; another week, it would be painting. Later still, she experimented with jewelry making, pottery, and photography.

Roxanne knew that she wanted to quit her job, but she was all over the place with her options. She found that she was quite good at just about everything she tried, and this only perplexed her even more. Her energy was far too fragmented to come up with a specific goal, much less a plan, so we explored her options.

We started by determining what she enjoyed the most, which was jewelry making. We then devised a specific goal and a plan that helped her to stay focused on this one activity. She signed up to participate in a craft show near her home a few months later, so she knew that she'd have to produce the inventory for it. This was exciting, and she spent her evenings and weekends creating beautiful wearable art. Her unusual designs were a big hit, and she signed on for several more shows. She also set up a website and added items to sites that sold original creations. Over time, she was making as much in jewelry sales as she had been at her secretarial job, and she was able to move on to doing her art full time.

Roxanne needed to look at her options objectively. She had to reign in her scattered energy and then create a plan to get going. Once she did that, she became motivated and focused—and her intention to follow through to the end brought her the results that she wanted. The bottom line is, whether you're starting a business or organizing a party, a workable program is the springboard for success.

YOUR INTENTIONAL ACTION PLAN

The following fundamental considerations will help you create both a plan and a clear conscious intention.

1. Know your goal.

Just as a map is seldom helpful if you don't know your destination, you'll never be able to move in the direction of success if you don't have a clear picture of your desired goal. You must think long and hard about both what you want and the process of getting there. It helps to write down *all* your options, so use both your intuition and your common sense when considering your goal alternatives. Be sure what you want resonates with your heart, your talents, and your lifestyle. Let yourself see all the details of your desired outcome clearly. Without a specific goal, you'll never be able to create a workable plan.

Remember to pick a path that sparks your passion. The more you love what you do, the more your energies will align with the powers of the Universal Laws. This is a lightning rod for synchronicity, that magical place where intention meets reality. The Universe will support your choice to pursue a goal that honors you and represents your heartfelt desires.

2. Find out exactly what it's going to take to reach your goal.

There's always a part of the planning process that requires a period of investigation. You may have a general idea of the groundwork necessary to reach the destination you have in mind, but make sure you get detailed information that you can incorporate into your plan. Talk to people in your chosen field; if possible, try to find someone who's willing to mentor you and give you sound advice.

Do plenty of research. For example, if you want to become a lawyer, surgeon, or licensed psychologist, you'll have to find out what degrees you'll need and which colleges offer them. You'll also have to learn what's required to get into those institutions and how much they cost. If you want to open a store, you'll need to decide what products you'd like to carry and find out where you can get them wholesale. You should also check out possible locations and investigate the retail history and spending patterns of the area. Every goal requires prep work, whether it's education, experience, or seed money. Find out what's involved now so that you won't have too many surprises later on.

3. Write a detailed action plan.

Once you find out what your dream will require, you need to put all the steps together so that it makes sense for you. Draw up a general timeline outlining your desired outcome in terms of the long-term, short-term, and immediate needs. Your long-term goal is the ultimate outcome you're working toward. The short-term ones are the significant steps that get you there, and your immediate missions represent the action that you need to take each day to keep moving forward.

For example, when I'm working on a book, the desired outcome is the finished and edited version. My long-term goal is the rough draft; in the short-term, I need to complete the chapters; and my immediate objective is to research the details and write, write, write. When I'm working under a deadline, I even try to figure out how much I'd have to produce each week in order to get the project done on time.

4. Remember your energetic action steps.

In your plans to achieve success—whatever your goal may be—your energy production should be considered daily as well. Meditate regularly to create a calm and peaceful life-force vibration. Affirm yourself and your power. Look in the mirror and acknowledge your worthiness. Be careful not to get urgent about your process or your goal, but work your plan with patience and peace. These energetic approaches will serve you well however long it takes to arrive at your desired outcome.

In setting up your timeline, you need to be realistic and flexible. Things may take longer than you think, or they might go more quickly, but *some* action needs to be taken every step of the way. You may have to make phone calls or write e-mails or do research of your own. Write those specific points down and weave them into your daily intentions. Having a structured plan will keep your focus from becoming fragmented and keep you from falling into old distractions. You don't have to turn your world upside down. Even doing a little something each day will keep the momentum going and show the Universe that you are serious about making your dreams come true. Soon you'll be able to match your action with your intention, the next necessary step to success.

Affirmations for a Productive Plan

✦ I am willing to lay the necessary groundwork for achieving my desired goal—no matter how extensive that may be.

✦ I prioritize my goal, and I know that I can create a practical plan that I can work on consistently.

✦ I set up my long-term, short-term, and immediate goals, including energetic techniques like affirmations and meditations to create a peaceful pursuit.

✦ I am creative, resilient, and flexible. I am open to all the options and abundant outcomes that the Universe has to offer.

✦ I open my heart, my mind, and my life to all the wonderful assistance of the Universe. I know that I am worthy.

✦ ✦ ✦

Chapter 21

Take Action Every Day

The Third Step to Success

Each of our acts makes a statement as to our purpose.

— LEO BUSCAGLIA

A plan without action is just a meaningless daydream. When you take the first step, the real work begins, and the positive energy that you create here will be the biggest accelerator to creating a real outcome. No matter where you are in your journey, whether at the very beginning or near the finish line, there should be some action that you can take today to move closer to your goal.

This means that you must be ready to *actively* involve yourself in each part of the process. Are you willing to do whatever it takes? Are you committed to doing the work—be it creative, clerical, sales, educational, managerial, grunt work, or anything else that your goal may require of you? If you're not ready to do the labor, you're not willing to see the success.

This is why it's so important to think your goal all the way through. Some people are great when given direction but can't make the jump to self-motivation, while others are wonderful creators but terrible at marketing—especially when it comes to selling themselves. And many individuals are powerful initiators yet unfortunately lack the follow-up to see their plans through. All the stages of your goal require action. You may be able to delegate parts of it, but ultimately you must be responsible for making your dream a reality.

I once saw an interview with the successful novelist Jackie Collins. The interviewer asked what her reaction is to those people who say, "Romance novels are so easy! Anyone could write one." She responded, "Let them!"

It's a breeze to say that something's easy as long as you're not doing it; the hard part is taking the action and getting it done. You can talk all you want about what you can do—or even what you'd like to do—but until you actually *do* it, the talk is just hot air. Stop giving lip service to your plans, and start taking the consistent action necessary to make your goal a reality. To prioritize the kind of time and effort this will take, your goal must be important to you—at least as significant as the other time-consuming requirements of your life.

People often confuse importance and immediacy. They think that if something needs to be done right away, it must be more important than what can be easily put off. Having a lot of tasks that need to be done can give you feelings of immediacy and even urgency—which can unfortunately be misinterpreted. The laundry and the dishes may need to be done, but are they more important than working on your goal?

If you allow all the little tasks of life to become your priority, you'll never set aside enough time to consistently work on what really matters. You could go from morning to night taking care of your daily activities without ever giving a single thought to your goal. And when you throw in endless distractions and mind-numbing indulgences, you can completely lose sight of the dream.

Keep the Universal Laws in mind. Today's action (or inaction) is an energetic cause. Since every effort expands your intention in the energetic realm, no activity toward your goal should ever be considered a waste of time. All that you do broadcasts your vibration and focuses your consciousness creation, so even if it's just a quick phone call, a deep breath, or an affirmation, *do* something different—something meaningful—now.

It's time to create balance in your life and set your priorities in a way that will reflect what's *really* important to you. If your dream is worth achieving, then it's worth taking daily action! Even if you have a long-term goal that seems very far away, don't put off the preparation. Take some action today. Even if you feel you've completed much of the work, don't stop now. There may still be something else that can move you forward.

TIPS FOR TAKING ACTION

Review the following pointers often and keep going until you reach your ultimate outcome. Use your Success Journal to address the issues that call for written answers.

- **Clearly define the action needed for each step of your plan.** Create specific intentions for each immediate and short-term goal within the long-term timeline.

- **Make a motivation list, a list of *all* the reasons you want your desire to become a reality.** Write down every wonderful thing that it would bring to your life. Be conscious not to discount the present value of your life while you're looking at the future blessings. But when you find it difficult to get excited about all the work you have to do, read your list. It will inspire new energy and renewed determination.

- **Structure some kind of action into your daily schedule.** Make it a logical amount of time considering your schedule. If you plan several hours that you don't have, you'll end up doing nothing. Even if it's just 10 minutes, try to book it at the same time each day, when you know you'll be focusing solely on your goal and free from distractions. Keep in mind your personal energy patterns. If you know that your energy fizzles out in the afternoon or evening, don't place your most important tasks there.

- **Review your daily action plan at least once a week.** Reevaluate it as you complete each task. Give yourself more time when you need it, but if you do get done with a short-term goal earlier than expected, move on to the next item on your list. If you find that unexpected tasks pop up, be open to inserting them and be flexible with your expectations.

- **Create a little inspiration notebook.** Carry it with you and add any new ideas or points of inspiration if something comes to mind. You may be surprised that something far-fetched could be unexpectedly helpful in the future.

- **When confronted with obstacles or distractions, reread your personal intentions—all of them.** Remember the success intentions you wrote down at the beginning of your journal? Turn to them when you need to rekindle your motivation. If you haven't yet written those down, do so now. They'll help focus your consciousness on your long-term goal.

- **Take time each morning to visualize *today's* action.** Picture when and where you're going to do what you need to, and see yourself engaging in the activity with enjoyment. Don't just apply this to your goal actions; see yourself engaged in all the activities of your day with happiness and fulfillment. At the end of the day, visualize the joyful completion of specific activities yet to come.

- **As you're falling asleep, take a few minutes to envision your desired end results, and let that image go with trust and patience.** When your goal comes to mind during the day, let yourself get excited about it and say this affirmation: *This or something better is coming to my life.*

The emotional choices of loving self-talk and a trusting, peaceful mind are powerful actions that should be woven into your daily life. In fact, they should become a way of life for you, creating a foundation of brilliant yet gentle energy that will align your technical action with the dynamic forces of Universal intention, accelerating your happiness and ultimate success.

Affirmations for Successful Action

✦ Today's action creates tomorrow's results. I choose to take some sort of action now.

✦ I live a balanced life and weave my goals into my other priorities in equal measure.

✦ I make considered choices about what to focus on and work on every day. Action turns my desires into reality.

✦ Each morning, I take a few moments to visualize what I'm going to do that day. I make my daily life and my goal activity a peaceful pursuit.

✦ I am always patient and persistent. Every day, I take some action in the direction of my own goals. I know that my desires are already taking shape in the energetic realm.

✦ ✦ ✦

Chapter 22

Let Go of Attachment without Stopping the Action

The Fourth Step to Success

Relinquish your attachment to the known, step into the unknown, and you will step into the field of all possibilities.

— DEEPAK CHOPRA

For some people, this is the most difficult step to understand because they become very attached to their goals. They often think that this will motivate them to persevere, and they fear that letting go will cause them to give up, but just the opposite is true. The more needy you are about your goal, the more your desperation will make you miserable, sabotaging your success and killing your motivation to persevere.

Your persistent action starts with your attitude, not your attachment. Are you determined or desperate? Determination is an approach of *calm but continuous action*. It allows you to concentrate all your effort into creative productivity instead of emotional unrest. This resonance is centered, balanced, and focused—and it produces results!

Desperation, on the other hand, moves you out of focused action and into emotional reaction. It causes you to linger in fear and apprehension, a consciousness that blocks both action and creativity. This endless agitation eats up your energy and requires even more effort. And when you project a desperate vibration into the energetic realm, it can only create that kind of reality. As difficult as it may seem, you must let go of the feeling of desperation.

Thoughts such as *I can't be happy without this* or *I'll never be a success without that* only make you miserable, while broadcasting very ugly signals of longing and need. They absolutely ruin your sense of balance and your energy of presence, causing striving and anxiety. They are based in the conclusion that you simply can't feel happy or successful now. Your desires will be repulsed by this vibration, and your negative results will only lead you further into desperation. Your fear that you can't be happy will become a prophecy fulfilled.

> You must let go of the urgency and cast out any thought that attaches your potential for happiness to the achievement of any external thing. Release desperation by defining your goal as something that enhances rather than completes you or your life. Be patient and trust in the Divine timeline. You'll attract what you desire when you trust, let go, and choose to create joy each day.

YOUR DAILY DOSE OF VITAMIN E

Your success is a big commitment because to get where you want to go, you need to maintain a high level of energy, one that will accelerate the productive times and stimulate you when it's slow. You can maintain this high energy with a daily dose of excitement, which I refer to as "vitamin E." This attitude is the fuel of your intention; it's motivating and invigorating, and it needs to be renewed often. Get excited about your goal, and visualize it as already achieved. Smile and feel your enthusiasm moving through you. This activity isn't just silly daydreaming; it stimulates brain chemistry and focuses consciousness creation. But your intention for excitement must also be applied to your everyday life *and* to all the actions that your goal requires.

This was a problem for a friend of mine who always wanted to write the "great American novel." He's extremely witty, eloquent, and urbane and could easily see himself as the next Hemingway. He dreamed of becoming a best-selling author, going on the talk shows and wowing everyone with his literary genius. There was only one problem: he hated to write!

Whether he lacked the self-discipline or just couldn't muster up enough interest in the process itself, he was never able to compose anything of length or substance. He still talks about the novel that's in his computer, but until he can create real enthusiasm for each present step of the journey, he's never going to make this particular dream come true.

So when picking out your goal, you must ask yourself, *Do I really enjoy what's required to get to the outcome?* This is the key to staying active yet unattached: get excited about the process itself! You may be thrilled by the image of your successful outcome, but can you generate the same buzz when you see yourself doing the work that it takes to get there? If you visualize yourself winning a marathon, can you also imagine yourself training hour after hour, day after day, repeatedly pushing through exhaustion and pain? If you can envision yourself being promoted to vice president of your company, are you geared up to put in the overtime hours and take the risks that others may be afraid of? If you dream of acting on a hit television show, are you also willing to take acting lessons and show up at cattle calls with hundreds of other hopefuls, praying for that callback but willing to deal with the rejection?

And if, indeed, you are capable of seeing yourself engaged in all the arduous tasks involved in the process, can you then take it even one step further? Can you see yourself *enjoying* the work and doing it for its own sake? In other words, would you still get excited about it if there were no fame or fortune at the end? This is what the Law of Pure Desire is all about. When you find the process itself engaging, you bring your life energy to it every day. Picture yourself happily engaged in the action of your goal, and *then* picture the happy outcome, too. Hold these images in your heart and mind, and let them be your guides.

CHANGING YOUR GOAL:
Moving On Is Not Giving Up

So what do you do if you find you can't get excited about the process—or even believe in the goal? Well, if you find yourself in either of these positions, it's time to think things through again. It doesn't mean you're a failure if you realize you don't enjoy the work. It just means you picked something that didn't truly resonate with your heart and with your truth. And if you simply can't believe this particular outcome is something you can do and you want to do, you'll have to investigate if this is just a limiting belief, as we'll discuss in Chapter 26, or is it true in your heart of hearts? If this is a firm belief that you can't seem to budge, it may be time for you to look for a new goal.

Whichever is the case, it doesn't mean you're giving up, it just means that you're honoring yourself, your inclinations, and your intuition. Let it be okay to look into alternatives, but ask yourself first: *What calls to my heart? What would I enjoy doing? What do I see as truly possible for me?*

When I asked my friend, the aspiring novelist, what he would enjoy doing just for the experience of it, he said painting. He told me he had already taken classes and painted often just to relax. I had never known this before, so it surprised me when I visited him and saw several beautiful sketches and drawings that he was planning to put on canvas. He realized then that letting go of the writing goal was what he was meant to do, and he created dozens of beautiful pictures that were displayed at a one-man show and were praised and desired by everyone there! This was more fulfilling than any novel could have been, and in his process, my friend found the action that he loved so much, he didn't attach or even think about the outcome. In fact, that joyous action each day was the outcome of happiness itself, something that motivated him and made him feel like a success every time he finished a painting!

Let yourself be honest and flexible about what excites and motivates you. See if you can find a goal that uses your talents and brings you joy and motivation. This is the first step to continuing determined and peaceful action.

TIPS FOR TAKING ACTION WHILE LETTING GO OF ATTACHMENT

There are several things that you can do to move out of a desperate orientation into a happy and active pursuit of success.

- **Tune out your negative thinking.** Whenever you notice yourself in an unpleasant energetic state, change the stations on your cognitive radio. Imagine yourself pressing the Seek button on your thoughts, and keep going until you find a thought that resonates with the higher vibrations of trust and determination. Try to let everything else go because negative thinking simply cannot produce positive results.

- **See the value in your process.** Whatever action you're engaged in—whether you're taking classes or putting in overtime—never view the path to your success as a burden. Be willing to engage in the process for its own sake. Look for pleasure and joy in all that may be required to reach your goal—and in your whole life!

- **Affirm yourself, your future, and your worthiness several times a day.** Acknowledge your resourcefulness, strengths, and capabilities, and always know that you deserve the very best.

- **In all your actions and decisions, maintain your honor and dignity.** No matter what may happen, never lose sight of this guiding principle. Success that costs you your integrity or dignity is not an achievement but a profound personal failure.

- **Keep working on your confidence.** It isn't possible to be happy, active, or successful when you're always down on yourself, so get rid of the doubt and self-criticism. Believe in yourself and your ability to make your own dreams come true—and determine to keep taking action until they become a reality.

- **Start to notice the many ways that you're already a success.** Congratulate yourself on the value that you've created in your life—and on the gifts that you bring to the world. Decide to make your biggest success the mastery over your own energy and consciousness. Then every other achievement will follow.

- **Learn how *not* to be *un*happy.** Self-love and optimism are the mental foundations for real joy. If you have trouble being happy, look at how you feel about yourself and what your general outlook on life tends to be. Choose to release the thoughts that make you miserable. Look for the images, memories, and positive expectations that you associate with a happier state. Breathe, smile, and shift your focus as you choose peace of mind instead of worry and doubt.

- **Laugh and smile more, even when you may not feel so inclined.** Smile every day and find joy in the little things. When you are more spontaneous and playful, it projects an irresistible energy!

- **Be the person you want to become—right now!** How would you feel if all your dreams came true? Would you be more joyous, playful, and loving? Choose to be all that—and even more—beginning today.

Your personal energy ignites the beacon of your truth for all the world to see. It's the vibration of your inner light that creates the real image you send out. If you feel that you've been dimmed by disappointment or urgent desperation, it's time to change all that and quite literally take "charge."

Charge your energy with excitement and imbue your intention with the sparks of purpose and determined action. At every opportunity, alternate your current from lack to have, from pessimism to optimism, and from doubt to self-trust. Every single choice to switch these vibrations creates another positive impulse and shines a brighter beam throughout the world, accelerating your success with unattached enthusiasm and joy. When you connect a genuinely joyous effort with the image of your successful completion, your intention will be focused, your energy will be brilliant, and your action will bring results!

Affirmations for Unattached Action

✦ Every day, I take calm and focused action. I remain determined, peaceful, and directed.

✦ I release urgency and live with patience. I create a happy life and see myself as a success in all the self-honoring choices I'm already making.

✦ I pursue my goal with open receptivity. I am always willing to receive.

✦ I engage in every action for its own sake. I see purpose and joy in the process.

✦ No matter what any future outcome may be, I choose to live with happiness and appreciation now. Every day, I notice all the things I already have to be grateful for!

✦ ✦ ✦

PART V

The Three Unseen Assistants to Success

It's undeniably clear that energy is a fundamental part of the workings of the Universe. Countless unseen forces move within and around us, impacting our experience of life itself. But in addition to the vibrational forces we've already talked about, there are three unseen assistants that abide in the energetic realm. They're the vibrations of the spirit, and their energy is so powerful that it would be a serious mistake to ignore their help and presence.

Spiritual energy moves through all creation. In fact, it's the most dynamic force of both the natural and preternatural worlds—and it's capable of bringing unlimited joy, assistance, and accomplishment. Consciously connecting with this unfathomable power is the single most important thing that we can do with our lives, and though it's one of our most valuable tools, it's so often the least prioritized. Even the spiritual part of our own identity is easily dismissed—mostly because it just doesn't seem as important as our physical or material needs. We're so busy trying to make money in order to be happy that we disregard one of the most profound sources of contentment available to us!

The world of spirit is filled with abundant joy and unlimited resources. Its energy is both local and nonlocal, individual and Universal, present and infinite. Each spirit being—including you—has a specific identity, yet can't be separated from any other individual or even from the source and flow of all creation.

These are all very heady concepts, but they must be considered because this spiritual vibration is where the "magic" comes from. When you connect with this overwhelming Universal force, you attach yourself to the source of all things wonderful. In the joy of this brilliant connection, you create miracles, and you realize that you are a miracle yourself! In fact, the ethereal and physical realms are spectacular beyond our comprehension, and when you resonate at the level of the spirit, your vibrations open your life to all that is beautiful, bountiful, and joyous.

Chapter 23

Your Higher Self

The First Unseen Assistant to Success

The Source is unlimited. It knows no boundaries; it's endlessly expansive, and endlessly abundant. . . . Discarding doubt is a decision to reconnect to your original self.

— DR. WAYNE W. DYER

The spirit world provides us with wonderful energies that have the highest intentions and the power to assist us in achieving our goals—and the closest and most immediate of these helpers is actually your self! This identity is your soul, also known as your spirit self or your higher self. (It's not "higher" because it floats above you or is somehow better than the rest of you; it's called this because it vibrates at a higher frequency than your physical self does.) You forge your connection to both the Divine Presence and the great abundance it can bring through your soul, and this is also how you can access all the information, power, and resources that you'll ever need.

Your spiritual self knows that its essence, and very existence, is unlimited and eternal. It realizes that its expression doesn't end with this life, which is but a fleeting whisper of thought in the long and glorious journey of being. The realization of this truth brings a pervasive sense of calm and safety to your everyday experience, one that transcends your perceptions of limited time and restricted opportunity. Your own spirit opens you to the infinite and unlimited reality that is present even in the here and now.

Without this eternal definition, time is your enemy. You may become desperate, anxious, and controlling—with the emotion of fear as the electrical undercurrent of your life. This energy fills your personal pursuits with an urgency that sabotages the very happiness you seek. Embracing your timelessness radically changes your human experience of fear, integrating a broader, more peaceful approach to everything—including your goals.

HIGHER SELF, HIGHER POWERS

Your higher self is more aware of what you need than your mind is. It has all the solutions that you seek and access to great fields of information anytime you desire. It's also capable of any strength you'll ever need, but you must open yourself to receiving its power. When in doubt, ask it to bring you the trust and peacefulness that comes from releasing worry. If you're confused about your options, ask your higher self for the intuitive wisdom to know just what to do—and for the courage to follow through.

Every personal characteristic is available through these vibrations. Attributes such as confidence, wisdom, courage, determination, love, and hope are all within your spirit self. Even if you feel as if you've never experienced some of these before, your eternal soul has, carrying that knowledge and those emotional experiences with it throughout time. And it's willing to bring these wonderful qualities to you whenever you need them—in any situation, at any time.

The Hologram of Your Higher Self

From quantum physics to biomechanics, the hologram has been used as a model for such complex things as the nature of the Universe and the workings of the brain. A hologram is a three-dimensional picture that's created when a laser beam is split in two; the first beam is reflected off an object, and the second beam is directed to collide with the light of the first. The "picture" on the film—or plate—is a record of this light-interference pattern. Unlike a normal negative, the holographic film looks like a mishmash of circles, rings, and wavy lines. However, when another laser light is beamed through that film, a three-dimensional picture is formed and projected, revealing all aspects of the original subject. A hologram isn't limited to two dimensions; the picture shows what's behind and on every side of the object being photographed.

The fascinating properties of this phenomenon don't stop there. If you were to cut the holographic negative into pieces, an entire three-dimensional image would still be revealed by directing a laser through any of the fragments. No matter what scrap you chose or how small the piece—or its place on the film—the hologram would reveal the entire picture: front, back, and sides.

This irreducible, three-dimensional element is why the hologram is used to represent the many nuances of consciousness and why it's an apt representation of how your individual consciousness works in the world. You're like that wavy, undefinable picture on the film because your full consciousness isn't visible on the surface. It's only when you shine a light on your own true nature that you see the real and full picture of your consciousness creation. It's not just your individual desires or intentions that get projected out into the world; it's the many dimensions of your personal consciousness that represent the full reality of your eternal life.

You can call up any energy or power you need at any time with this holograic visualization. Start by relaxing and breathing deeply. Then visualize a beautiful sphere of light at your heart center. See and feel that light moving up and out through your crown chakra at the top of your head until it is just above and in front of you. Look up at this beautiful, three-dimensional image of your higher self. Let yourself feel the incredible love and power radiating outward. Know that this brilliance is your true eternal self, capable of providing any quality you desire.

Continue to look up and take a deep breath, naming the emotion or quality you want. For example, you might say, "Peace." Whatever you need, name it and call for it from the light of your powerful higher self. Feel that energy filling your heart and whole body. Breathe deeply and relax into the sensation, meditating on the feeling. Experience the energy you named growing within, filling you, lifting you up, and making you relaxed, certain, and free.

Allow yourself to do this process with any quality you desire to experience. Whether it's courage, confidence, strength, trust, understanding, grace, compassion, persistence, discipline, purpose, dignity, or anything else, relax and repeat the name of the characteristic. Sense the feeling coming from your higher self. Soon you will feel that power growing within, and it will be fully yours.

Attracting Success Holographic Meditation

You can use a meditation that expands on this technique to enhance your power of attraction. Visualize the holographic sphere of your higher self coming up from your heart center and rotating just above and in front of you so you can see its beauty and feel its powerfully magnetic characteristics. Think about the resonant qualities you want to project to the world—energies like confidence, self-love, and deserving. Even if these are emotions that you haven't often experienced personally, your higher self knows what they feel like and can project these irresistible vibrations far and wide, attracting the very people and solutions you need to bring you success.

When you have sensed these vibrations radiating outward, take a moment to send this beautiful hologram out into the Universe where your highest vibrations are projected in every direction. You start to see lights on the horizon coming toward the light of your own higher self. These are the solutions you seek being drawn to you by the radiant vibrations of your own soul light, and they are already entraining with you in the energetic realm. Knowing that, you can release those lights back to their sources and bring your higher self hologram back to you.

When you do, take a moment to pull down this beautiful light filled with all the higher qualities and emotions you desire. Let yourself feel the confidence, love, courage, and profound feelings of deserving filling you up and radiating outward in a brilliant light that is irresistible.

This is a very powerful yet easy meditation. You can do the basic part of it, just calling one quality when you need it, or you can call up all the strength and brilliance your soul carries with it at all times, sending it out into the Universe to magnetize your desires. There are two meditation audios in the bonus download, "Attracting Success" and "Attracting Love," that use this holographic projection technique. I was inspired to create this process when I was going through my second divorce, and although I didn't think I wanted to marry again, I knew I'd be dating, and I only wanted to attract the highest and best from another. I knew I needed to project the highest and best energies of myself. I started doing this meditation in April, and I met my present husband in July.

In addition to this technique, there's also a wonderful affirmation that's taught by a friend of mine who's a truly inspiring counselor and lecturer in Lily Dale, New York. At his seminars, Tom Cratsley encourages people to tap into their souls' magnificent powers by using affirmations that start with the phrase *I open myself to my spirit's capacity*. They end with a specific intention to learn, change, heal, or receive—whatever may be needed at the time.

This is a dynamic way to connect with your own inner strength. No matter what you have to do, you can use this intention to achieve it. To begin, relax and breathe deeply; then meditate on your heart center and feel your power growing there. As you do, consider the issue you're dealing with and affirm your specific spiritual focus.

Use it for anything you need. For example, you could affirm: *I open myself to my spirit's capacity . . .*

- to release worry
- to trust and be peaceful
- to forgive myself
- to receive guidance and inspiration
- to finish this project
- to sleep peacefully and wake up refreshed
- to believe in myself
- to speak my truth

You can rely upon this powerful technique whenever the need may arise. It reminds you that you are not alone, and you have unending options in personal strengths, positive emotions, and creative intentions. Remember to choose them!

The dignity and strength of the spirit are core parts of the human experience, far greater than fear. In fact, your higher self is the part of you that feels no fear and knows no boundaries. It's your soul's identity that brings unending resourcefulness to your life. In addition to all the qualities you'll ever need, this aspect has access to all the wisdom of the infinite and eternal Universe.

You're one with the Divine mind, and this source of all knowledge is available to you even now. Your essential self is a wellspring of information, so ask your questions, quiet your mind, meditate, and listen to your intuitive responses. Whenever you need to make a decision or get clarity about something, request the information and ready yourself for the answers that you'll certainly receive.

BECOMING INSPIRED

What happens when you define yourself according to the expansiveness of your soul instead of the limits of your body and mind? It opens you to Universal inspirations. There are countless cases of people who've been truly inspired at unexpected times. The fields of science, art, literature, and even finance are filled with stories of apparent miracles. These moments are energetic responses that come at a time when the higher self resonates with the spirit of the Universe. In fact, the very word *inspire* means to be "in spirit."

This isn't necessarily a mystical process, although it may seem that way. The cosmos is filled with information and boundless creativity. Like the morphogenetic fields that carry the energy of emotion, great fields of data also carry the eternal wisdom and knowledge of all ages—past, present, and future. This is always available through your resonant connection with the Universal flow. The only thing that stops you from tapping into it is your own resistance. Obstacles may come in the form of doubt and distractions, but once you let these energetic blocks go, you'll find the answers that you seek coming to you in truly unexpected and mystical ways!

I believe this synchronicity with the Divine mind is the source of countless inventions, discoveries, and even great works of art, music, and literature. One particularly astounding inspiration happened to California chemist Kary Mullis, when he invented the polymerase chain reaction (PCR), arguably one of the most important breakthroughs in understanding and decoding DNA.

In his book, *Dancing Naked in the Mind Field,* Mullis tells the story of how he'd been working in the lab trying to find a solution to DNA identification with no luck. One day he left the lab and drove to his cabin in Anderson Valley, California. Looking up at the hills and the blossoms of the buckeye trees, the solution suddenly became clear to him. In a split second, he was inspired with the answer, and he pulled over to write it out.

When he got back to the lab, he tested the potential of this solution that was a bolt of inspiration. He later said it was so simple that he couldn't understand why no one had come up with it before. But the information had been locked up in the morphogenetic fields, waiting for his matching resonance to tune in to it and take it away.

Mullis had been truly inspired. The answer hadn't revealed itself in the lab, while he was poring over his notes. It came to him as he was driving his convertible, blissfully looking at the beautiful trees dotting the hillsides. He'd been seeking the answer, and he was relaxed and open to receiving. The solution was there waiting for him, and his desire and intention moved the information from the energetic realm into his reality.

This revelation brought him the Nobel Prize, and its influence has spread throughout the world. The process that resulted from his discovery has totally shifted the understanding of DNA, helping predict and save people from genetically predisposed diseases and radically changing forensic criminology.

Mullis isn't alone in this type of experience. Writers, artists, inventors, and people from all walks of life throughout all periods of time have experienced the magic of spontaneous inspiration. Einstein often said that his greatest solutions came at times when he wasn't thinking about the problems. Thomas Edison kept a cot in his laboratory, and he reported that he frequently got the answer he was looking for upon waking from a nap. You can get inspired, too, if you simply relax, open up, and ask.

Let Your Higher Self Do the Work

One way to tap into this amazing power is to get more and more comfortable with tuning in to your intuition. To do that, you need to quiet your mind and listen for answers; then you've got to be willing to recognize and follow the guidance that you get. Learn to listen to your gut feeling more often, and start to distinguish the difference between the voice of intuition and that of fear. Sometimes they can sound so similar that you have to go deep within and listen to your heart to know the difference.

I once met a woman who was scheduled to be on the airplane that was blown up over Lockerbie, Scotland. Her intuition compelled her to delay her departure by just a few hours, yet another part of her hesitated to pay the extra money for rescheduling. Listening to her higher self and letting go of the monetary fear saved her life.

> To increase your intuitive connection with the Universal flow, calm your energy and release your concerns. Learn to relax and let go of all the hurry and worry you may be feeling. These are the vibrations that throw you off your spiritual connection. Regular meditation and peaceful reflection will connect you to a higher source and move you into the peaceful current of Universal guidance, love, and information.

Whenever you're in need, think about the issue you're working on and ask your higher self for help. When you go to bed at night, send your spirit out into the world to do your work for you. Whether it's convincing someone of the efficacy of your ideas or just getting you the specific information that you need to proceed with your goal, your soul has more power than you know.

As you fall asleep, direct your higher self to move out into the Universe on your behalf. The first time I did this, I was very young and motivated by what I realize now was a very superficial intention. I had a crush on a young man who knew me but had never made any moves to get closer. So, I thought I'd try this process to initiate some action. As I was falling asleep, I'd direct my higher self to go talk to him and tell him, "You really want to ask Sandy out." I did this every night for about two weeks, not feeling any desperation, just amusement and curiosity to see if it would work.

Well, it did! I ran into him at a party of a mutual friend, and he asked if I'd be willing to go out with him. I'm happy to say I was much more impressed by the process than I was with that date.

Now, that may seem like a silly and meaningless example, but I have to tell you, I have used this process since then for all sorts of things—including getting my wonderful publisher, Hay House. Right before sleeping, I'd send out my higher self to talk to the people involved and to convince them that my book had value. There was no coercion, just a gentle word or two from my spirit to the spirit of the person I was visiting. It took about three or four months, and again it was simply a quiet intention before falling asleep, not something I dwelled on or brooded about or even thought about during the day. It was something I gave to my spirit to spread the word, another little technique to accelerate the energy of my desire, which helped to make it a reality.

You can use this technique to accelerate your intentions, too. Just consider the outcome you want to achieve and the names of any people involved. As you slip into sleep, gently guide your higher self to take a short message directing the right person to be open to your intention. If you don't know the name of the person, you can name the company or even the department you have in mind. Do it without attachment and release it with joy and patience. Keep a notebook by your bed so that you can write down any impressions that you may have during the evening. Even your dreams may have the answers you seek, so jot them down and remain open to seeing the truth within.

The spirit energy that's always with you is a part of both your present and your eternal definition. You'll never be more in spirit than you already are right now. Your soul doesn't get greater, more powerful, or wiser when it's released from your physical body; it just becomes less encumbered by physical distractions. Right now, your essence has the power to tap into the fields where all wisdom is stored, and it can connect with all the energetic realms. So, ask your higher self for help, but don't stop there. Send your request out into the world—you may be surprised by the responses you get!

Affirmations for Connecting with My Higher Self

✦ Every day I am becoming more and more aware of my own eternal spirit. I live in the peace my spirit brings.

✦ I am open to my own soul's beauty, grace, and receptivity. My spirit brings me great connections and wonderful assistance all the time!

✦ I open myself to my spirit's capacity to love and be loved, to create, to trust, and to receive.

✦ More and more, I am listening to my intuitive voice. Inspiration comes in many ways and at unexpected times, bringing knowledge and guidance each day.

✦ I release worry and worldly concerns, and I embrace the peace and power of my eternal identity.

✦ ✦ ✦

Chapter 24

Angels, Guides, and Loving Spirits

The Second Unseen Assistants to Success

Outside the open window
The morning air is all awash with angels.

— RICHARD WILBUR

A huge part of the energetic realm is the spirit world, which is wider and more populated than most people could ever imagine. In addition to the energy of your own soul, the energy of every other individual pulsates through time and space. Unseen entities smile upon you, willing to assist you in a myriad of ways even now. These beings, including angels, guides, loved ones, and other caring hearts of the energetic realms, are always vibrating their messages of love and assurance in your direction.

ANGELS

Though these entities are often the most dismissed, their energy can be some of the most dynamic forces that we can align with. Throughout history and many religions, angels have been believed to be the servants of God and helpers of humankind. Don't ignore this astounding power because you feel that it's just too religious or weird. If there's something you want to do or achieve, call on the angels for help. As with all kinds of assistance—spiritual or otherwise—you have to ask in order to receive.

There are many stories of angelic presence in all sorts of situations. A friend of mine who works in a somewhat hazardous factory job told me that he asks the angels to protect him whenever he goes to work. One day, a fire broke out, and the smoke was so thick that he couldn't find his way to the exit. He heard someone call out his name, telling him to follow their voice. He continued to do so, and when he got to the door, he found he had escaped the smoke and fire, but there was no one to be seen.

An Olympic ice-skater once told me that she calls upon the angels all the time. She often feels them dancing with her on the ice, even lifting her up when she performs her jumps. Another friend who was a pilot for a small commuter airline once found himself in the middle of a huge storm over Lake Superior. His 12-passenger plane went into a nosedive, and although he and his co-pilot tried with all their might, they couldn't seem to pull the aircraft out of it. He called out, "Somebody help me," and suddenly he felt two strong arms helping him bring up the nose of the plane, allowing him to finish the flight and get his frightened passengers safely to their destination. He had never believed in angels before. In fact, he often laughed at the mention of them. But now he was convinced that they were the very source of the power that saved all 14 lives on the plane that day!

These people—and so many more—have asked for help from angels, and they certainly got it. Open your heart to them. But assistance from the spirit world isn't limited to the angelic realm.

GUIDES

Put your requests out there because countless guides are willing to help. These assistants may be teachers, saints, or other spiritual masters. Comedian Danny Thomas learned this firsthand, and his one request ended up saving countless lives.

In the early 1940s, Thomas was having a great deal of difficulty trying to make it in the entertainment business. He'd done radio work and stand-up comedy, but he wasn't making enough money to support his growing family. He and his pregnant wife were expecting their first child soon, but he had only $10 in his pocket and didn't know how he would pay the $50 hospital bill.

While praying at his local church, the priest spoke of St. Jude—the patron saint of hopeless causes. Thomas asked the saint for a sign to help him find his way in life and know whether to stay in entertainment. He decided that if nothing happened with his comedy and singing career soon, he'd give up on his dream and get a regular job.

Not long after that, Danny received his sign—a radio gig that more than covered the hospital bill he'd been worried about. The signs kept coming in the form of a Hollywood agent that was drawn to him, being cast in several parts on radio shows, then his two-hit television series. He also founded a very successful production company that created many popular comedy shows and brought him great wealth.

When Danny asked for St. Jude's intercession, he said that he would build a shrine in the saint's name to thank him—and he did much more than that. In 1960, he founded the St. Jude Children's Research Hospital for children with catastrophic illnesses. Even before the hospital opened its doors in 1962, the organization was already hard at work to raise funds and award grants for medical research. Started under the auspices of Danny Thomas's personal funding, the policy was created that no child would ever be turned away for lack of funds. Even today, families never receive a bill for treatment, travel, housing, or food.

This amazing place is considered the leader of childhood cancer research today. The treatments they've developed have helped push the overall childhood cancer survival rate from 20 percent to more than 80 percent. In the decades since its founding, countless young lives have been saved. The spiritual help that Danny

Thomas sought from St. Jude so long ago is now bringing answers to the prayers of families from all over the world. He was awarded the Congressional Gold Medal for his humanitarian endeavors, and the World Health Organization has named St. Jude's as its first Collaborating Centre for Childhood Cancer, hoping that together they can increase the survival rate even further.

St. Anthony, the patron of lost things, is a guide I often turn to. You can call upon him to find anything you've misplaced. Invoke him while thinking of the missing item, and you should soon get an idea that leads you right to what you're looking for. Here's an invocation you can use: *Dear St. Anthony, come around. Something's lost and must be found.*

I turn to St. Anthony all the time, not just for lost items but also for assistance in locating information or support. I even asked him to help find our adoptive children and bring them home. Over the years, I've called on St. Anthony so often that now I just call him Tony!

A few years ago, I was giving a lecture to a rather large audience, talking about spirit assistance and telling a few stories of how St. Anthony has helped me. When I gave the invocation, a lot of people wrote it down, but one woman went running out the back of the auditorium. After I finished my lecture, this same person came up to me and apologized for leaving. She told me that she had to call her sister right away to tell her about St. Anthony.

This woman's sister had lost their grandmother's engagement ring, which was an expensive antique that was also very dear to them both. She recited the invocation over the phone, and then they both said it out loud together. Immediately, her sister got an image of a drawer in her dresser. She opened it—and the ring was sitting right on top! She couldn't understand it, because she'd looked there a dozen times before.

The woman concluded her story by saying, "We were so surprised!" I told her not to be so stunned because I hear that kind of story all the time, and St. Anthony is known to be a loving, supportive soul. She answered, "Oh, I'm sure that's true, but we were surprised because we're Jewish!"

Rest assured that the spirit world is nondenominational and willing to assist all who will open their hearts to them. I talk to a diverse group—from Buddha to the Holy Spirit, from Sai Baba to my beloved grandmother Anna. You can ask for help from anyone in spirit, too, Ascended Masters, saints, prophets, angels, or any of your loved ones.

LOVED ONES AND OTHER SPIRITS

There's a well-known story about Enrico Fermi, the acclaimed physicist. Tragically, Giulio, his beloved brother, died when Enrico was only 14 years old. After this loss, Enrico threw himself into reading old physics books as a coping mechanism for his grief.

Toward the end of one volume, his sister noticed something peculiar about it. She asked him how he could understand a book that was written entirely in Latin. He told her that he understood everything in it, and he hadn't even noticed that it was in a language completely unfamiliar to him.

Some people who know the story say that it was Enrico's deceased brother who translated the work for him. Others believe that he was helped by an angel, and some are convinced that he simply had an inner knowing. Whatever the source of his miraculous comprehension, he used it to become a leader in nuclear and radioactive science at a very early age.

Don't be afraid to ask for help from all possible sources. Request answers and success! It's well known that Cornelius Vanderbilt consulted a spiritualist for advice on business investments. He went on to amass a fortune and founded a university.

Wherever the aid may have come from, all these stories have one thing in common: The assistance that was needed didn't originate in the mundane, physical world. It came from the energetic realm that's home to the unseen forces and loving personalities who have our best interests at heart. Our angels, guides, and guardians move freely in—and have influence over—both the physical and energetic worlds, so let yourself open your heart to their presence. Place pictures of your loved ones and even of the angels around your home. Speak to them and ask them questions. The answers may come at any time and in surprising ways. Astounding information and assistance vibrates all around you. In a world of pure potential, all that you'll ever need is right at the edge of consciousness, waiting for you to open the door!

PLANTING YOUR ATTRACTION INTENTION IN THE ENERGETIC REALM

You can align your energy with the incredible power of spirit and accelerate your goal achievements through the simple technique of attraction intentions. This process can be used to help manifest anything you desire, such as a promotion, a new job, a new love, a place to live, or even just a wider network of friends. It involves a bit of writing and a few minutes of meditation, but it has truly incredible effects. Here's an example of how the process would work if you're looking for a new job.

At the top of a blank page in your journal, write the sentence, "I am attracting the ideal position (job, career, etc.) that . . ."

After this introduction, go down the page and list all the qualities that you want in your ideal job. Make sure you list things like: *is interesting and enjoyable, has a supportive boss and friendly coworkers, is in a good location, has a comfortable environment, provides great remuneration and all the benefits I desire, makes me happy to go to work, has room for promotions, offers a great retirement, brings me lots of friends, fun and interesting activities.*

You can tweak the list as time goes on and you realize more details that you want to attract. You can even add things like *short commute* or *working from home*. Remember, you always want to attract a position that honors you and resonates with your heart *and* your highest intentions.

As I said, this process works for anything. If you want to attract a new residence, new love, or something else, you would put a top sentence about attracting the ideal home, partner, friends, literary agent, lawyer, realtor, doctor, or whatever you may need. Do only one list per page, writing down all the qualities you desire.

Plenty of people write lists of what they desire then do nothing with them. Unfortunately, they're missing one of the most important pieces, the incredible power of spirit. Once you've written your attraction intentions, don't set them aside and never think about them again. Nor should you read them every single day. If you obsess about what you want to attract, that only stimulates the Law of Paradoxical Intent, making you more desperate and *urgent*, and that needy energy will actually block your intention. The solution is to focus only a little bit on your attraction intentions in a way that engages the unlimited power of spirit.

Here's what you do: Once or twice a week before going to bed, take out your list of attraction intentions. (If you've written multiple lists, do one at a time.) Spend a few minutes just before bed where you scan your intention and all the details on it. Read it and put its energy in your heart center. Then, as you're falling asleep, call upon your own higher self or your spirit and angel friends to take your intention to the energetic realm. Visualize yourself handing your intention over to them, asking them to carry it to the field of pure potential where *they* will be putting their own energy and high intentions into it as well.

Each specific intention will be vibrating in the Universal flow of all possibilities, projecting your desires into time and space. Then the ideal solution or person that matches the specific vibrations you listed will be drawn to you and your intention in the energetic realm. Through the process called entrainment, your own personal resonance will connect with the ideal partner, job, home, or friends based on their matching energies to your intention. As that resonant connection grows stronger, that ideal person or solution will be drawn to you in real time and space.

Now, you must remember two things with this process. First, when you send the angels or spirit friends out into the Universe, let your intentions go as well. Completely release them with total trust and surrender; don't brood about your goal or let yourself feel urgent about it. Instead, create an attitude of joy and appreciation for all that you *already* have and for *all* that spirit is doing to help make your dreams come true.

Second, you must support your energetic intentions with your choices in your daily life. If you ask for a new boss that respects and honors you, you must consciously choose to respect and honor yourself. If you ask for a loving, supportive partner, you must choose to support, care for, and prioritize yourself, both in your self-care and in your self-talk. When you yourself project a positive energy *and* you have your spirit friends planting your goals in the energetic realm, the results are amazing. This combination of personal and spiritual powers, whether you're using this technique or just asking for inspiration, will lead you in dynamic new directions, bringing abundant happiness and joyous blessings to every area of your life!

Affirmations for Connecting with Loving Spirit Energy

✦ Loving assistance often comes my way. I am open to receiving the guidance I need at just the right time.

✦ Angels grace my life with kindness, inspiration, and compassion. I am protected and well cared for.

✦ Whenever I have a question or concern, all I have to do is ask. I always receive the answers I need, and I am grateful.

✦ Connecting with spirit brings power, purpose, and clarity to my life. I release doubt or hesitation and I make heart-to-heart connections with ease.

✦ The Universe is filled with spirit's loving intentions. I now align my own loving intention with that amazing power and abundant flow.

✦ ✦ ✦

Chapter 25

The Divine Presence

The Third Unseen
Assistant to Success

We are so filled with trouble that the Divine Melody is never heard. If we could see . . . if we could understand, if we only realized the presence of the All, what could we not do?

— ERNEST HOLMES

The Divine source of all creation exists in every wave and particle of the cosmos. This compelling energy is the heartbeat of life and the birth of all things—including every success. As such, that Presence needs to become a real and viable part of your life. If you dismiss this amazing force, your dreams may die merely from spiritual starvation. But if you see the Divine as a giver of life and co-creator of your existence, you'll forge your energies with unlimited power and create a consciousness of peace and tranquility that permeates your entire existence.

This shouldn't be just an idealistic approach, but rather a heartfelt experience, a process where you ask for and receive God's loving influence every day. The personal dignity inherent in human life comes from the soul's origin, and it reveals the real nature of our eternal truth. This connection transcends all problems, lack, and worry. It brings a greater sense of peace and constancy, one that always draws you back to your source and your solution.

You can't separate who you are from who *You* are. If the Divine Presence isn't integrated into how you truly feel about yourself, then the most attractive vibration of the Universe will be blocked within. This is the major malady of humankind: all over the world, millions of people feel their vital source energy dammed up in their own broken hearts. It's a painful, sinking heaviness of loss that can drive you into desperate longing for external gratification in such things as addiction, acquisition, and escape. But no amount of outward pleasure will ever satisfy an empty and unconnected soul.

YOUR TRUE IDENTITY—
YOUR SPIRITUAL DEFINITION

How would you define yourself? When I ask my clients this, they usually respond with statements like, "A woman who has three children and who is a teacher in Texas." Or "A single man living in New York working as a stockbroker." But these statements, though they may describe your present circumstances, fall far short of truly defining you.

To arrive at your truth, you must define yourself as spirit first. In this definition, your worth isn't based on externals, but on your Divine legacy. You are holy and so is your life. To dismiss this rejects your sacred identity, which is the real source of personal success. You must see your value and the worth of your eternal life, finally letting go of judgment and conditional self-acceptance because such material measurements consistently deny the innate holiness of your human self. The living presence of the Divine within is your ultimate source of worthiness, and when you embrace this truth, the world will enfold you in its blessings.

JOURNAL FOR SUCCESS

In this simple but important journal exercise, you will write a *spiritual* definition of yourself, listing your observations of your true identity. It could start with something like the following examples, but please create your own statements.

- I am an eternal being whose life pre-existed this life and goes all the way back to the creative source of Divine Consciousness.

- I am a child of God, and by virtue of my Divine legacy, I am unlimited in power, value, and deserving.

Add more of your own observations, and when you're done listing your defining truths, expand them into present intentions and affirmations, such as:

- I am connecting more and more with the Divine power within.

- Every time I pass a mirror, I will stop and see, feel, and sense the beauty and value of my own eternal soul.

- I honor myself and my soul's truth. I release judgment, doubt, and limitation, and I acknowledge the value of my eternal life.

When you define yourself by your spirit's Divine connection, you know that your spiritual and personal success are intrinsically linked to your true self-regard. You're a child of God, a manifestation of that eternal love and light, and how you treat yourself is a statement to God about your capacity to love one of His children. Would you let someone talk to your child the way that you've been speaking to yourself? When you criticize yourself, God is asking you, "How could you treat My beloved child this way?" Your judgment denies the eternal spirit of your life, and if self-loathing and self-condemnation are allowed to continue, they'll wall up the light within you until your magnetic energy is as dense and dark. But you don't have to live in the self-degradation that belies the expansive beauty and deserving of your real identity anymore.

THE SACRED PRAYER OF MIRROR AFFIRMATIONS

People resist seeing the truth of their Divine legacy and value because they have embraced their human limitations for so long. But seeing this intention as a central goal could lead to the fulfillment of every other goal in your life. And recognizing the unlimited and eternal identity within can be a magical first step in making all your dreams come true.

This is how and why mirror affirmations can create an irresistible force in the momentum of your attraction. You may recall that there are three powerful energetic forces that project a truly beneficial resonance in the process of mirror affirmations. But there is an expansive spiritual vibration that magnifies that value beyond measure. When you look in the mirror with a genuine intention to open your heart to the worthy and powerful identity within, you shift the very core of your consciousness and become the generator and receiver that reaches everywhere all at once. Your Divine understanding connects you in unfathomable ways with the very power of the Universe.

With this as your perception, your mirror affirmations become a deeply feeling experience, a sacred prayer to the eternal and Divine source that is your truth and your most profound identity. The choice to acknowledge this allows you to see yourself and your life in a different light.

This is not just mindless lip service to a lofty yet meaningless practice. Nor is it a desperate attempt to use yet another technique to try to get what you want. It is a profoundly authentic intention to stop, look into your own eyes, and see the light of eternity there. This valuable and beautiful light of your own soul longs for you to recognize your truth. Turn your mirror affirmations into a sacred prayer to the Divine within you—to your Sacred Self.

Open your heart to connect with your Divine legacy, the ultimate source of your deserving and receiving. After all, the joys of success, love, and real gratification can't flow freely to you without a deep sense of worthiness within. Once again, a shift of energy is required. Moving closer to the Divine necessitates retreating further from self-criticism and dismissal. Consistently shift your negative definition and choose higher perceptions of yourself. To open yourself up to God, let go of inner conflict, embrace peace and trust, and view your life in the light of eternal understanding.

This is your soul's point of view, an authentic vibration that embraces an understanding of the *real* value in life. The soul may not prioritize material acquisition, but its ability to see the joy and grandeur of the little experiences of life opens you up to all the blessings that this world can offer. All it takes to achieve that power is to connect your heart with the Divine within and all around you.

THE DIVINE HEART

The path to the Divine isn't a long road—just the distance from your head to your heart. Don't look for heaven in the sky above you because your connection can't be found up there. Instead, meditate on your own heart center. Breathe slowly and deeply and ask to feel the eternal light that already resides inside you. See it growing within and radiating outward, connecting you with all the other lights of Divine Love. This is the nature of the vast soul of creation: we are all beams of that bright source, joined together in God's infinitely brilliant vibration.

In addition to daily meditation, another way to connect with this powerful presence is through sincere and heartfelt prayer. This has long been known to be a force of healing, protection, and inspiration, and it's also a great conduit to the Divine. A prayer said with a genuine heart reaches the unknown recesses of the energetic world, often bringing results that nothing else could have created.

I keep a prayer list in the front of my journal, on which I place the names of people or situations that may need healing or a resolution. I speak to God about those names each morning, and at night I spend time sending loving intentions to all those situations. I focus on my own goals, but I also include more global issues, such as help for the homeless, healing for the sick, and peaceful resolution to hostilities. I also add an invocation for loving assistance to be sent to all those who have nobody to help them.

Whatever you're praying for, your words and thoughts don't have to be formal or creative; they just need to be straight from the heart. Let yourself open the channels of communication when you want to release habits or need to heal; ask for what you want, and give thanks for what you have. Prayers of appreciation and thanksgiving are the whispers of love returned to the granter of all wonderful gifts. Express that gratitude in all that you do, and it will become a living invocation. When you see the Divine in every experience, you realize that your whole life—every activity—can be a meditation or a heartfelt prayer.

There are many stories of athletes, inventors, business owners, rock stars, actors, and countless others who attribute their success to their relationship with God. Don't look at this merely as sappy sentimentality. The unlimited power of the Divine, the creative source and resonance of all the Universe, is your greatest supporter and the most loving, willing co-creator in your individual destiny. Open yourself to this connection, and you'll feel life-changing power in each breath. Truly great things can happen in your life, too—in fact, there's no greater joy than a heartfelt connection to the peace and presence of God.

Affirmations for Living in Divine Presence

✦ I release fear and self-criticism. I am blessed with the love of God, and I deserve to love myself.

✦ All joy, success, and peace of mind flow in Universal abundance to my life. Endless blessings come to me now.

✦ I see the Divine in all people. Loving Divine Intention connects us all.

✦ The love of God fills me up. My life is a meditation and a peaceful prayer. I embrace my own loving connection to my Source.

✦ Divine Consciousness vibrates in my body and my life, bringing me life-changing power, healing, and joy.

✦ ✦ ✦

PART VI

The Two Obstacles to Success

Sometimes your pursuit of success seems to be met with one obstruction after another. Things just keep going wrong, your timing is off, the economy goes bad, or other things get in the way. You don't seem to make the right connections—or perhaps the people involved keep messing up.

These obstacles may be circumstantial, and they may even be cyclical. After all, everything in life moves through cycles. Winter is a time of decrease; summer is expansion. Don't fault yourself for hitting bumps in the road. Instead, look at the situation around you and the energy and patterns within you.

You do have influence even over cycles and obstacles—if you take your time and approach the issues more consciously. Whatever may be going on, you can change your energetic response and your own mental reactions, and in this way, break through two of the greatest blocks you'll have to deal with in pursuing your success.

Life is a process, a continuous stream of experiences—both good and bad. Energetically speaking, it's not so much what happens to you as how you respond to it that makes the difference. No matter what occurs or how long your success may take, you can choose to keep taking action, not only in the direction of your goals, but also in terms of your own consciousness and energy production. Whatever obstacle may arise, you need to remember that even a little shift in conscious thought can create a significant—and even immediate—transformation in your life. Now and always, you have the power to make that change and see your goals blossom into beautiful reality.

Chapter 26

Engaging in Limiting Beliefs

The First Obstacle to Success

Believe that you will succeed. Believe it firmly and you will then do what is necessary to bring success about.

— DALE CARNEGIE

It's clear that your beliefs are the generator of both your energy and your life force, so there's no greater factor determining your success. The two most damaging notions are conclusions of doubt and limitation. Just think about how the former affects your consciousness: your brain can easily be convinced that what's merely perceived is actually real, so if you doubt that you can succeed, you'll create that in your consciousness—and then your consciousness will create it in your reality.

If you want the forces of the Universe to help you achieve what you desire, you must choose to live according to the unlimited truth of Universal abundance. You could make all the plans and take all the action necessary, but if you have a limited mindset, or even one of doubt, you simply won't be able to get the world to respond. If your energy is full of fear and limitation, you'll be

255

fighting the flow, constantly struggling against the tide. It's time to decide: do you want to focus on limitation or expansion?

The real path to success comes from choosing strong, optimistic convictions. Everything about your consciousness creation is formulated in your beliefs. They're the source of your daily thoughts, which create your personal energy. Healthy cognitions create positive results; unhealthy ones create a dark broadcast that can lead to unhappy outcomes.

> The Laws of the Universe and the unseen forces are very clear. You will achieve what you believe—not what you want, desire, or hope for. There's no variation on this truth. Your beliefs are the fuel of the cosmic engine, your manifestation machine. If you embrace limiting assumptions, you'll project a consciousness of limitation and attract further restriction. But unlimited beliefs will produce boundless results and open your life to abundant receiving.

STOPPING SPONTANEOUS NEGATIVE LOOPS

Our negative thoughts pop up whether we want them or not. You could be going along, involved in a task, and suddenly have an unpleasant assumption appear. Sometimes it may be just a fleeting thought, but often the negativity is totally overpowering, filling your mind with so much dread and doubt until it seems as if there's nothing you can do to escape it.

When that happens, you have to consciously shut down that thought pattern and start all over with a new one, and once you get that established, you have to be determined to block all the damaging fears that may continue to pop up. In fact, you can create your own positive defense. I've done it myself, and I've taught the following process to clients who've used it to intervene in all sorts of situations.

Positive Visualization: Rise Above It!

Take just a few moments to do this simple process to gain a new perspective about the issue you may be concerned about.

Sit comfortably, and take a few deep breaths. Drop your shoulders and relax the muscles in your body. Visualize yourself as a tall, strong tree, standing over the people and situations around you.

See yourself growing stronger and taller, going up and up till you're looking way down at the people and the situation. The people look like ants and the situation is so small, you feel far above it and unphased by it. In fact, even the clouds of your own negative thinking have blown away, making you feel free and powerful in the bright light of the sun. The difficulty feels so small now, and you are so strong and capable.

Feel that strength filling you up. Know that you can see everything from a different perspective now, one where you have the power and peace of mind!

This process will help you cement new thoughts and empowered sensations in your own consciousness—and in the Universal flow as well, sending positive vibrations out into the energetic realm. If you keep doing this every time you have a difficult situation or negative thought, it will only be a matter of time before a new dynamic energy becomes present in your life.

You can use this technique whenever you're facing (or even thinking about) a problem or having a limiting belief. Your mentality creates your reality, and you can choose this positive mindset at every opportunity. Rise above the walls of anxiety that are blocking your success. Create new neural pathways and see each thought of limitation floating away as you get stronger and greater than anything that may come your way.

You can consciously reverse your old conclusions of doubt and limitation. No matter what you've believed in the past, you must rid yourself of these old, nagging thoughts now. You do have the power to let them go, and it's the only logical choice. Even if you feel compelled by habit or superstition, your negative beliefs can be replaced by new patters of trust and optimism simply by choosing (and repeating) the true observations of unlimited power.

TRUTH OR SCARE?

The following list represents the most common limiting beliefs regarding the issues of success, and these conclusions don't represent your truth; they only represent the misinformation of others. Such thoughts are not only energetically damaging but also harmonically destructive, throwing you out of balance with the Universal flow. To get back into harmony, you must believe something more honest and empowering. Stop deceiving yourself with old lies and start living in your power. Recognize the unlimited potential within yourself, your world, and all your personal pursuits.

Which of these beliefs do you find yourself engaging in the most? Identify the ones that you've had, and then write your new truths on index cards. Carry these with you and read them as often as possible. You can use the thought restructuring sheets process from Chapter 8 in which you write your negative concerns in a left-hand column then a positive option for each in a right-hand column to get clarity. Add an optimistic image when you're reading—even if it's just a simple vision of you in a favorite place, smiling and being happy. Visualize this picture, accompanied by your new belief, whenever you catch yourself engaging in a thought that you're trying to refute.

Limiting Belief: I'm not good enough (smart enough, attractive enough) to make it. I don't deserve to succeed.

Personal Truth: I am good enough (smart enough, attractive enough) to succeed. I deserve all the good things the Universe has to offer. I believe in myself and my ability to create a great future.

Limiting Belief: I need to be perfect. Everything I do has to be perfect. I have to be accepted by everyone.

Personal Truth: I accept myself. I can learn to accept who I am and what I do without any judgment.

Limiting Belief: How can I succeed? I've never really been successful before.

Personal Truth: I release the past and let it go. Today is a new day; this is a new thought. With every new moment I create a positive new energy and a strong belief in myself.

Limiting Belief: I don't have enough money (education, luck, looks) to succeed.

Personal Truth: I have all that I need to succeed. I have all the resources I need to create the great future that I want.

Limiting Belief: Life is hard. There aren't enough good jobs (women, men, opportunities) to go around.

Personal Truth: The Universe is abundant. There are plenty of wonderful jobs (women, men, opportunities) for everyone to have a successful and happy life. I am attracting those abundant opportunities now. There's always plenty for me to enjoy.

Limiting Belief: Things always turn out badly for me. If it weren't for bad luck, I'd have no luck at all.

Personal Truth: I choose to acknowledge all the good I have in my life. I am attracting more and more happy circumstances. I am truly lucky and blessed.

Limiting Belief: My present life isn't good enough. I have to do or be something different—or have more to be good enough.

Personal Truth: What I am doing now is valuable and worthy, and so am I. I choose to see myself as successful right now. I see the value in everything I do, and I attract more to me.

Limiting Belief: I have to compete every day. I must constantly strive to be better. I can't accept myself just as I am.

Personal Truth: I am valuable just as I am. I don't have to do or be anything different. Every day, I choose to acknowledge my value more and more. I am learning to accept, believe in, and appreciate myself in every present moment.

Limiting Belief: The world isn't safe; life isn't safe; love isn't safe. I can't trust myself to handle things. I'm miserable!

Personal Truth: I can trust myself and know that I am safe in the world. It is safe for me to accumulate wealth and to love and be loved. I live my life to the fullest with joy and peace.

Limiting Belief: I can't be happy until I succeed. I have to worry and hurry to make this happen.

Personal Truth: I choose to feel good about myself and create happiness in my life right now. I know that a peaceful, happy attitude attracts greater success and joy to me, so I create that every day.

These are just some of the limiting beliefs that you may find yourself engaging in. Can you think of more? Jot them down in your journal and be sure to write the countering statements with them. Carry those positive thoughts with you and repeat them until they become your spontaneous reaction. This isn't just busy-work; it's a crucial part of your positive energy production. The process of manifestation is so strongly linked to your thoughts and beliefs that you simply can't continue to engage in limitation without attracting more restricting people and situations to you.

BLOOD TYPE: BE Positive

Some people define themselves through their limitations. Their negativity seems deep within their nature, in their very blood! They're so steeped in their own fears and anxieties that it never even occurs to them to respond in a different, more positive way. Whether you engage in this type of chronic misery or only have the occasional fleeting doubt, you must use your power of choice to take a different energetic path.

Limited thinking is just another habit, a deep form of worry that can be addictive, and when you throw anxiety at a problem, the energy of that obstacle only increases. No amount of fretting, fear, or doubt will ever help create a positive solution; it just increases the difficulties you're already upset about. You must *infuse* your life with an affirmative way of looking at things that represents your truth.

Changing your thoughts and beliefs may seem like a big task, but in the long run, it takes far less effort to do so than to continue living under their negative influence. Do *not* look at this as impossible or even unrealistic. Limiting beliefs constrict your reality, and there's no getting past the energetic walls they set up around your present happiness and your pursuit of success.

It's your belief system that causes the most chronic suffering in your life. It's not the dead-end jobs, the bad relationships, or even the lack of money—though these are the things you may focus on most. But it's the hopelessness that comes from fear and judgment that makes you the most miserable. Don't stay stuck there any longer! Choose to let go of despair and embrace the truth of your unlimited potential. The resulting feelings of joy and freedom will empower you more than you can ever imagine.

I often relate an interesting story at my seminars that demonstrates the power of belief. It's about a father who took his son to see the circus back in the days before the arenas, when the circus was popular and the show went from town to town, taking the big tents with them. In one of these villages, a father took his son to see how the workers set up the big top. They watched as the elephants were put to work dragging the heavy canvases and lifting the huge center supports that were as large as telephone poles.

Naturally, the boy was amazed at the animals' incredible strength. But later, when they went back to watch the circus, they saw that the elephants were tied up. Each one had a rope around one ankle tied to a wooden stake to the ground. When the boy saw this, he asked his father why the beasts didn't just snap the rope or pull the stake out of the ground. After all, earlier that day, they'd had the power to lift huge poles and pull the heavy tents.

The father explained that when the elephants were babies, one ankle was chained to a steel rod in the ground. Whenever they tried to walk away, the chains stopped them in their tracks, and they soon learned that when they were tied down in this way, they couldn't leave. This became their guiding belief system and their physical reality. Even after they grew to a huge size, they lived their entire lives based on their baby-elephant beliefs. Their existence was limited—not by their truth, but by what they were taught. It's time to ask yourself, *What baby-elephant beliefs are you holding on to?*

What limiting thoughts are keeping you tied down? What personal powers are you dismissing just because you were taught at an early age that they didn't exist? Whatever you've been taught, you can teach yourself something new and true right now! You're more powerful than you know. You're unlimited in the ability to change your thinking, and this gives you the ultimate strength: the power to change your reality. It's time to get rid of the chains of misinformation that somebody used to hold you down when you were young. It's time to live in your true power and believe in your unlimited potential.

The Universe says "Yes!" to what you believe—whatever that may be. Whether positive or negative, your ongoing conclusions will lead to the outcome of your dreams and desires. When you choose to break through your habitual, self-imposed limitations and open yourself up to abundant belief, the Universe will say "Yes!" to a joyous life now and endless blessings to come.

Affirmations to Release Limiting Beliefs

+ I release all doubt. Whenever thoughts of limitation come to mind, I release them and see myself rising above the situation I'm thinking about. I am strong and free.

+ I release all worry and live in trust. I have all the power I need to make my dreams a reality. I am capable, strong, confident, and worthy.

+ The Universe is abundant: I believe in the availability of my goal, and I know there are many ways to happiness.

+ There is nothing that I can't conquer. I am unlimited in my power to change my thinking, energy, and reality.

+ I open myself to my spirit's ability to break through limiting thought patterns. I free myself from doubt and worry and choose positive, trusting, and nurturing thoughts instead.

+ + +

Chapter 27

Giving Up Too Soon

The Second Obstacle to Success

While one person hesitates because he feels inferior,
the other is busy making mistakes and becoming superior.

— HENRY C. LINK

Many people never arrive at the achievement of their goals because they simply give up when the going gets tough. Real achievement takes time, energy, focus, and patience. Your willingness to persevere needs to be constant because it may be the only thing that sees you through the tough times.

You should always have grand ambitions—and you should also be willing to invest the time, effort, and flexibility into making them come true. Be careful not to latch on to only one option or outcome since this creates an urgency that sabotages the momentum of your intention. You need to be persistent but relaxed, focused but flexible—both with your plans and with your goals.

I recently heard a good metaphor for this type of mindset. Whenever a plane takes off, it has to declare a destination and file a flight plan, but sometimes things happen that may necessitate unexpected changes, such as bad weather or technical difficulties. The aircraft has to go around the storm or perhaps even land at an entirely different destination.

Your pursuit of success may take a similar turn. The destination is your goal, and the flight plan is your course of action. At any time, you may be compelled by circumstance, necessity, or even inspiration to make important alterations. Whether it's just a slight variation in your route or completely reconsidering your destination, you need to be willing to make the necessary changes.

In 1914, Bruce Ismay's goal was to have the largest, most luxurious cruise liner to cross the Atlantic. There were warnings of icebergs, but no adjustments were made in the speed of the ship or its route. Far from reaching his goal, Ismay's brand-new, state-of-the-art ship, the *Titanic*, sank on its maiden voyage, bringing more than 1,500 passengers and crew members (and Ismay's business and reputation) down with it.

Don't sink your hopes and dreams in the icy waters of inflexibility and urgency. You may have to change direction—or even your ultimate destination—but if you're willing to reevaluate, reconsider, and adjust, you'll be able to see your destiny revealed. Stay open to the many options that the Universe has to offer, embrace them, and keep on going. Your determination will pay off!

STAYING POWER

There are countless cases of people who refused to give up despite difficulty and defeat. Here are just a few of them:

- After coming to Hollywood and playing bit parts, Clark Gable was told by a major movie producer that he would never have "leading-man" appeal. He went on to star in one of the most iconic lead roles in cinema history—Rhett Butler in *Gone with the Wind*—and was known as "the king of Hollywood" in his prime.

- Nelson Mandela spent 27 years in prison due to his efforts to end apartheid in South Africa. In the next four years after his release, apartheid was officially ended, he received the Nobel Peace Prize, and he was elected president in South Africa's first democratic election.

- Michael Jordan was cut from his high school basketball team.

- Stephen King had been writing for 20 years without successfully publishing a novel. He made ends meet with jobs at a laundry and then a high school. While working on a new story, he got so disgusted with his writing and so defeated from rejection that he threw it all away. His wife saved those pages from the trash and helped him finish what would become his novel, *Carrie*—the first of his many megasellers.

- Dr. Seuss's first book was rejected 27 times. After finally being accepted and published, he worked tirelessly to create dozens more books, which have sold millions and enriched the lives of children all over the world.

- Jerry Seinfeld was panned by the critics when he first started doing stand-up comedy, yet he went on to star in one of the most popular television comedies of all time.

- Conrad Hilton originally tried to buy a bank, but when the deal fell through at the last minute, he bought the hotel he was staying at instead. He spent the 1920s creating the successful Hilton brand of hotels, with multiple locations across the state of Texas. Then the Great Depression hit, and he struggled for years, deep in debt and on the verge of bankruptcy. Now the Hilton brand of hotels is worth billions of dollars, with hundreds of locations all over the world.

These are just a few of the countless stories of people who kept on going in the face of difficult—and sometimes seemingly unbeatable—odds. If you refuse to quit, your own story can join these; and your name can be added to the list of people such as George Washington, Charles Dickens, Albert Einstein, Florence Nightingale, Joseph Pulitzer, Abraham Lincoln, and Oprah Winfrey. These determined individuals refused to let adversity get them down.

THE BUNNY OF SUCCESS

A famous advertising campaign for a popular battery company features a little pink toy bunny rolling through all sorts of challenging circumstances. Undaunted, the rabbit spins on its heels and "keeps going and going." Your pursuit of success needs to be driven by the same kind of undaunted energy and intention. Where your dreams and desires are concerned, you need to be the bunny!

To help you along the way, here are some strategies that can keep your intentions moving forward and your energy in excited action.

- **No matter what happens, never let self-doubt seep in.** There's no room for self-criticism in the intention to pursue success. Your consciousness and energy *must* resonate with courage and determination—no matter how long it takes. Keep affirming!

- **Always remember that your success doesn't depend on any one event.** Never make a single project or issue mean too much. This only creates a desperate energy that pushes the desired outcome away. There are always alternative options, so if something doesn't work, pick another and keep going.

- **Don't be impatient.** Pace yourself and follow up on your plans while you enjoy the process—and your life. Your peaceful and persistent energy will do more to attract success than any individual goal.

- **Drop the conditional self-acceptance.** Stop comparing yourself to others, or being envious of them; those behaviors make you small and unattractive. When you live unconditionally, you attract in the same way.

- **Don't focus on what's going wrong; concentrate on what's going right and try to reproduce it.** When something doesn't work, let it go and renew your resolve, redirect yourself and keep going.

- **Live in appreciation.** Notice, acknowledge, and celebrate all that you have in your life. Dissatisfaction expands, so look around you and choose to be satisfied.

- **Create a timeline, but don't set time limits.** If something takes a little longer, that's okay. You may have to adjust your plans. Don't give up; be patient and flexible.

- **Let go of regrets.** Longing to change the past adds to resistance in the present. Stop brooding about old mistakes and look forward instead.

- **Get out of your comfort zone.** Take risks—do something new, different, and daring! Let go of your fears and take a chance.

- **Never define your setbacks as failures.** Failure has often been called just a high-priced education. By eliminating what doesn't work, you can figure out what does—and move even closer to your dream. And you always have the option to change dreams.

- **Be honest with yourself.** Be realistic about what you need to alter. Change can be safe and bring success, so always be flexible, open, and honest.

- **Keep your courage up**. Never see problems or setbacks as reasons to return to those old limiting beliefs. The Universe is abundant; face your future without fear.

- **Never lose your sense of deserving**. Whatever may happen, you are still worthy of having the best. Always acknowledge that, affirm your deserving, and be willing to do what it takes to make it happen.

- **Don't quit!** Keep persevering no matter what. Have faith, and be open to options and wondrous opportunities. See every day as a miracle; see yourself—and your precious life—as a miracle, too!

I had a gardener friend who grew a rare bamboo plant that took quite a long time to mature. The roots grew first, and then much, much later, the plant would come. She was diligent, though, watering the empty ground, weeding around it, and even talking to it in order to nurture the plant that was on its way.

Her friends and family thought she was silly to do this for more than four years with no apparent results. They told her that she was taking care of empty ground, and they wondered why she couldn't see that the plant was obviously dead. But she kept going because she knew the special requirements of this particular species.

Finally, in the fifth year, the bamboo sprouted. In fact, it grew nearly 50 feet in the span of one year! All the time that she'd been cultivating it, that plant had been setting down deep roots strong enough to support its rapid growth.

Cultivating your success takes the same kind of diligence. *The work you're doing may not be yielding visible results right now, but it's setting down roots equal to the size of your success.* So, be patient and keep going. If you create a sturdy foundation, your success will rise and be strong, abundant, and beautiful for all the world to see!

Affirmations for Untiring Perseverance

✦ No matter what it takes, I am willing to persevere.

✦ I am firm but flexible, determined and dedicated. I continue to act and feel joy and excitement in each action.

✦ I see any difficulty as just a new opportunity. I renew my strength and redirect my focus at every turn.

✦ As I move toward my goal, I reevaluate and make any necessary adjustments. No matter what, I review what needs to be done, and I keep on going.

✦ I release impatience. I cultivate an attitude of appreciation and success in everything I do. I trust in myself and in my ability to create a great future.

✦ ✦ ✦

PART VII

The One
Path to
Success

As you fall into a greater harmony with the unseen forces and Universal Laws, you'll undoubtedly feel your energy shifting. You'll begin to notice your consciousness changing, and in time, the external variables of your life will follow suit. But the most important transformation will be the emotional quality of all that you experience, the pervasive joy that fills your life.

This process of flowing energies and attitudes creates a domino effect in terms of your manifestation. As you change your perception, you become happier, which shifts your personal energy and eventually alters what you attract into your life. In this way, the bottom line of continual and unlimited successful manifestation is the ongoing intention to create happiness in the here and now. Be the success you want to become; live with the joy you want to achieve. Don't wait a moment longer to embrace the attitude that your life is a blissful adventure—even now.

Chapter 28

Living with a Joyous, Successful Consciousness

The One Path to Success

*. . . exhilaration in life can be found only
with an upward look. This is an exciting world.
Great moments wait around every corner.*

— RICHARD M. DEVOS

How has your day been? Were you as happy, peaceful, or joyous as you'd like to be? If not, what do you think it would take to make you feel that way? Take a minute to consider the answers to these questions right now, and write them in your journal. Be honest with yourself because your success may hinge on your answers.

Maybe you think that it would take having more money, more stuff, or perhaps a romantic relationship to make you happy; maybe you believe that having a new job or a whole different career could bring you the joy and fulfillment that you seek. If so, be careful! These thoughts will only make you miserable in the present, sabotaging both your energy and your pure intention. The paradox is clear: your conclusions about what you need in order to be content may be destroying any possibility for real joy right now. Look at the way you view your life and ask yourself: are you creating an empty, aching consciousness of need that will prevent the very things you seek from coming to you?

Don't confuse the acquisition of wealth and material goods with being happy. Energetically speaking, money doesn't bring you bliss. It's your happiness that brings the abundance! The joy that you already have in your life magnetizes the things that you think will bring more pleasure. This is good news because with this attitude, you no longer have to wait to be happy. In fact, in order to create a truly successful consciousness, you can no longer delay the choice to enjoy your life.

This can all seem like hard work if you're not accustomed to it. Some people don't even know how to be genuinely happy—they never saw it in their childhood or learned how to engage in it as adults. For these individuals, unhappiness becomes a way of life, and as strange as it may seem, the familiarity of that state creates its own kind of "comfort," causing people to *want* to maintain the status quo. This self-perpetuating misery may seem to be the path of least resistance, but it takes much more energy and effort to maintain a lifestyle of bleak dissatisfaction than it does to learn to become content.

The effort to create joy should be a lifestyle, not a single intention attached to the achievement of a single goal. Yet many people are so desperate for material things that they don't even expect or desire to be pleased until they're able to get just what they desire. This is an emotionally immature approach to life. It's the adult version of a kid saying, "I'm taking my ball and going home." If you don't get what you want, and you refuse to get into the game, you're isolating yourself from Universal flow and blocking the happiness that you'd be able to experience if you'd just let go and enjoy the moment.

This reminds me of an experience that I once had with my nephew when he was about three years old. I'd taken him to a restaurant, and while we were waiting for our food, he took out the action figures that he carried everywhere with him just in case he wanted to play. Among them were monsters and other gross-looking creatures, as well as about a dozen X-Men of various sizes and colors.

He began to set the X-Men up for their never-ending battle with evil, when his face suddenly got sad, and he frowned. He folded his arms in front of him and said, "I'm not playing." When I asked him why, he told me that he'd left his Wolverine at home. I pointed out that he had many other very strong and equally powerful combatants, but he still refused to play.

After a few minutes of silence, I said, "Okay, let's forget about that and play the happy game." To do this, we'd each take turns listing the things that we enjoyed. It always started out in a rather sane manner, as we'd list things such as snowball fights and hot fudge sundaes. Eventually, however, we'd invariably break down into utter silliness as we listed things such as snot sandwiches and spider-gut soup.

My nephew loved to play the happy game, but this time, he didn't budge. I tried to coax him into it by saying, "Come on, don't you want to play the happy game? We can get really gross. It'll make you happy!"

He just sat there and shook his head. Finally he said, "Without my Wolverine, I don't want to be happy!" He'd rather mourn the loss of something missing than enjoy what he had or even choose a fun option.

Surprisingly—and unfortunately—this response isn't limited to children. There are plenty of joyless adults who feel the same way. If they don't have exactly what they want, then they flat out refuse to be happy at all. Their grown-up versions go something like this: "If I don't have a husband, how can I enjoy my life?" or "If I don't get the money I want, I'll never be able to be happy."

Why is it so difficult to delight in our present experiences? Even in the face of difficulty, we can still shift out of two important negative patterns. The first is the decision to judge instead of value. This creates a sort of pleasure gap between our expectations of happiness and our actual experience of it.

Our second error is living in envy instead of appreciation. This can become a chronic, debilitating syndrome where our consciousness is focused on what other people have and what's wrong with our lives. This approach causes our happiness to be eaten away by a gnawing resentment over what we lack.

THE PLEASURE GAP

People tend to look for fun in the extraordinary activities of their lives, often completely dismissing the potential for joy at any other time. This creates a greater and greater split between the quality of their daily routine and the experience of their more "special" times. Think of the consciousness that this produces concerning your day-to-day existence! If you only glamorize the unusual and dismiss the pleasures of the mundane, you can't help but experience a gaping emptiness for the majority of your lifetime.

The pleasure gap exists when you see relatively little value— and even less hope for joy—in the endless series of the daily activities and tasks of life. But you can find happiness when you choose to treasure *all* the experiences of your life. You can bring an attitude of playfulness—a fresh, lighthearted approach—to everything, including your everyday actions. This can't just be an occasional priority. It needs to be an overarching intention, one where you begin and end your waking hours in the energy of appreciation, no matter what that day entailed.

It's time to fill in the pleasure gap, bring delight to every moment of your life, and make all your experiences special. Always release the perception that life is a burden; it creates far too dark an energy for the Universe to have a positive response. Choose to look at your activities in an entirely different way, knowing that your path is filled with opportunities to experience moments of peace and value—even today, even now.

There's a Zen proverb that says, "Chop wood, carry water." This simply means that all of life can be a meditation, an opportunity to see peace and beauty in even the smallest details. This is the ultimate expression of the energy of appreciation, and it creates an easy, fluid consciousness that prioritizes present peace as the purest form of success. A poem called "Hyacinths," written in the Middle Ages, expresses this sentiment well:

> If of thy mortal goods thou art bereft,
> And from thy slender store
> Two loaves alone to thee are left,
> Sell one, and with the dole
> Buy hyacinths to feed thy soul.

Because of their amazing scent, hyacinths are one of my favorite flowers. Every year, I buy some at the grocery store and bring them into my house, and they fill the place with the sweetest smell of spring. It's amazing how such a little thing can bring so much joy and gratitude! No matter the season, you can always look around and ask, *What feeds my soul?* Think of the wonderful energy you'll create if you can experience all your life with an attitude of peaceful appreciation. Your resonance of inner happiness will be downright irresistible!

The pleasure gap creates a huge polarity in how we experience life. It keeps us suspended in chronic discontent, filled with all-or-nothing thinking, dragging ourselves through meaningless days, waiting for something better to come along. But we need to remember that no matter what's going on, the *only* time we can choose to create joy is the present.

Bridging the pleasure gap doesn't mean indulging in physical desires or distractions all the time; it's a deeper contentment, one that comes from a profound appreciation of the here and now. Real happiness is a choice—not something we simply fall into, and it's a choice we must make over and over again. In choosing to be cheerful and appreciative now, we create the energy that perpetuates happy emotions always and everywhere.

In the London underground—the network of subways that move beneath the sprawling city—there's a sign and audio anouncement that say, "Mind the gap," warning people of the space between the platform and the train. It's time for you to mind the *pleasure* gap. Make sure that you're not missing real opportunities for peace merely due to your refusal to honor your life as being special every day. It's your choice: you don't have to wait; you can dare to be happy now.

THE SALIERI SYNDROME

The 1984 Oscar-winning movie *Amadeus* was a fictionalized version of the life of Wolfgang Amadeus Mozart. In addition to demonstrating Mozart's genius, it relayed the story of a man named Salieri, a composer who was a contemporary of the title character. He was acclaimed at the Vienna court, but according to the movie, he felt very envious of Mozart's talent. In time, he became obsessed with this self-assigned competition, and it made him more and more miserable. He felt as if he couldn't compete with the beauty of the other man's compositions, and it ruined his ability to be happy.

Although many historians disagree on the actual relationship between the two, this story is a great metaphor for the misery that a lot of people feel today—that is, the competitive attitude that engenders envy of those who have something we want. Rather than diminishing through the years, this emotion seems to be increasing and spreading to people of all ages and in all places. In fact, as more individuals become wealthy and their riches are displayed for all to see, it creates a *Why not me?* mentality. But wanting what others have eats away at your present peace. It translates into chronic, agitating dissatisfaction, an undercurrent of energy that can doom your intentions for success.

Envy causes you to bitterly compare yourself to those who've achieved what you haven't. This bitter, depressing focus results in self-judgment and disappointment in the present and hopelessness about the future. It's the ultimate paradox that this obsessive concern with lack only increases it. The negative energy seeps into your consciousness and can become a way of life, until all you can see is the emotional debris of constant dissatisfaction. Emotionally, energetically, and every which way, envy is an abyss of misery.

There's an old adage that says: "If you find yourself in a hole, stop digging." This is good advice when it comes to this wretched pit. If you already feel as though something's missing, this longing will only dig you deeper into that reality, but you can rise out of the hole by shifting your focus. After all, if that which you focus on expands, you certainly don't want to keep concentrating on what you lack and what others enjoy. That obsessive energy only sends more good things *their* way—not yours!

Instead, you can view others' lives and be happy for them. More important, you can look at whatever *you* possess and be pleased for yourself. You no longer have to hold on to the belief that you need more to be content. Instead, you can embrace the understanding that you'll get more as you welcome joy. It's your beliefs, not your material goods, that bring you pleasure.

Success is a matter of interpretation. Instead of perceiving yourself or the events of your life as "not enough," you can choose to see yourself and your life in a more positive way. Even this choice is a huge success! And if you keep making it, if you continue to find the little joyous nuances throughout your days, that ongoing successful attitude will bring more happiness to you.

Remember, if you're unhappy, it's not only because you don't have the right job, car, relationship, or house; it's because you don't have the right attitude or belief. When you look around and feel blue, you don't need to change the circumstances of your life—at least not right away. Start by changing what you make it all mean. Choose to see genuine value within and around you—right now.

This shift in energy is a critical step to creating a success consciousness. Stop being a prisoner of your own limiting beliefs; refuse to be a victim of longing and lack. You have the power to end the envy and break free from the patterns of negating yourself and your life. You have the option to enjoy the present and bridge the pleasure gap. It's time to let go of the old desperate striving, the judgment, and the exhausting competition—and to finally understand that your only point of potential happiness is in your chosen perception of this present moment.

THE HAPPINESS FACTOR

Your consciousness is always in the process of creating! You need to direct its energy to the emotions and experiences you want, not the conditions you're trying to get away from. If you keep focusing on your problems, that's just what you'll attract—more problems. Instead, you must direct your attention to your solutions. Imagine good results and visualize positive outcomes, all while you're living with genuine happiness as your present point of view. Every time you get out of your own way and stop dismissing and denying the happiness you could already have, your willingness to see the good things within and around you directs the Universe to send more.

Success is a result of how you experience your life—not just in the pursuit of your dream, but in the routine procedures of your life. The motivation for every personal goal is the desire to find joy, but real achievement comes from choosing that on a daily basis. *Happiness is the factor within the equation, not the product of it.* You must activate a joyous approach to your life if you want to create a truly dynamic success consciousness. This is so important that it must be the first thing you try to succeed at if you want to go any further.

A successful life has two requirements:

- **You must be willing to let go of the things that are keeping your energy down and making you unhappy.** Although this includes patterns like self-sabotaging distractions and addictions, the two most important blocks that you have to be willing to release are judgment and fear of the future. True happiness can't co-exist with these kinds of thoughts and the emotions they create. You must be relentless in your refusal to engage in these energies; so every time you catch yourself making a judgment, being self-critical, or envisioning a catastrophe, do an immediate intervention. Repeat: "Stop. Release. Breathe." Say this right out loud if you can, but at the very least, say it in your mind. Afterward, take a deep breath and let the thought go. Do this as often as necessary until your refusal to fear or judge becomes a spontaneous reaction for you.

- **You must appreciate as much as you can about the present while continuing to work on your goals of the future.** This kind of gratitude comes from choosing to see the value of your entire life and your true self even now. You can keep moving toward your dreams, but you can't withhold your appreciation, waiting to bestow it upon a future event. Present gratitude is like a fuel in the rocket to your dreams. It has to be given lavishly, genuinely, and unconditionally *right now.*

In both the book and film *The Wizard of Oz,* Dorothy, the Scarecrow, the Cowardly Lion, and the Tin Man are desperately searching for the Emerald City. They're all looking for different things to make them happy, and they're told that the great and mighty Wizard who lives there can give them those things. When they arrive at their destination, they find that he's just an ordinary man hidden by smoke and mirrors and a frail little curtain.

In our search for success, we, too, are looking for the Emerald City. Like Dorothy and her three friends, we believe that the solutions we seek are in some far-off achievement, some distant, conditional goal. If we maintain those false assumptions, we'll set out on a journey where we'll be forced to face tornadoes of desperation, wicked witches of worry, and the flying monkeys of our own fears. We can continue to pursue that path, or we can choose to learn now what it took Dorothy a harrowing trip to find out:

the solution is—and always has been—within ourselves. *Happiness is not a future event; it's a present choice. Success is not a specific outcome; it's a way of life.*

HAVING FUN IN THE UNIVERSAL PLAYGROUND

Something that helps project the highest energy is having an attitude of playfulness when it comes to everything you do. This is a lighthearted and joyous intention, an approach that can bring a more high-spirited resonance to your life. Instead of looking at the day before you and seeing only endless drudgery, you can decide to have fun—and even play. Let go of your dread over tasks at work or menial chores at home. What kind of energy does that approach perpetuate in your life? Instead of complaining about having to clean the house, acknowledge your appreciation for having a home!

> Engage in your tasks with more creativity and enjoyment and look for the beauty in your environment. Listen to inspiring or exciting music; buy yourself flowers. Have some fun and dance and sing as you work. Remember that more than anything else, it's your daily energy that defines you—and determines your destiny.

If you can find absolutely no pleasure or value in the task that you're doing, bring joy to your mind by remembering something wonderful from your past or by reviewing your appreciation list. Recall a happy place, a fun time, or a special person, and bring renewed satisfaction into your life. Be more spontaneous and playful with your intentions. As you go through life, try to take things less seriously and less personally. Don't make everything mean so much!

Let go and live with joy. Intend to have more fun in your life. Affirm: *I am open to seeing more joy and being more playful in my life. I am always free to smile and enjoy.* Make this choice and soon you'll start to see a real difference in your attitude. The first time I tried to interject the energy of playfulness into my tasks, I was doing laundry. I'd always seen this as a tedious chore, so I wanted to change my energy around it.

Since nobody was home, I danced with the basket and started talking to my clothes, asking them if they had any ideas that could make this task more fun. I actually said this right out loud! Thankfully, they didn't answer, but this was kind of silly and fun, so I decided to continue. I proceeded to tell them that they were going to get a bath and feel so good after they were clean.

But then, when I was moving everything from the washer to the dryer, I realized that one of my favorite purple socks was missing. I held up the one I'd found and started interrogating it, asking, "What did you do to make your mate want to leave you? I saw you wrapped around that underwear!"

This made me laugh! I was doing the laundry and giggling. (Of course, I was also glad that my clients couldn't see me at that moment.) That experience not only changed that day for me, it also transformed my attitude about doing the laundry and so many other domestic chores. I realized that I could enjoy, instead of dread and despise, so many things that had seemed like meaningless busywork before. And while this may seem truly silly, it can completely alter your energy. It's not just the energy of the task that changes, it's your whole resonance of attraction! So let yourself have fun for a change—a real and significant change!

THE QUANTUM TICKLE

Laughter is a monumentally attractive energetic vibration, and it should be practiced as often as possible. Studies show that this is one of the few activities that stimulate electrical impulses in all parts of the brain. In addition, it sharpens your thinking, enhances creativity, reduces stress, increases energy, and makes you more productive. Experiencing laughter on a regular basis increases serotonin levels and gives you a greater sense of well-being. It also sends positive energy out like a rocket!

So give yourself permission to let go and really whoop it up. Rediscover the child inside you. Take a selfie of yourself making a funny face, and if you're brave, send it to your friends so they can laugh, too. If it doesn't come naturally at first, trick yourself into being happy by faking a smile. Your brain doesn't know the difference. It will still produce endorphins, lifting your mood and changing your personal resonance. Most important, this will alter your perception—which shifts your consciousness creation.

I once took a seminar where the class was told to start belly-laughing, creating that sound that comes from deep within and shakes your whole body. We were not told a joke or shown anything funny, so we looked at the teacher like he was spouting nonsense. He kept insisting, so we started, and soon we found ourselves laughing about the laughter! He kept it going for a half hour then explained the chemical and energetic efficacy of it all.

Let go of your old inhibitions and take the risk to have more fun. Choose to laugh and smile every single day. These choices don't take a lot of effort, but they pay off in creating a blissful consciousness and a hugely happy, magnetic energy.

Many studies have shown that smiling, even when posed, increases endorphin production, elevating feelings of well-being and happiness. The influence of facial expressions on our emotional experience is known as the facial feedback hypothesis. So, although you may think that the reaction of smiling is caused by happiness, it is equally true that the emotion of happiness is stimulated by the conscious choice to smile. As simple as this is, it is truly a powerful intention in terms of your resonance and life-force projection.

So, when you're thinking, "What can I do to make things better?" You know the very least you can do is choose to smile. And don't forget the Easy Alpha Affirmations from Chapter 2, which only take about 10 seconds. With just a smile, raised eyes, a deep breath, and a few simple words, you can completely shift your emotional vibration!

The intention to cultivate light-heartedness right now isn't a cliché; it's energetic power. Living in joy raises your resonance and matches the very emotion you're trying to achieve through success. This entraining of emotional vibration is the most dynamic way to bring that achievement to you. The energy of the Universe is clear: your attitude about your life will shape it.

You have the choice to shape your destiny through pessimism or optimism, drudgery or enjoyment—and you make that decision many, many times each day. Set yourself to creating joy and delight, and the Universe will respond with blissful returns. Always keep in mind that a truly vibrant consciousness of success is sparked by these daily renewals of optimism, smiling, laughter, self-love, and joyous energy in the here and now.

QUANTUM CHARISMA

When you think of people who have charisma, certain characteristics come to mind. They possess a joie de vivre, or joy for life, that infects everyone around them and everything they do. They have high energy, enthusiasm, and peaceful dignity that pervades their life. You, too, can create this kind of attitude now, completely changing the direction of your life. Your power of choice is your ultimate liberation—you can select joy, peace, and enthusiasm in every thought and perception. Since patterns of attraction always operate through the movement of energy, this is the highest vibration you can choose.

Your consciousness is your order form in the Universal catalog because it reveals just what you choose to prioritize most. Whether your focus is enduring lack or unlimited abundance, the Universe will surely fill your order, so never define yourself by the problem. Hold an unwavering focus on the solution. Remain single-minded in your determination to engage only in honoring, self-loving, unconflicted thought, and your pure purpose will connect you with Divine Intention and Universal flow.

Every change you make will alter your conscious direction, and even a little modification in consciousness can create a huge shift in your reality. The world is full of endless options, and the great field of all possibilities wants to send your dreams your way; stop resisting and open yourself to receiving. Your willing, ongoing intention of appreciation will create an open, flowing channel to the source of all success.

When you align yourself with the unseen forces and the Universal Laws, the sparks of success begin to fly. There's a current in the air that's quite literally electric. This is your quantum charisma—your relentlessly optimistic energy combined with a clear, conscious intention—and it's your most powerful force for successful manifestation. This pulsating power is with you at this moment, and it can align with the unlimited, abundant potential that the infinitely vibrating world has to offer. When you discover the bliss and beauty that is now and always within you, you'll have already achieved your *quantum success*—joyous appreciation for yourself and for every precious moment of your life!

Your present bliss is the beginning and the end of your success, and it's time for you to rise to meet your greatest dreams fulfilled. Your destiny is already taking shape in the energetic realm. Witness the miraculous energy within and around you, and before too long a future full of miracles will unfold.

Affirmations for Living with a Success Consciousness

✦ Every moment of my life is special. Joyous appreciation is my constant choice.

✦ Now and always, I am willing to change any negative, fearful, or limiting thoughts. My present optimistic consciousness and my own happy energy are my greatest success.

✦ Everything that I think and do provides an opportunity to succeed right now. Today I live with joy.

✦ I value myself and my life. I choose to affirm myself and see all the ways that I can succeed at being happy now.

✦ I choose to bring an attitude of playfulness and joyous appreciation to my life. I smile and laugh more. I have more fun, and take more risks. My life is a happy adventure!

✦ ✦ ✦

CONCLUSION

The power of the Universe is your power.
The light of the Universe is your light. The energy of all time
and all space vibrates within your eternal consciousness,
always engaging you in elegant acts of creation.

You're creating your future right now, diligently working at the destiny factory, churning out bits of energy, information, and expectation that will all be assembled into your own vehicle of future experience. It could be a cheap lemon that always needs to be repaired, or it could be a beautiful luxury car that runs like a top and gives you a joyous ride to magnificent destinations. It's totally up to you because you're the one that builds it, assembles it, and drives it forward with every moment of your life.

For that reason, it's important to remember all that we've discussed here. You live and move within the very real patterns of the energetic world, so don't dismiss it as too unrealistic. What's impractical is continuing along the same old lines if they haven't yet gotten you where you want to go!

CONSCIOUSNESS QUICK-SHIFTING FOR SUCCESS

When you're bored or down or upset by something specific, you don't have to stay in that difficult place. You can shift your energy and consciousness quickly by doing (or focusing on) something else. Here is a short list of easy, quick-shifting steps:

- Sometimes all it takes is movement and deep breathing to turn your energy around. Get up, stretch, and yawn—even if you may not feel like it. Hop on one foot, look in the mirror, and make funny faces at yourself. Breathe, smile, and laugh—know that this creates much better energy than frowning and worry.

- Listen to your favorite music and sing along. Combine this step with the previous step by dancing to the lively, happy tunes that you enjoy the most. This activates your mechanical and acoustic energy, lifting your emotional and electromagnetic resonance as well.

- Stop what you're doing and say some quick affirmations, such as: *I can change my mood. This moment is valuable. I have power, and I am choosing to use it now! I can do all these easy things to change my energy and attract greater success right now!*

- Change your activity. Make a phone call to a friend. Go somewhere else or do something entirely different. Distract yourself with a book or a video or a podcast—even if it's only for a little while.

- Take a happiness vacation. Whenever things get hectic, take a few moments to do the following meditation:

  Let go of all concerns. See them lifting up and floating away. Take a deep breath and feel your consciousness dropping gently into your heart center. Take a moment to recall something or someone that you truly appreciate—perhaps a favorite vacation spot, a sport you enjoy, a beloved friend, or a funny incident. Take another deep breath and repeat the word peace *or* joy *as you picture this happy image in vivid detail. Let yourself sense the happiness and peace growing in your heart center, gently filling your body and mind. Feel the loving, blissful energy expand, and your joyous memory will shift your consciousness deep within.*

- Put happy pictures around you, including pictures of joyous memories, favorite places, or beloved friends and family. Consider getting a digital frame. As the pictures in the digital frame rotate every minute or so, it will catch your attention and draw you in to each joyous memory.

Affirmations for Quick-Shifting

✦ The quality of this moment is up to me. I have the power to shift my focus to something happy now.

✦ I have the option to change my energy now—to move, breathe deeply, laugh, affirm, and visualize a joyous image.

✦ The quality of my life is up to me. Now is the best time to take control and make myself happy and grateful.

✦ Today I'm going to play the game of "quick-shifting." I turn any negative focus around by choosing things like deep breathing, smiling, quick affirmations, pleasant distractions, music, dancing, laughing, and happy visualizations.

✦ I affirm myself and my life! I remain true to my intention to create many successful moments of joy and optimism every day.

Let yourself engage in all these processes for as long as it takes. Try to reread this book at different stages in your success pursuit. You'll find that different information will resonate with you at each stage. Keep up with the visualization, affirmation, and journal exercises, and remind yourself of all the powers you have at your disposal. There are three absolute musts you want to take control of in order to change your future now.

✦ ✦ ✦

THE THREE KEYS TO DESTINY CREATION

All the powers are vital in establishing a dynamic destiny, but three fundamental forces of your nature should never be overlooked. In fact, they're so important that they should be reexamined every day—if you're having a hard time, do it every hour or even more often! The following tips will help you use them to their fullest extent. As you go through your routines, always keep in mind these three central keys to destiny creation: consciousness, energy, and intention.

Consciousness

Your consciousness creates your reality, so it's important to think about what you're most conscious of. This means developing a real knowledge of where your mental focus is much of the time. When you concentrate on the value and joy in your life, those experiences will expand and keep on expanding to the degree that you continue to prioritize them. Remember these pointers to keep yourself on track:

- **Don't be a consciousness zombie.** Wake up to what you're thinking about and how that's going to impact your energy. Only you can take control of what you're conscious of; you don't have to stay stuck in your old thought patterns.

- **Keep reminding yourself of your consciousness options.** Instead of obsessing about what's going wrong, shift your focus to what can go *right*. Lock on to that assumption, and determine the action you can take to make it a reality.

- **Always hold a positive perception of yourself in your mind and heart.** Whenever you get down on yourself, remember your new positive self-perception and loving definition of yourself. Be very careful not to fault yourself for your difficult experiences.

A common misconception is that if anything goes wrong, it's all your fault—energetically or otherwise. Let that go and start considering where you want to go from here.

- **Choose to be much more conscious of what you have than what you lack.** Always make it a priority to acknowledge the good things—big and small—that you have. In this way, you'll continue to manifest more abundance and blessings in your future. And don't forget to also acknowledge the goodness within you. Remember, you are an eternal being, a child of God, deserving of all the wonderful things the Universe has to offer.

- **Create exciting images of a happy and successful self and future.** Make these images bright, clear, and close to your heart; breathe deeply as you experience their joy and excitement. When you visualize the future outcome; take a moment to hold a happy memory image in your mind and heart as well. This will spark very real reactions in your neural pathways, your neurotransmitter production, and your conscious expectations.

- **Investigate your real expectations.** Turn any pessimistic conclusion about future possibilities into an optimistic one. Remember that the world is full of endless opportunities. Expect the best, and know that your consciousness can create it.

Energy

You're always in the process of transmitting and receiving energy. Your life force is broadcasting at every moment. Even now, your thoughts, beliefs, and emotions are sending out very specific signals about who you are and what you're willing to accept in your life. If you want to attract successful situations and people who will help you create them, your resonance must vibrate with healthy beliefs, positive thoughts, and genuinely joyous vibrations.

- **Always be aware that you're in the process of energy production.** Even if you're not conscious of it, you're still generating it. As often as possible, engage in the kind of thoughts and beliefs that generate positive and attractive vibrations. If you catch yourself in an old negative pattern, don't judge yourself, just choose to switch to a more trusting approach.

- **Always choose to support, encourage, and believe in yourself.** The energy of confidence begins with self-honoring. Your choice to engage in thoughts or activities that are dishonoring to you invites the world to do the same. Know that you deserve your own high regard, so affirm your belief in yourself and your worthiness every single day.

- **Choose optimism!** There's absolutely no energetic value in a pessimistic outlook. No matter what's going on around you, you can look past the problems and open yourself up to receiving the solutions. Think about how well things could go, and then take action in that direction. If you find yourself in a dark and difficult place, increase your neurotransmitter intentions. Do them many, many times a day along with your other affirmations. In time, you will feel a shift in moods that will carry you to happier feelings and outcomes.

- **Find your real purpose.** Remember that part of your mission is to connect with your spirit, so let yourself learn more about who you are and why you're here. And once you've found out, honor that and open up to all the guidance and inspiration that's available to you from the energetic realms.

- **Stay present!** Energetically speaking, your power base is only in the current moment. Remember that each new second offers a fresh opportunity to change your consciousness and energetic vibration. Even if you were filled with negativity just a moment ago, you can choose another vibration now. Forgive yourself, and let go of the past. Use the power of the present to manufacture a brilliantly beautiful future.

- **Live in the power of love and deep appreciation.** These are the most attractive energies you can project. Remember the influence of the simple word *love;* send it to yourself, to the people you're with, and to the projects you're involved in. Live with gratitude for all that you have and all that you are. Say *thank you* to and for the little things. Your intention to acknowledge and give thanks magnetizes even more to be grateful for.

Intention

Your intentions direct both your energy and consciousness, thus creating the focus of your life goals. Real success is purely motivated, never driven by fear. When you pursue your goals in order to enhance a purposeful and joyous life, your intentions will direct the bountiful Universe to assist you in every way possible.

- **Never intend your goals to be the *only* source of your happiness, self-worth, or self-definition.** This is guaranteed to create urgency and desperation, highly toxic energies of paradoxical intent that will push your dreams away. If you find yourself thinking that way, release the thought and reclaim your power and freedom of choice.

- **Consider your intentions seriously—whether they concern your professional pursuits or daily activities.** Give thought to why you do things, and then ask yourself whether the actions you take resonate with you and bring you a sense of purpose, happiness, and fulfillment. When the energy of your action aligns with your heart, it becomes one of the greatest forces of manifestation!

- **Make sure that you're not engaged in conflicting intentions.** If you want to succeed at something in particular, you need to be sure you want it on every level. Know that you deserve it, and believe that you are capable of achieving it—and that the Universe can provide! Also intend to enjoy your ongoing process. Don't cancel out your Universal order with contradicting fears, dread, and doubts.

- **Surrender any emotional attachment to your goals.** Let go of need, urgency, and desperation; be patient but persistent. Look for the satisfaction in the process, and you'll see real value in the end.

- **Live with conscious intention every day. Intend to live with joy!** Whether you're just doing a mundane task or you're engaged in the pursuit of your dreams, do it with a clearly happy intention. Aim for value, peace, and loving appreciation in your everyday life.

- **Create a daily intention to connect with your loving source, the Universal Intelligence, the all-compassionate heart of God.** The more you make this heartfelt purpose an active part of your daily life, the more your energy will resonate in harmony with the abundant field of all possibilities.

SHARING SUCCESS

All three of these things—consciousness, energy, and intention—go into determining your own personal success, but never forget that your vibration also expands in the world to create the shared destiny of all humankind. The nonlocal nature of this influence means that you have power everywhere. In fact, your higher intentions have as great an impact on the success of our species as they do on your own life.

Every bit of energy that you project moves all humanity in one direction or another—toward love and success or hate and destruction. Every thought of judgment or self-criticism accelerates the negative momentum in the world, while each caring focus accelerates the positive as well. Even just the intention to cease the struggle in your own mind works to end the conflict elsewhere in the world. This is the undeniable reality of the M-fields of shared consciousness: we're all constantly contributing to the consequences of our species, determining outcomes near and far. As each of us learns to vibrate on a more loving level, we'll not only unfold a more brilliant destiny for ourselves but also bring a higher, brighter vibration to the destiny of all humankind.

GOOD VIBRATIONS

Remember to live and move in optimistic and trusting choices. In all that you think and do, always consider your affirmative and nurturing options. Start with the statements at the end of each chapter, then add your own. Keep in mind that every present moment holds an energetic opportunity for you, so always choose an uplifting perception of yourself, your goals, and your world. Affirm your life every chance you get, and the Universe will respond in wonderful ways.

Don't dismiss this approach as an idealistic fantasy; it weaves together irresistible forces that align personal and Universal vibrations with strength and purpose. Your energy vibrates relentlessly through every single cell and experience. Your many options to resonate at a higher, brighter level never stop—not even for a moment. Right now—and every now—you can make a choice that has the power to change your life forever, so decide on an attitude filled with excitement, joy, and expectation. Rise above your old, unhealthy patterns and resonate with a new belief in yourself and in your unlimited world. Live with the image of your brilliant future floating all around you, and you'll find yourself immersed in that reality before too long. You design your destiny every moment of your life. Be the bliss you long for, and untold beauty and blessings will be yours!

INDEX OF ENERGY-SHIFTING
TRUTHS AND TECHNIQUES

These processes will expand your energetic options, shift your life-force resonance, and accelerate your desired outcomes. They are arranged by both name and topic.

affirmations
  affirmation saturation, 98, 154, 165
  alpha affirmations, 19–20
  Easy Alpha Affirmations, 19–20
  Energetic Vortex of Mirror Affirmations, 164–65
  for a Power Consciousness, 105
  for a Powerful Presence, 182
  for a Powerful Purpose, 176
  for a Productive Plan, 207
  for Attractive Energy, 116
  for Charismatic Confidence, 156
  for Connecting with Loving Spirit Energy, 244
  for Connecting with My Higher Self, 235
  for Dynamic Magnetism, 25
  for Endless Appreciation, 194
  for Healthy, Happy, and Powerful Choices, 136
  for Letting Go, 93
  for Living in Divine Presence, 251
  for Living in Harmony, 54
  for Living in Love, 145
  for Living with a Success Consciousness, 289
  for My Expanding Influence, 70
  for Overwhelming Optimism, 167
  for Pure and Powerful Intentions, 126
  for Pure Desire, 34
  for Quick-Shifting, 293
  for Real Commitment, 202
  for Right Action, 62
  for Successful Action, 213
  for Unattached Action, 222
  for Untiring Perseverance, 271
  mirror affirmations, 164–65, 248–49
  neurotransmitter affirmations, 97–98
  receptive affirmations, 161–64
  Sacred Prayer of Mirror Affirmations, The, 248–49

Appreciating the Future: Power Up Your Visions of Success, 191–93
appreciation
  Appreciating the Future: Power Up Your Visions of Success, 191–93
  appreciation journal, 188
  Heart-Centered Shift, 191
  sharpen your skills, 189–91
  Stop, Drop, and Crop, 190
attachments, letting go of
  Changing Your Goal: Moving On Is Not Giving Up, 218–19
  Tips for Taking Action While Letting Go of Attachment, 219–21
Attracting Success Holographic Meditation, 228–30
attraction intentions, 242–44
attraction quotient
  Attraction Quotient Quiz, 113
  Change Your Energy, Change Your Results, 115–16
brain frequency
  Easy Alpha Affirmations, 19–20
  Change Your Biochemistry for Irresistible Attraction, 97–99
  Shift Your Self-Image: Creating New Neural Pathways of Self-Confidence, 154–55
Change Your Biochemistry for Irresistible Attraction, 97–99
Changing Your Goal: Moving On Is Not Giving Up, 218–19
Consciousness PIE, 99–105
Consciousness Quick-Shifting for Success, 291–93
constructs
  Constructing a New Approach, 39
  Understanding Constructs, 38-39

Easy Alpha Affirmations, 19–20

Energetic Vortex of Mirror Affirmations, 164–65

Freezing Names, 141

gratitude (see *appreciation*)

Happiness Vacation, 292

Happy Memory Imagery, 98, 295

Heart-Centered Shift, 191

higher self
Attracting Success Holographic Meditation, 228–30
Hologram of Your Higher Self, The, 227
Let Your Higher Self Do the Work, 232–34

Hologram of Your Higher Self, The, 227

intentions
attraction intentions, 242–44
Planting Your Attraction Intention in the Energetic Realm, 242–44
pure intentions, 121–23
Releasing Conflicting Intentions, 124
Shift to a Determined, Pure Intention, 121–22
Tips for Powerful Intentions, 125–26

Journal for Success, 6–7, 23–24, 31–32, 33, 43, 49, 67–68, 81–82, 87–90, 111–12, 122–23, 131–35, 160–61, 174–75, 181–82, 188, 201–02, 247

Let Your Higher Self Do the Work, 232–34

love
Love as a Directed Energetic Intention, 144
Meditation: Surround It with Love, 145

meditations (see also *visualizations*)
Attracting Success Holographic Meditation, 228–30
Happiness Vacation, 292
Meditation: Surround It with Love, 145
Meditation: Your Sacred Identity, 52–53

neurotransmitter affirmations, 97–98

Planting Your Attraction Intention in the Energetic Realm, 242–44

Positive Visualization: Rise Above It, 257

Quantum Tickle, The, 285–87

receptive affirmations, 161–64

Releasing Conflicting Intentions, 124

Sacred Prayer of Mirror Affirmations, The, 248–49

self-image
Constructing a New Approach, 39
Creating New Neural Pathways of Self-Confidence, 154–55
The New You Is Waiting, 84
Your True Identity—Your Spiritual Definition, 246–48

Shift to a Determined, Pure Intention, 121–22

Shift Your Self-Image: Creating New Neural Pathways of Self-Confidence, 154-55

Stop, Drop, and Crop, 190

thought restructuring
Releasing and Rewriting Toxic Thoughts, 80–85
Thought Restructuring Sheet, 83

tips
Consciousness Quick-Shifting for Success, 291–93
for Powerful Intentions, 125–26
for Taking Action, 211–12
for Taking Action While Letting Go of Attachment, 219–21

Venting Letters, 85–90

vision boards
Appreciating the Future: Power Up Your Visions of Success, 191–93

visualizations
Attracting Success Holographic Meditation, 228–30
Heart-Centered Shift, 191
Hologram of Your Higher Self, The, 227
Imagery Is Everything, 101–03
Meditation: Your Sacred Identity, 52–53
Positive Visualization: Rise Above It, 257

Your True Identity—Your Spiritual Definition, 246–48

SUGGESTED READING

Answers from the Ancestral Realm, Sharon Anne Klingler.
Carlsbad, CA: Hay House, 2023

Beyond the Quantum, Michael Talbot.
New York, NY: Bantam, 1988

The Biology of Transcendence, Joseph Chilton Pearce.
Rochester, VT: Park Street Press, 2002

Dancing Naked in the Mind Field, Kary Mullis.
New York, NY: Pantheon Books 1998

Elemental Mind, Nick Herbert.
New York, NY: Penguin, 1993

Energy Medicine, Donna Eden with David Feinstein.
New York, NY: Putnam, 1998

Happy for No Reason, Marci Shimoff.
New York, NY: Atria Books, 2009

Higher Purpose, Robert Holden.
Carlsbad, CA: Hay House, 2022

The Holographic Universe, Michael Talbot.
New York, NY: HarperCollins, 1991

Intuition & Beyond, Sharon Anne Klingler.
London, England: Random House UK, 2002

The Law of Higher Potential, Robert Collier.
Tarrytown, NY: Book of Gold, 1947

Molecules of Emotion, Candace B. Pert, Ph.D.
New York, NY: Scribner, 1997

Power Words, Sharon Anne Klingler.
Carlsbad, CA: Hay House

The Power of Intention, Dr. Wayne W. Dyer.
Carlsbad, CA: Hay House, 2004

Quantum Reality, Nick Herbert.
New York, NY: Anchor, 1985

The Quantum Self, Danah Zohar.
New York, NY: Quill, 1990

The Spiritual Universe, Fred Alan Wolf.
Portsmouth, NH: Moment Point Press, 1999

Taking the Quantum Leap, Fred Alan Wolf.
New York, NY: Harper & Row, 1989

ACKNOWLEDGMENTS

I'd like to gratefully acknowledge and send my loving appreciation to the following:

To my dear family: Benjamin Earl Taylor, Jr.; Vica Taylor; Jenyaa and Ashley Taylor; Sheri Klingler; Devin Staurbringer; Yvonne and Earl Taylor; and Kevin and Kathryn Klingler.

To the family of my heart: Bayley Van Rensselaer, Marilyn Verbus, Ed Conghanor, Julianne Stein, Melissa Matousek, and Tom and Ellie Cratsley.

To my wonderful publishing family: Reid Tracy, Margarete Nielson, Patty Gift, Nicolette Salamanca Young, Tricia Briedenthal, Bryn Best, Steve Morris, Matteo Pistono, and all the wonderful people at Hay House.

To my office family: the ever-indispensable Rhonda Lamvermeyer, Bayley Van Rensselaer, and Marilyn Verbus.

To my spirit family: Anna and Charles Salvaggio, Ron Klingler, Sarah Marie Klingler, Rudy Staurbringer, Flo Bolton, Flo Becker, Louise Hay, Tony, Raphael, Jude, and the Holy Spirit of all life.

To the Divine Consciousness that lives in all things and loves in all ways.

Finally, to you, the reader: Thank you for your light in the world. May God bring you happiness and abundant blessings always.

ABOUT THE AUTHOR

Sandra Anne Taylor is the *New York Times* best-selling author of *Quantum Success*—now updated and republished as *Unlimited Abuncance*—along with other titles, including *Your Quantum Breakthrough Code, Secrets of Attraction, Secrets of Success, The Hidden Power of Your Past Lives, 28 Days to a More Magnetic Life*, and *The Akashic Records Made Easy*. Her oracle decks, *The Energy Oracle Cards, The Quantum Oracle*, and *Energy and Spirit Oracle* reveal both universal influences and upcoming events with amazing accuracy. Her most recent deck, *The Past-Life Energy Oracle*, uncovers powerful karmic influences along with present healing and future direction. *The Priestess of Light Oracle*, with renowned artist Kimberly Webber, channels the sacred wisdom of nature and spirit animals. *The Akashic Tarot* (with Sharon Klingler) opens the records in stunningly predictive and inspiring ways. Sandra's books and cards are available in over 32 languages worldwide. Listen to Sandra's inspiring podcast, *Energy Activation*, on mindbodyspirit.fm or wherever you get your podcasts.

For more information about Sandra or to contact her, please call (440) 871-5448 or go to her websites: **www.sandrataylor.net** and **www.starbringerassociates.com.**

Hay House Titles of Related Interest

YOU CAN HEAL YOUR LIFE, the movie,
starring Louise Hay & Friends
(available as an online streaming video)
www.hayhouse.com/louise-movie

THE SHIFT, the movie,
starring Dr. Wayne W. Dyer
(available as an online streaming video)
www.hayhouse.com/the-shift-movie

***

8 SECRETS TO POWERFUL MANIFESTING: How to Create the Reality of Your Dreams, by Mandy Morris

EMBRACE ABUNDANCE: A Proven Path to Better Health, More Wealth and Deeply Fulfilling Relationships, by Danette May

INFINITE RECEIVING: Crack the Code to Conscious Wealth Creation and Finally Manifest Your Dream Life, by Suzy Ashworth

MANIFESTING YOUR MAGICAL LIFE: A Practical Guide to Everyday Magic with the Angels, by Radleigh Valentine

POSITIVE MANIFESTATION JOURNAL, by the editors of Hay House